Open Secrecy

Open Secrecy

HOW TECHNOLOGY EMPOWERS
THE DIGITAL UNDERWORLD

Isak Ladegaard

UNIVERSITY OF CALIFORNIA PRESS

University of California Press
Oakland, California

Library of Congress Cataloging-in-Publication Data

Names: Ladegaard, Isak, author.
Title: Open secrecy : how technology empowers the digital
    underworld / Isak Ladegaard.
Description: Oakland, California : University of California Press,
    [2025] | Includes bibliographical references and index.
Identifiers: LCCN 2024047439 (print) | LCCN 2024047440 (ebook) |
    ISBN 9780520397286 (hardback) | ISBN 9780520397293
    (paperback) | ISBN 9780520397309 (ebook)
Subjects: LCSH: Dark Web. | Computer crimes. | Black market. | Data
    encryption (Computer science)—Social aspects. | Information
    technology—Social aspects.
Classification: LCC HV6773 .L33 2025 (print) | LCC HV6773 (ebook)
    DDC 364.16/8—dc23/eng/20250118
LC record available at https://lccn.loc.gov/2024047439
LC ebook record available at https://lccn.loc.gov/2024047440

GPSR Authorized Representative: Easy Access System Europe,
Mustamäe tee 50, 10621 Tallinn, Estonia, gpsr.requests@easproject
.com

34 33 32 31 30 29 28 27 26 25
10 9 8 7 6 5 4 3 2 1

Contents

Illustrations

Introduction

In 2010 an entrepreneurial bookseller in his late twenties launched a side project that had long been on his mind. "The idea," he wrote in his diary, was to "create a website where people could buy anything anonymously." His creation was Silk Road: the world's first sophisticated e-commerce market for banned goods and services. Its maiden product was a packet of homegrown psychedelic mushrooms he had grown in a cabin in remote Texas. Soon, hundreds of drug dealers across the world had signed up on Silk Road and started selling cocaine, methamphetamine, ecstasy, cannabis, and heroin to faceless customers. One of the drug dealers who used the website told me that the ability to trade on a secure online marketplace had transformed his long-standing business: "You can make structured plans, attainable goals, you can expand in a controlled manner." Another dealer, who cooked his chemical drugs at home, said he never had any in-person contact with market actors or other criminals.

Over the past ten years or so, people like them have used the administrative capacities of digital platforms to actively undermine state control. Their remarkable accomplishments—documented throughout this book in analyses of three empirical cases—reveal an uncomfortable truth: no one is in control of the consequences of information technology. Right now, millions of people are working together in communities that state actors see as destructive but are unable to stop. What I call "open secrecy" combines mass communication tools and anonymity, or pseudonymity, often based on encryption. This mix enables groups to create and maintain large alternative worlds, in which they can talk about banned or controversial matters, collaborate on problem solving, disseminate solutions, and transfer capital, all while masking their real-world identities, when necessary. With open secrecy, shadowy groups can operate without crippling concerns about state power, expressed through law enforcement crackdowns or corporate regulation.

Silk Road was remarkable when it arrived because it looked and worked like eBay and Amazon—complete with product categories, star ratings, and a digital shopping cart. The difference was that encryption technology protected its users from surveillance. Their communications, money transfers, and online personas were brazenly public yet difficult to tie to real names. Silk Road was open and secret at the same time. It showed us a version of reality in which drugs are treated as ordinary consumer products. When the FBI arrested the creator in a San Francisco library in 2013, the game was up for him, but not for the world he had created. In the weeks that followed, thousands of market actors used their ability to communicate and collaborate in open secrecy to create and migrate to a new market, aptly called Silk Road 2.

The marketplace launched to much fanfare in the digital underworld and soon facilitated millions of dollars' worth of trade. After about a year law enforcement shut down this market too, but by that time it no longer mattered. Silk Road users had learned from their struggles, figuring out how to leverage encryption to protect private and public messaging, how to cover their real-world identities, and how to preserve their pseudonyms and online relations, which enabled them to move around like shadowy nomads, hopping from dark market to dark market, secret website to secret website. In responding to challenges, users became stronger, more flexible, more resilient—and very difficult to stop. Occasional arrests are made, as people make human mistakes and leave digital trails for the police. But used correctly, the technology that enables open secrecy is solid.

In 2025, more than a decade and a half after the Silk Road digital marketplace arrived, drug e-commerce is still going strong.

The same tools have been picked up by actors in other domains and parts of the world, such as free-speech activists in the East. In later chapters I explain how, around the same time that Silk Road was created, a group of programmers in China discussed ways to circumvent state censorship of the internet. One developer had created a tool to do this for himself, and he and his peers worked to improve it. This nascent community expanded over the next ten years or so, and their tools became increasingly sophisticated, even though the central government in Beijing tightened internet control and law enforcement managed to track down some of the group's members. Or perhaps the tools got better *because* of police pressure? Like the digital drug trade, the Chinese anticensorship community survived the crackdowns that targeted it. Its members learned from their setbacks and carried on in more sophisticated ways. In a testimony to the quality of their work, one of their anticensorship algorithms was recently used by Google to help Iranian protesters connect to the open internet. Another organization that has learned from this community of free speech activists is the Tor Project—a New Hampshire–based nonprofit organization that provides anonymization tools to the global public.

The story is complicated further by how open secrecy has also empowered the far right. White supremacists have harnessed open secrecy to expand recruitment, cloak and grow fundraising, spread hateful messaging, and coordinate antisocial activities of anonymous troll armies. As the destructive capabilities of far-right extremism became increasingly evident—with innocent lives lost in terror—technology companies booted many far-right users off their platforms and cut off support, but with open secrecy they could bounce back and now they operate in a decentralized space that is increasingly independent of mainstream services. For instance, the social media site Gab, popular among far-right actors, returned when it was rejected by mainstream app stores for promoting hate speech and was dropped by its domain hosting provider and payment processors, after one of its users murdered worshippers at the Pittsburgh synagogue Tree of Life. The platform was reconstructed using open-source code and now stores and hosts its own data, meaning Gab can remain operative even if technology firms refuse to sell it their services.

If neither law enforcement agencies like the Federal Bureau of Investigation and the National Crime Agency in the West, resourceful autocracies in the East, nor Big Tech can stop shadowy groups that operate in open secrecy, then who can? Who will? The answer is clear: no one. Connected, tech-savvy groups can roam freely, confidently, and they have already started to change the internet and by extension the world we inhabit. People in the openly secret underworld often express an ethos of resilience and emboldened underdogness. After migrating from Silk Road to a new drug marketplace, one person expressed this sentiment, saying, "You can't kill an idea." On the developer platform GitHub a similar defiance was on display when a Chinese anticensorship software developer was caught by the police and ordered to resign. One of many supportive comments read: "Ideas are bulletproof." And, soberingly, the same sentiment surfaced when the operator of the far right–friendly platform Gab responded to shutdown efforts in a message to his followers: "You can't stop an idea."

New technology often reproduces social structures, but once in a while it stimulates real disruption, real change. Open secrecy is such a force: by undermining the state's capacity to maintain social control, it further diminishes the prospect of a future characterized by orderly progress. Our attention is warranted.

1 Invisible Forces of Liberation and Control

The wireless information streams in our homes and offices arrive via long, onerous underground journeys, sometimes beneath the great blue oceans, where thick cables are visited by repair operations and Russian spy submarines. The lines connect cities, countries, and continents, and meet in places like the Cairo Internet Exchange and DE-CIX in a dull Frankfurt neighborhood. Thinking about the internet's intestines helps us understand that although the network is a bustling, chaotic, and seemingly unstoppable digital world, it is also a physical system in need of maintenance and protection, a web of cords that has been put together by engineers and tucked away and then guarded by state actors and private firms.[1]

Technology tends to become more opaque, clean, and abstract as it advances. It is no coincidence that in *Her*, director Spike Jonze's shockingly prescient portrayal of the near future, the heartbroken protagonist befriends an artificial creature that is not a metallic doll with an awkward stride but an enchanting voice who speaks to him through his earbuds. In the film's cityscape—an aesthetic blend of Shanghai and Los Angeles—pedestrians walk on footbridges, above and away from road traffic, and just like cars are absent from the morning commute, big-screen devices are gone, yet everyone appears to be continuously connected. Technology that is both out of sight and omnipresent, it is suggested in the film, is more advanced and sophisticated. Computers will soon be embedded in our furniture and woven into our clothing, and internet signals are already everywhere, all the time.[2] As Bill Gates once said, "The advance of technology is based on making it fit in so that you don't really even notice it, so it's part of everyday life."[3]

A case in point are the artificial minds we can access through our gadgets. Their sorcerous capabilities are brought to life by a simple button push, or a voice command, and their responses come quickly and with ease, but they were trained on troves of information and are powered by data centers the size of football fields. As for the internet, it might become hard to find the physical network even if you dig underground in search of cables, as companies launch satellites that form networks in Earth's lower orbit to literally beam Wi-Fi–like connectivity from the sky. And once something disappears into our surroundings, we often stop questioning its existence, its purpose, what it does to us, and whether it could or should be different. Systems out of sight and mind, like that techno future envisioned by Gates, are difficult to critique and challenge, which is why concealed power structures are stronger than the ones that are right in your face.[4]

Technological advances often reproduce the world as we already know it, even if they offer new ways of doing things. For instance, in the internet's early days, there was a lot of hope (and hype) about what the global network could do to reduce inequality. Top universities started to offer free online education, which could potentially help historically disadvantaged people who would struggle to navigate the admission process or afford an in-person college degree. Today, a mathematically gifted kid who lives in impoverished conditions in northeastern Russia can in theory make herself employable in the current AI boom by studying "Machine Learning with Python" at the Massachusetts Institute of Technology. But, as it turns out, people who enroll in free online courses are not like the Russian kid;

rather, they are folks who reside in wealthier neighborhoods that have higher levels of education compared with the general population, at least in the United States.[5]

I have audited a few open online courses myself. This is partly because I'm curious and enjoy learning—traits that feel intrinsic to who I am—but that attitude, as well as my interests, have grown out of things I have already had the opportunity to do, study, and think about. I also have time and energy available for exploring potential side projects that is unavailable to many. The *digital divide* that was once about unequal access to computers and fast internet is now about know-how coupled with the disposition to use available technology to explore, play, and learn—which often overlap.[6] The AI revolution will likely be another chapter in the same story—access to machine intelligence will, despite talk about universal utility, primarily benefit tech-savvy or at least tech-interested people. But sometimes the internet and related technologies, and how people use them, *do* produce real social change. This book is about one such transformation that is happening without anyone really noticing.

We are now used to, perhaps even a bit bored by, the modern idea that technological development drives us forward. When people get access to useful tools that they can adopt without too much fuss, they will employ them to get stuff done more efficiently, and their lives will be slightly altered, often by "optimizing" some kind of task.[7] Widespread adoption of simple but useful technology is in large part how the Industrial Revolution started—more so than lauded acts of invention—and industrialism and a new capitalist hunt for productivity gains helped turn us into the modern people we are today: future-oriented and aspirationally rational.[8] But tech-driven transformations are full of unintended consequences and rarely work out in the way people expect, and that's where to look for social change. As Marshall McLuhan famously argued with his somewhat confusing phrase "the medium is the message," the real power of technology lies in the subtle and often unacknowledged developments it brings to human interaction and social structures.[9]

I claim that the connectivity enabled by underground cables, signals in the air, and software engineering enable activities that undermine a key characteristic of modernity—states' ability to govern through centralized data collection and administration. State sovereignty is already under attack on numerous fronts, perhaps most of all by globalization, for instance, as companies, people, and capital move across the world, even cutting ties to the physical territories from which they emerged.[10] I claim that state power is further undermined by the digital disorder brought about by open secrecy.

More Is Different

Social movement scholars have documented how people use information technology to garner support for their causes, organize action, and disseminate and leverage collective emotional energy, such as outrage about the status quo and hope for a better future.[11] Information technology, they say, is liberating, empowering. Others have argued that technology is a source of power that primarily benefits those who already have plenty of it. They say that we live in an increasingly dystopian era of mass surveillance, as the content people generate and the digital trails that they leave behind by living their lives are collected and analyzed. Information technology is the public administrator and policeman's dream, as turning messy social life into measurable activity with extensive data categories for citizens is central to modern statecraft, and private enterprises have figured out how they can turn data into profit, often in the name of convenience.[12] My position is the middle ground: information technology undoubtedly empowers group activities, which are often prosocial, such as when people protest a repressive regime. But the same liberatory force has a darker side, because the newfound capacity for communication and collaboration across time and space also strengthens harmful and dangerous groups.

People who violate norms or laws have always used technology to evade punishment, so perhaps nothing fundamental has changed, just like internet access has reproduced existing patterns of inequality? Perhaps the contest between agents of social control and shadowy groups remains the same never-ending game of cat and mouse? That has been the story thus far. For example, illegal drug markets have remained small, because growing too fast and too large brings unwanted attention; survival has depended on keeping trade within personal networks.[13] Only powerful criminal syndicates like the Italian mafia have been able to operate global, large-scale networks for shadowy matters.[14] But with open secrecy this ability has been "democratized." A tech-savvy group of friends or early collaborators can now build a social network, launch their own cryptocurrency, and implement encrypted communication lines. If the team remains small, their project is a mere experiment, they're just gangs with computers, but if they gain a large following of anonymous actors, they can grow out of their digital basements into a community that has power, something that can act out and live on beyond its founders. Scale matters—more is different. For example, a city is not just a village with a lot more people in it; it's a different thing, it's more complex, erratic, capable, and resilient. Cities have outmuscled nations and outlasted empires.

The practical ability to operate in open secrecy grew out of developments in hardware and software technology, which have made it easier for people to remain anonymous or pseudonymous, while talking to each other and working together, expanding their projects, maintaining personal networks, recruiting participants, and broadcasting their goals and accomplishments. Openly secret groups have organizational capacities that we associate with modern states—they can initiate and maintain large-scale projects with strategic coordination, even when contested by powerful forces such as law enforcement. When people are digitally connected, feel empowered by anonymity or pseudonymity when needed, and are determined to reach their goals, they now have the tools to work together, over country borders, across years and even decades, resolving setbacks and recruiting members along the way. If openly secret networks are kicked off a site or banned from a service—for instance, as private firms are pushed to get extremism off their platforms—or if states take a more direct approach and apprehend or arrest people, the targeted groups can relocate, verify their online personas, discuss their challenges, broadcast communications to their followers, brainstorm problem-solving, rebuild their world, disseminate ideas and solutions, and carry on.

I've included three real-world examples of open secrecy in this book. In the United States the pseudonymous operator of Silk Road, who facilitated millions of dollars of illegal trade over the internet, repeatedly announced and promoted the market's accomplishments online. His follower did the same with Silk Road 2, now even on social media, seemingly in part to poke his nose at law enforcement. When the market was shut down by the Federal Bureau of Investigation, the reconstruction also happened in public. On the other side of the planet—or rather, from many different parts of the planet—a vibrant, global community of pseudonymous software developers created, maintained, and distributed anticensorship tools through open code–sharing platforms. In both cases people carried on even as key figures were targeted by police and/or vanished. In yet another example, far-right actors responded to regulatory pressure by soliciting cloaked cryptocurrency donations, rather than mainstream payment options, rewrote their platform with open-source code, and moved their data off the cloud to private servers.[15]

Other examples of open secrecy that do not feature in this book include file piracy networks, child pornography rings, and "sharing" of academic work like college textbooks and peer-reviewed journal articles.[16] These domains have been studied as separate cases but not as a phenomenon. These underworlds are morally very different, of course (perhaps with child pornography at one end of the spectrum and college textbook piracy at the other), but the domains are similar in that open secrecy has enabled them to remain active for years, in some cases decades. The resource-intensive efforts to stop them have resulted in platform closures, service bans, arrests, and long prison sentences, but these policing "successes" matter little because the communities can carry on, publicly and covertly.

Open secrecy undermines the modern state's ability to achieve its administrative goals through surveillance—not as in counterterrorism and CCTV (closed-circuit television) at the corner store, but the systematic collection and storage of information on citizens that has been a central force of modernity and transformed social life over the past several hundred years and more recently transmuted consumer markets into data-generation industries.[17] Such information collection and control undoubtedly continues to characterize modern life, but open secrecy helps people carve out spaces for dark underworlds where they will continue to live, hidden in plain sight, regardless of what state actors do. Open secrecy, in other words, diminishes state sovereignty. Open secrecy is a value-neutral force of liberation that renders conventional social control strategies ineffective and tells us, shows us, that the ability to steer society in a particular direction, which has always been a daunting challenge, is complicated further by the empowerment of shadowy groups.

Studying Open Secrecy

I started collecting data for this project as a journalist in Oslo, in 2013. I wrote several articles about e-commerce of banned goods and services, and interviewed drug dealers and customers. One interviewee, a seller of 2C-B (a chemically synthesized drug with psychedelic effects), told me through encrypted messages that he was "cooking" at home, did all transactional work online, and sent his products by post. He never met a drug-market person in real life. He continued his operation for years after we spoke, and word is that he retired orderly, by choice, as what two people called a "legend." He was what Walter White could have been—without all the violence and destructive hunger for power—and his story suggests that e-commerce tools widen access to trade in the underworld. If you're tech-savvy and have the know-how to make chemical drugs, you can set up shop and operate a global drug distribution operation, even if you lack the capacity for physical brutality.

When I moved to Boston for graduate studies, I was determined to continue studying this digital underbelly, now with academic rigor and patience. I set up a system for systematic data collection in my weathered Allston apartment, and every morning for the next ten months or so, I'd wake up, stretch a bit, walk up to a desktop computer on my wobbly IKEA dresser, and execute a python script that downloaded data from several drug e-commerce markets. This routine annoyed my partner but built the empirical foundation for numerous research papers. I gradually realized that underneath all the drug-trade stuff there's a bigger story about a more consequential phenomenon: the combination of mass communication and anonymization tools, which enabled people to operate on public websites, with verifiable, secure pseudonyms, and build things together, broadcast ideas and emotions, develop personal ties, and foster communities. This open secrecy, as I ended up calling it, is a value-neutral force of liberation and organizational action that undermines the sovereign state—the steward and protagonist of modernity.

Years later, now an assistant professor at the University of Illinois, a friend told me that the digital underworld of drugs I'd written about reminded her of censorship circumvention in China. I investigated and realized that she was right. The circumventors operated in a globally dispersed ecosystem of transgressive software development, and its longevity suggests that not even the Chinese Communist Party can stop openly secret networks. Then, on January 6, 2021, I found my third empirical case, back in the United States. The siege on the Capitol and the mainstreaming of the far right that had enabled it was a stark reminder of how open secrecy's empowerment of shadowy groups can, notwithstanding the positive connotations of liberty and social movements, be unambiguously antisocial. I scraped data from Stormfront, the KKK-affiliated online community, and when a far-right scholar encouraged me to go further, I decided to include the Daily Stormer and Gab, so my analysis captured the digital far right's three largest domains.

My preferred data-mining approach for all three cases analyzed in this book—digital drug trade, anti-censorship development, and the digital far right—was to first use Python to generate lists of all the URLs I wanted to download (e.g., discussionthread1, discussionthread2, and so on). I then wrote additional scripts to download the html files to my disk, and a third set of scripts to scrape, clean, and wrangle the downloaded content. I also used TelegramScrap, developed by ECM Silva, and data from Gab was purchased from Open Measures.

Most of the computational tools that textbooks discuss are quantitative, but in my view it is bad practice to do any kind of text analysis without actually reading at least some of the material, and ideally a lot of it.[18] All of my quantitative analyses in this book—for instance, measures of how software development practices changed after a police intervention or how the far-right's hate changes its focus over time—were both preceded and followed by careful reading of relevant conversations between people.

The chapters on the digital far right include findings from a novel text analysis approach that I developed in a recent research project.[19] My goals in the different analyses I conducted are explained in those chapters, but many of them are based on measures of extremism in all the written posts and articles that I had collected from the three sites. I operationalized extremism as how often people used extreme keywords in their messages. For example, someone who frequently referred to the conspiracy theory that the United States is actually a Zionist Occupation Government (ZOG) would be considered conspiratorial, and if the talk about ZOG increased over time in the person's posts, that would be considered an increase in extremism.

How did I find keywords for my topic models (where one was "conspiratorial talk," another "talk about Black people," etc.)? I first used a simple neural net model (word2vec) to convert the collected far-right text data—tens of millions of posts—into a word embedding, which maps every single word in the data in a multidimensional vector space based on the words' contextual co-occurrence in the corpus. This process took more than a week. Next I used my own list of seed words for each topic (e.g., seed words for the "white race" topic included "whites" and "white_nationalism") to identify semantically related terms (such as "aryan"). All discovered words that could have multiple meanings were evaluated. For example, when I wanted to measure the prevalence of talk about Black people, I wasn't sure if I could use the word "black," as it could refer to many things (black metal, black hole, etc.). But my reading of three hundred randomly selected examples of that keyword in its context showed that in more than nine out of ten cases, the word did indeed refer to Black people and is thus a valid measure of that topic. This inductive approach to topic word discovery helped me discover dozens of words to include in my topic dictionaries that I would not have found on my own, such as local slang for different racial and ethnic groups (which I will not reprint here) and particular concepts that carry important meaning (e.g., different words for people who sleep with nonwhite people).

I have included methodological footnotes when I deemed it important to explain how I arrived at estimates or findings, but I also strived to keep such details to a minimum, and the measures as simple as possible, to focus on the story that I tell through my empirical analyses. I have, however, maintained the same academic rigor of my scholarly training and my peer-reviewed journal articles throughout the work on this book. For instance, whenever I present qualitative findings, such as quotes from drug-trade or far-right discussions, I have without exception read (and reread) far more than what I present, and I never cherry-picked statements.

My approach to qualitative content analysis is to first immerse myself in the data at hand and read until the content starts to feel repetitive and no salient findings or patterns emerge—a sign that data saturation has been reached. I then start over and read the same content again with a focused perspective, looking for specific examples that, when combined, represent broader themes in the data. For example, when I wanted to understand how far-righters talk about race following a specific terrorist attack, I read hundreds of posts about key incidents—which were carefully selected to be representative of terror. I read the content several times and included quotes that captured the sentiments in the bigger dataset.[20] I also conducted interviews—twenty-three in total. These participants were recruited through theoretical sampling—I asked people who seemed like they might be able to provide valuable insights and perspectives on puzzles that emerged from the project, such as why drug-market actors spent so much time talking to each other when e-commerce enabled impersonal exchange, or how hackers ended up carrying on the work after losing peers. As I believe is best practice in mixed-methods research, I crisscrossed between reading and counting patterns, and talking to people, which allowed the different types of inquiries to inform each other.

The chapters that follow include many quotes. Most have been trimmed and slightly edited for clarity and/or to protect participants, as linguistic idiosyncrasies can potentially aid identification. I include citations if I use material that is publicly available (e.g., social media posts or letters from a court case), unless the content is drawn directly from my own archival data mining research or interviews. When I use pseudonyms, they are *additional* pseudonyms for accounts that no longer exist. For sources that are still active online (e.g., on GitHub or Stormfront), quotes are anonymous, unless the source is a convicted criminal (like Dylann Roof) or is or was a public or publicly known figure (like Andrew Torba and Clowwindy).

My goal is not to collect evidence of amoral activities but to examine and elucidate structural patterns that can help us understand how information technology contributes to social change by undermining state power. That is, the book's three cases are different, and while I certainly have my views on them, their similarities are more important. They all illustrate how, for better or worse, the combination of openness and secrecy enable novel organizational forms that make human societies harder to govern. Even the world's most resourceful organizations in their respective domains—such as American and European law enforcement, the Chinese Communist Party, and Big Tech—are unable to halt their influences. That's open secrecy.

2 The Three Acts of the Information Age

Act One: The "Premodern" Internet

Humanity is part of a small group of mammals that use technology to navigate their environment—monkeys and whales do so too—and might be the only species that uses it to create entirely new universes.[1] My household joined the internet when I was about eleven. I remember the thrill of creating a new persona and the allure of finding out who was behind the chat room usernames (ASL?). The opportunity to speak with people from different parts of the world was particularly appealing for a child in a Norwegian town with a population of fifteen thousand. I somehow ended up befriending a thirty-something man from São Paulo, who said he liked the band a-ha and Morten Harket. We spent hours chatting, and eventually he sent me an envelope with what appeared to be photographs. I opened it and found a shot of him wearing a white T-shirt and entirely ordinary shorts. It was all very innocent. I think.

The ability to communicate with globally dispersed strangers was magical and way more tangible when the internet first entered homes in the 1990s, as it had to be dialed up over twenty-nine melodic seconds that seemed full of struggle. The technology that made it all work was constructed by researchers in academia and industry who had been bankrolled by the US military, who wanted an effective communication system that was spread across multiple hubs and was thus resilient enough to survive a nuclear attack. Early internet funding was diverted from a missile defense system project.[2] As the Cold War ended, cyberspace developed into an anarchistic world reminiscent of premodern cities, where there was no centralized planning or rule. Instead, life was locally organized (e.g., in online communities). Generally the chaos worked for people who lived in it—people knew where to go to find what they were looking for, and like other "foreign" cultural worlds, local symbols and norms made sense to the people who inhabit that world and "get it," even if it might seem incoherent and meaningless to outsiders.[3]

The individual and collective autonomy and organizational capabilities enabled by the internet should make governments afraid, some argued, as people could now build communities on their own terms.[4] The internet is a decentralized communication system without an overarching institutional shape—and thus people can add new networks to existing ones as they see fit or partake in online communities centered on things they find important and meaningful. Technologists like Michael and Rona Hauben marveled at these newfound possibilities. They predicted that with information technology available to everyone, we would create a free and better world in which we all belonged, regardless of race, class, or gender. People would consider strangers their compatriots, because online we live next door to every other netizen in the world, and we can all hang out, much like I chatted with my pal from São Paulo.[5] The internet was thus the start of a new and better way of living. The state might have driven its mechanical development, but the people took over and built a global, chaotic universe with scattered meeting points, unique cultural diasporas, and novel ways of living together.

But predictions are risky. For example, AT&T initially believed that only businesses would be interested in the telephone.[6] What was once one of America's largest technology companies, Digital Equipment Corporation, didn't think anyone would want a computer in their home.[7] The Nobel laureate Paul Krugman famously said in 1998 that the internet would fail, as it "becomes apparent [that] most people have nothing to say to each other."[8] The Haubens were also wrong: The internet did not become the global, über-diverse community that they envisioned, because people prefer conversation partners who agree with their own political and ideological leanings—that is, people who are like themselves.[9] Even people who actively seek out difference often just want a little bit of it—they want the comfortably exotic.[10]

However, echo chambers are not all bad: homogenous groups can bring fresh perspectives to the world as people are more likely to speak out in a safe place, where they can raise and discuss rough and newfound ideas. These alternative perspectives can expand the culture's broader argument pool.[11] Sites where anonymous or pseudonymous people can talk openly about things they otherwise want to keep hidden—digital backspaces—has been a central feature of the internet, empowering spatially dispersed groups whose members engage in stigmatized but harmless behavior (such as sexual kinks) but also dangerous ideas (such as justifications of violent extremism in the name of Islam or white nationalism). These cases suggest that the internet's force of liberation should not be read normatively, even if the word "liberty" has so many wonderful connotations.

The internet is a portal to many universes. Bored in high school, I joined one discussion board devoted to Norwegian hip-hop (which is better than you think)—it had its own memes, one of which even ended up on a T-shirt. (Its appeal was that only a few hundred people in the world would get the joke.) Two decades later, when I asked my students at the University of Illinois which online worlds appeal to them, most seemed to have found at least one that was valuable to them, and several mentioned a musical subgenre with more cultural clout—K-pop—which has become what it is today largely owing to its tens of millions of tech-savvy and intensely devoted followers, who appreciate its novel mix of innocence and cool.[12] In the words of one American fan, a Black woman from Mississippi: "Getting into Korean culture was a way for me to see a different world."[13]

Communities that are primarily online have been referred to as "virtual"[14] places in which people are "alone together,"[15] but the reality of a community should be measured by the reality of its consequences—the extent to which it has a genuine and demonstrable effect on its members.[16] By this definition, there is no doubt that online communities are as real as any place-bound ones: they display strong group norms of support and reciprocity, sometimes extraordinarily high levels of empathy among members, and relationships that can be deeply meaningful, foster committed and continuing interaction, and organize collective action, even if participants remain at home.[17]

I grew up when internet usage was expensive and on the clock, so my main pop-cultural snorkel was television. I loved watching it so much that my father, who was furious about my addiction to the "the box," as he called it, removed it for a year. Draconian or not, he did have a point: TV watching is primarily a passive practice. The internet is different. Connected people can team up, communicate, make something that's valuable to themselves, their peers, larger interest networks, and perhaps even global audiences.[18] In the early 2000s, computers' capacity for content creation—now turbocharged by AI—was heralded as a way to challenge the dominance of the mass-media conglomerates that had consolidated during the Reagan and Clinton eras.[19] *Time* magazine was oddly prescient when in 2006 it declared that the Person of the Year was "You."

"You" can be plural, and the internet has undoubtedly empowered collective actors. American K-pop fans, for example, have used their energy, social media acumen, and organizational prowess not only to support their idols by making particular songs go viral but also for political purposes—for instance, when they signed up for free tickets to a Donald Trump rally and then failed to show up to leave the arena empty, spammed an online birthday card for the same man, donated $1 million to Black Lives Matter groups, and flooded trending white supremacy hashtags with fancams, short videos, or animated images of performers.[20] When the Dallas Police Department asked people to report "illegal activity from [BLM] protests," K-pop fans crashed the app. User @ygshit captured the spirit: "guys download the app and FLOOD that shit with fancams make it SO HARD for them to find anything besides our faves dancing." A few days later a similar app from the Grand Rapids Police Department was taken down after user @ngelwy posted: "you know the drill! SEND IN ALL OF YOUR FANCAMS!!! CRASH THE WEBSITE!!! PROTECT THE PROTESTORS!!!"[21]

The antigovernment protests and uprisings of the Arab Spring, beginning in December 2010 and ending in late 2012, is the canonical example of tech-aided social movements. An inexperienced Egyptian protester explained in an article in the *Cairo Review of Global Affairs* how she joined other demonstrators in Tahrir Square in early 2011 in part because social media made it easy to do so.[22] "There is no doubt," she wrote, "that social networking helped" catalyze the Arab Spring. By extending the public sphere to cyberspace, digital movements offer multiple avenues through which people can experience collective passion, cooperate strategically, share images and ideas, and express their commitment.[23] Social movements have historically been backed by resourceful organizations such as labor unions or fronted by powerful leaders, but digital, contemporary social movements are more likely to be (or at least appear to be) leaderless, as the individual protesters are given ample space to articulate their own idiosyncratic dreams and grievances on social media. This in turn invites a wider range of participation—which is particularly important for movements in our contemporary time, when class consciousness seems a distant hope, the influence of traditional institutions has waned, and people instead find meaning in alternative lifestyles.[24]

Digital collaboration can make a real impact not just by allowing people to express emotional sentiments that may resonate widely but also because people can build things together—another contrast with television. A mundane yet remarkable case is Wikipedia, which could not have been created without the information technology tools that enable collaboration among millions of globally dispersed people on long-term projects and complex tasks involving writing in a standardized style, resolving disputes, handling corrections, and dealing with acts of sabotage.[25] Although we now take Wikipedia for granted, it remains the world's largest and most accessible public summary of verifiable knowledge—a striking case of what people can accomplish together in the information age.[26]

Act Two: "Modern" Surveillance Ambitions

The widespread and unwavering belief in science as a tool for social progress first emerged with the mechanical wonders of industrialization in the late 1700s, at the advent of modernity. As people saw immense productivity gains from their implementation of new technology, they started to expect improvements in science, technology, and data-driven development of human societies, and at large, they anticipated a future characterized by order. The modern belief was that the human world was a big, complicated jigsaw puzzle, and if scholars, philosophers, mathematicians, and poets can put the pieces together, we will get the absolute truth about how the world works and what we should do while we're part of it.[27]

These delusions were tempered around the turn of the millennium as people became increasingly anxious about grand, global risks—such as nuclear meltdowns, terrorism, and environmental disasters—but the modern, optimist spirit was still strong in Silicon Valley. An example is this quote from a senior systems architect at a large technology firm, about the Internet of Things (IoT): "Ninety-eight percent of the things in the world are not connected. So we're gonna connect them. It could be a moisture temperature that sits in the ground. It could be your liver. That's your IoT. . . . We'll visualize it, make sense of it, and monetize it. That's our IoT."[28] The human world, it's suggested, can be turned into information bits that can be repurposed for a wide range of organizational goals. For example, data trails can help the police track down their targets.[29] They can also help grocery stores predict customers' pregnancies based on their shopping data.[30] Developments in artificial intelligence are driven by a similar perspective. For example, the mission of the company xAI, founded by Elon Musk, is to "understand the Universe," and to computer scientist and physicist Stephen Wolfram, the remarkable capabilities of human-mimicking AI models suggest that even how we think and make sense of the world may be governed by discoverable physics-like laws that can be analyzed by researchers.[31] Modern optimism about how technology can help us find missing pieces in that grand jigsaw puzzle prevails: with the help of data science, we can figure it all out.

Data about the world has always benefitted organizations, of course, but the omnipresence of the internet has made human life legible at an extraordinary scale, and data harvesting has become something of a moral imperative. Technology firms now say that big data, computational power, software innovations, and specific forms of digital skill can, will, and should transform the world. Call it the church of data science. Google, for example, makes many of its big and small decisions based on data instead of just leadership thinking. According to Marissa Mayer, a former executive at the company, the firm puts young and inexperienced people in charge of much more experienced engineers to keep the focus on the data: "Because [these managers lead] people who are so much more senior and more experienced, they don't have the authority to say, 'Because I said so.' They need to gather the data, lobby the team, and win them over by data."[32] A project manager who wants to implement new ideas can order up an experiment in which one of every hundred users gets an experimental version of her product, and if the results support her, she can use that quantitative evidence to push for her proposed changes. This organizational strategy ensures that decisions are not gut-driven but based on data.

It works well for product development. Steve Jobs famously said that his job was not to give customers what they wanted but to "figure out what they're going to want before they do," and technology companies have become really good at doing just that.[33] This is most obvious on social media platforms that are designed to keep us engaged, by selecting and deselecting bits of reality, for a representation of life that is not about accuracy but about user retention: increasingly, the entire digital world is composed of cherry-picked bits of reality that make life seem prettier, full of exciting news, livelier, more urgent, than it really is—reality is hyperreal. Algorithms, which have their own biases, make choices for us, in what we read online, what music we listen to, what's deemed important. This curated landscape shapes what we care about, how we think, what we like and dislike, and how we feel about ourselves.[34]

In addition to figuring out what people want and then giving them boatloads of it—an old practice mastered by the gambling industry— technology firms use data to shape our behavior.[35] Uber, for example, has implemented psychological gamification techniques to get its drivers to stay behind the wheel longer than they normally would. The platform adds a new ride to the driver's schedule before the current one is completed, making it easy to go right on to the next fare, much like how Netflix autoplays the next TV episode to encourage binge-watching; upon starting to log off, drivers are notified that they are ever so close to hitting a precious earnings target ("One more ride and you've earned $300 today!").[36] Off the road, Netflix correctly predicted that its show *House of Cards*, a remake of a UK series by the same name, would be a success because it had data on user preferences. They knew (1) that people generally completed work of the show's director, David Fincher, (2) that films with Kevin Spacey did well, and (3) that the original English version of *House of Cards* was a hit. As the company's chief communications officer said, "We know what people like to watch and that helps us understand how big the interest is going to be for a given show."[37] As the predictive model worked, we'll likely see another series that combines "famous actor," "director of captivating tales," and "British TV writing." We might even enjoy that new show more because it's comfortably exotic, and as we keep watching, we make the formula ever more accurate and more likely to influence future decisions at Netflix and elsewhere, perhaps to the point that we face an abundance of material that is always the same or gradually moves in a familiar direction, never steering off the safe, well-trodden path.

Aware of data's power but unsure of how to wield it, Big Tech frequently conducts experiments. In one such trial run, Meta presented about 690,000 Facebook users with either mostly positive content, such as posts from happy friends on vacation, or mostly negative content. The firm's researchers found that people exposed to positive stimuli were more likely to share positive posts themselves, and the others were more likely to share negative posts, suggesting that content curation influences how we feel—or at least the feelings we opt to express.[38] In another experiment, this one involving more than 60 million users, Meta researchers found that people who were presented with a list of close friends who had clicked on an "I voted" button were 0.39 percent more likely to vote than people who received a similar message without information about whether their friends had voted. That small number amounts to an estimated

60,000 people who were directly inspired by a Facebook message to go to the polls, plus another 280,000 who voted because of social contagion in the offline world.[39] For Meta and other tech companies the takeaway of this study was that social media curation can modify our behavior.

States have always had similar ambitions—they see data collection and management as means to expand and maintain power. Consider that modern European states invented surnames and permanent addresses to boost tax income and enable military conscription, or how they redeveloped messy, labyrinth-like streetscapes of premodern city boulevards—which were difficult to govern—in the name of public order.[40] In the contemporary United States the National Security Agency (NSA) and other intelligence agencies gobble down the data they can access legally, sometimes more than that, for fundamentally similar reasons—to make the noisy, messy world legible and thus easier to analyze and control.[41] Like surnames and residential addresses helped states keep track of people and their capital, digital identifiers in our computers and phones bring order to cyberspace. For example, as former NSA intelligence contractor Edward Snowden explained in an interview after disclosing information about NSA surveillance: "The movements of your phone are the movements of you as a person . . . every smartphone is constantly connected to the nearest cellular tower. Even if the screen is turned off, your smartphone is still screaming, 'Here I am! Here is my IMEI (Individual Manufacturer Equipment Identity), and here is my IMSI (Individual Manufacturer Subscriber Identity).'"[42] NSA's former director, Keith Alexander, justified the agency's intelligence systems in 2013: "[We] have contributed to understanding and disrupting 54 terror-related events—25 in Europe, 11 in Asia, and five in Africa and 13 in the United States. This was no accident. This was not a coincidence. These are the direct results of a dedicated workforce, appropriate policy and well-sculpted authorities created in the wake of

9/11 to make sure 9/11 never happens again."[43] Alexander argued that surveillance is worth the cost, and the intrusive feeling it generates in the public, because lives are saved. (He did not speculate about whether a different deployment of the agency's vast resources could have achieved a similar or better outcome.)

Information technology also helps states squash political dissent. China's expansive system of citizen surveillance, which dates back hundreds of years and currently involves tens of thousands of workers, has been given major high-tech updates for the internet age and has become, despite its considerable human and economic costs, better coordinated and equipped than any other autocratic surveillance system in history.[44] Yet the Chinese Communist Party (CCP) collects far more data on its citizens than it is able to process; a completely automated surveillance system "is still the stuff of science fiction."[45] Western states have similar challenges. In a public meeting at the Defense Innovation Board, Eric Schmidt, formerly Google's CEO and Alphabet's executive chairman, noted that the Department of Defense generates an enormous amount of data that it actually never uses because it doesn't know how to or what to do with it.[46] Both here and there, the availability of information and the lure of newfound means to mine and organize information on citizens appears to have fostered a compulsion to hoard it. I can relate. I learned how to code to collect data for my research on drug trade, and now that I have the know-how to mine data from online domains, I sometimes find myself thinking, what can I do with all the information that is available to me? What else should I collect? What can I do with what I have? Sometimes I tell myself: *stop*.

In both the East and West the symbiosis between firms and states deepened as they learned how to use data to achieve their goals. In China the National Intelligence Law of 2017 compels all local firms and entities to support, assist, and cooperate with Chinese intelligence by turning over data collected abroad and domestically, whenever asked.[47] Private enterprise doesn't face the same coercion in the United States, but the state has other means of achieving its goals. For example, the Central Intelligence Agency (CIA) has launched a venture capital firm (In-Q-Tel) to make it easier to invest in start-ups and thus access their innovative technologies.[48] The list of In-Q-Tel's beneficiaries is long: its website's snapshot of investments includes 750 companies, as of August 2024, and many others are kept secret. Big Tech leaders are increasingly onboard, and this didn't start with Trump. In 2019, Amazon's Jeff Bezos spoke at the Reagan National Defense Forum, arguing that technology companies need to help protect and advance US technological supremacy.[49]

Bezos said that "if Big Tech is going to turn their back on national defense, this country is in trouble," adding, "we're the good guys."[50] He had at least one private meeting with then–defense secretary James Mattis. Eric Schmidt helped found the Defense Department's Defense Innovation Board, which included Kurt DelBene of Microsoft, Milo Medin of Google, Marne Levine of Meta, and LinkedIn cofounder Reid Hoffman. Schmidt has called on his peers to see the government as a partner in research and development: "We are in a technology competition with China that has profound ramifications for our economy and defense. . . . Americans should be wary of living in a world shaped by China's view of the relationship between technology and authoritarian governance. Free societies must prove the resilience of liberal democracy in the face of technological changes that threaten it."[51]

The internet that the Haubens wrote about—a digital world characterized by anarchy, play, and creativity—is long gone. It has instead become a surveilled filterworld, closely watched by states and dominated by a few technology companies that share a zealous faith in data science's ability to map and make sense of social life. But the expanded surveillance has made some people really good at hiding, and as their methods disseminate, in part because people are fed up with being watched, the state is undermined.

Act Three: Late Modernity—A Digital Runaway World

Enthusiasm about the technology sector peaked around the release of the hit movie the *Social Network* in 2010 and petered out the same decade. Although Big Tech's platforms, gadgets, and services have become more or less essential for everyday life, they're also seen as intrusive, addictive, detrimental to mental health (in particular for teenagers), and so profitable that the firms that make them have been compared not to classic big companies like Ford or ExxonMobil but parasitic overlords bigger than capitalism and powerful nation-states.[52]

It's worth a quick thought experiment. If we define power as the ability to shape outcomes in your favor, what would you say is the most powerful entity in the world today: Apple or France? Only one of the two has a license to kill (a salient difference in perhaps a flawed comparison), but the point is that today's tech firms are in a league of their own. America's largest technology companies are so rich that the chief economics commentator at the *Financial Times*, Martin Wolf—who is not known for hyperbole—named them "masters of the universe" and called for more regulation, a rare sight in a business newspaper.[53] Wolf's critique was penned in 2017, before a global pandemic and work-from-home transformation made us even more dependent on technology and before the AI gold rush that started in late 2022. The market cap of the so-called Big Five—Apple, Alphabet, Microsoft, Amazon, and Meta—more than doubled from late 2022 to late 2024, from 6.4 trillion to 12.5 trillion.[54] The world's largest national sovereign wealth fund is by comparison worth $1.8 trillion.[55]

As noted, Big Tech shares some of the hubris of modern states, who relished their ability to build what they imagined to be a better world—for instance, through urban planning. A central flaw is the presumption that the experts in charge—be it modern state leaders or Big Tech CEOs—can forecast the future and realize their schemes.

Grand projects often fail and sometimes backfire in surprising ways, a realization that has fueled a late-modern skepticism of expert planning.[56] An example in the digital realm is how Meta tried to figure out what it can do with all the information they had access to; the company decided to make data available to the public, which would increase the number of bright minds digging through their datasets and thus speed up innovation. When something really clicks, they can emulate the ideas, much like how Amazon analyzes its data to see what sells and then introduces their own versions of the same product under an Amazon brand. In 2014 a data scientist named Aleksandr Kogan was hired by the British political consulting firm Cambridge Analytica to harvest data that was now there for the taking.[57]

Kogan created a Facebook app called This Is Your Digital Life—downloaded by about three hundred thousand people in 2014 and 2015—which collected data from not only those who installed it but also all the data of their friends. In total, Cambridge Analytica amassed information on up to eighty-seven million Facebook users, which helped the company dispatch targeted political advertising for their clients and possibly swayed the British electorate to the side of Brexit and American voters toward then US presidential candidate Donald Trump.[58] The scandal helped people realize that data science has no intrinsic moral compass, and that with the state-sized power of Big Tech comes state-sized disasters. Meta no longer makes its data easily available to third parties, but has the company really learned from its mistakes? The decision to invest tens of billions developing open-source AI models that are freely available suggests that it hasn't.[59] Inviting outside innovation is not a bad idea in itself, but we're operating on an unprecedented scale—projects that involve data from hundreds of millions or even billions of people should not be treated as just another experiment, because the consequences are beyond what we can imagine.

Big Tech's R&D will yield products that slot into familiar categories, such as virtual reality solutions for watching movies and holograms for video calls. I will probably end up using many of them. More concerning are the "unknown unknowns" in the tech sector's R&D—truly innovative innovations that use data in unexpected ways. Here's one example: The vehicles of Waymo, Alphabet's self-driving company, and Tesla have completed millions of miles on public roads in dozens of American cities, during which they recorded video of other cars, pedestrians, cyclists, and an unknown range of other variables. The primary point of collecting this data is to reduce uncertainties for their autonomous vehicles, in part by teaching them what to do when something unexpected happens, such as being run off the road by people who dislike having robo-cars in their neighborhood.[60] But the data—where people go, how they get there, what they do, who they're with, how they move their bodies, what they wear, and so on—will be used for other purposes, many of which are as yet unknown to the companies themselves. Godlike knowledge of human life in the hands of a few mighty corporations that innovate first and ask for forgiveness later and have the resources to fight regulation is concerning because we do not know what their engineers or third-party collaborators might do.

I wrote most of the paragraph above in 2019. At the time I thought I'd come up with a good example of how private data collection might one day be used in unforeseen ways, and I can now pat my younger self on the back. Tesla recently announced that the company will use its vehicle-training video data to help humanoid robots navigate the world: in the words of Tesla's former head of AI, Andrej Karpathy, the company's experimental robot "currently thinks it's a car," because it navigates based on the company's self-driving data.[61] It's possible that this development will be good for the world. Perhaps even likely. We don't yet know. But we do know that data collected by technology firms will be used in unforeseen ways, and we often won't know about it until after it has been done. Perhaps until after the *damage* has been done. Meta's former motto, for example—"move fast and break things"—would more truthfully be "risky bets with fingers crossed."

Cyberspace is now dominated by a handful of companies that maintain an outsize role in the economy while employing few workers and harvesting data from all of us, even past generations, for AI training. People know that they're being manipulated by addictive algorithmic feeds, seduced by convenience, and watched by eyes in the sky.[62] The mix of private wealth concentration, inescapable snooping, and the sense that the human world has become a lab for intelligence gathering and corporate product design has fostered a growing sense of disenchantment in the public, on both sides of the political spectrum. That's our present. That's the information age's third act. Representative surveys show that Big Tech, once seen as a beacon of innovation and a better future, is now seen as all too powerful.[63] And most people disapprove of mass surveillance.[64] When I asked my students at the University of Illinois to describe the tech sector with one word—be it positive, neutral, or negative—these were their responses:

greedy	intrusive	unethical
problematic	manipulative	naive
complex	invasive	double-edged
sneaky	shady	sword
stalkers	invasive	intrusive
entitled	unregulated	controlling
manipulative	powerful	controlling
complex	arrogant	problematic
corrupt	parasite	pervasive
disturbing	sleazy	manipulative

controlling	invasive	sneaky
two-faced	invasive	insidious
manipulative	corporate	shady

The three most common descriptors were *controlling*, *invasive*, and *manipulative*. My students are not representative of the general population, or even the student body at the University of Illinois where I taught this class, but the sentiment is widespread—a majority of Americans now worry about surveillance.[65]

It has been argued that contemporary surveillance systems are so opaque and complex that opting out seems futile.[66] But people are starting to figure out how they can hide. Millions have downloaded apps for protected messaging, and by doing so, they push back or at least nudge against the state-corporate surveillance symbiosis that dominates contemporary societies, as companies like Meta and state organizations like the NSA collect and analyze individual-level data.[67] For people who are involved in controversial or banned activities, contemporary surveillance is an acute threat to personal safety and organizational survival, and as I document in this book's three parts, the digital underworld has figured out how they can remain hidden.

Many readers may be prone to root for people who fight state surveillance, but this is not a story of good guys fighting "the system." Salient differences between my three cases—the digital drug trade, censorship evasion, and the digital far right—remind us that opaque networks can be both prosocial *and* antisocial. These three underworlds are similar in that they show how information technology empowers shadowy groups, even in a time characterized by mass surveillance and capitalist surveillance, and thus they represent a force of change that deserves our attention. Modernity made us think we could control human progress with technology, or at least keep it on the right course, and these ideas were in some corners reinforced in the early information age. But we are gradually being freed from that delusion. We now see that we live in what scholars have described as a runaway world, in which technological progress brings about unpredictable change, and the state is losing control of where we're headed.[68] Not even the world's most powerful law enforcements, governments, and firms can steer social change in the direction they prefer. But change is coming.

I   *Drug Trade on the Darknet*

3 *Illegal Markets Step Out of the Shadows*

A young Texan named Ross Ulbricht had big plans in 2010. He wrote on social media that he wanted to create "an economic simulation to give people a first-hand experience of what it would be like to live in a world without the systemic use of force." The following year, Ulbricht launched Silk Road, a new kind of e-commerce market that relied on anonymization software, cryptocurrency, and the hardworking employees of the US Postal Service (and soon their global colleagues) to enable exchange of banned products and services. It looked like a bare-bones version of eBay or Amazon. Silk Road was initially a one-man operation. Ulbricht personally answered user messages, fixed "constant security holes," and processed payments. "When the [payments] came into my local Bitcoin client, I matched them up with the amount and time of the purchase and did all of the necessary account adjustments."[1] Ulbricht promoted the market on a public forum for Bitcoin enthusiasts, characterizing it as a libertarian project with sellers and buyers finding mutually agreeable prices. "As of today, 28 transactions have been made! For those who don't know, Silk Road is an anonymous online market. . . . The general mood of this community is that we are up to something big. . . . Bitcoin and Tor are revolutionary."[2]

The response was broadly supportive, suggesting that Ulbricht's ideas were well aligned with the local community culture and the popularity of libertarian beliefs, held by roughly 20 percent of Americans.[3] It was libertarians who later campaigned for Ulbricht's release from prison. Donald Trump said he would free him if reelected, and when he was, he did. But back in 2011, the Bitcoin community was skeptical of Ulbricht's creation, although mostly on practical and not normative grounds. "What happens if a buyer ends up in jail and can't affirm the shipment arrived?" "[Or] just doesn't respond?" Ulbricht explained how the market's escrow system worked:

1. buyer places an order.
2. funds held in escrow.
3a. seller confirms shipment.
3b. seller never responds, buyer's funds are returned.
4a. buyer confirms delivery and funds are released [to the seller].
4b. buyer claims that the order never came. Buyer and seller have a few days to come to a resolution before admin will review the case and make a judgment.
4c. buyer never responds, funds are released to seller.

Escrow protected the interests of both buyers and sellers. Market order was further supported by conventional e-commerce solutions: vendor profiles and crowdsourced reputation data enabled buyers to make informed decisions.[4] When needed, Ulbricht could mediate disagreements and thus mitigate risks associated with nondelivery or nonresponse. His claim of having a staff was untrue at the time of his post, but after a few months, Ulbricht had hired a few helpers.

One concern in the responses in the same forum was the involvement of postal workers and delivery addresses:

MCDIRT: Does all this stuff just get shipped through the regular mail? I'm too paranoid to take the risk.

Ulbricht responded that buyers can simply "deny ordering anything," as "anyone can send anyone else anything through the mail." Moral concerns were also raised.

> TREADSTONE: Where do [you] draw the line, or is there even one? . . . If someone is cutting people up and selling their organs . . . is Silk Road going to delete the post?
> CREDO: Being against . . . laws that prohibit the free trade of particular plant products . . . is not the same as being against true crime.
> DIRECT: I would have to agree with that. Stealing someone's property creates a victim. . . . Growing something the state doesn't like and selling it is not a crime.

Posters agreed the line for permitted goods needs to be drawn somewhere, even in a market for banned goods. Ulbricht later clarified Silk Road's policy on the matter, in the market's own discussion forum.[5] Under a pseudonym he wrote: "Do not list anything whose purpose is to harm or defraud, such as stolen items or info, stolen credit cards, counterfeit currency, personal info, assassinations, and weapons of any kind. Do not list anything related to pedophilia." Ulbricht gave market participants a cognitive prosthesis by which they could navigate a morally contested realm.

User signups spiked when the first media report on the site was published in June 2011.[6] Two years later, when monthly trade on Silk Road had reached $7.5 million, I interviewed a man who had recently moved his "largeish" hash and opium business to Silk Road after "quite a few years" in the game.[7] The ability to trade in open secrecy had transformed the business. This man told me: "Our goals are different [now]. . . . Here you can make structured plans, attainable goals; you can expand in a controlled manner." He deemed digital trade safer than offline trade. "As for 'in real life' selling, that is a definite no [now], even to close friends, family . . . our security policy prohibits this strongly." Another seller I spoke with, a man who specialized in a chemically synthesized psychedelic drug, also had zero face time with his customers. "I don't talk to anyone outside of the markets, [and] I sell nothing offline," he said. "I have no desire to risk exposure in milieus the police might know of." For these two sellers and thousands more like them, open secrecy offered unprecedented opportunities for illegal business. Drug dealing was no longer limited to shadowy exchanges within personal networks, as it usually is.[8] Instead, masked buyers and sellers could trade publicly on the darknet, hidden in plain sight.

Accessing the Darknet

When I first wrote about darknet trade as a journalist in 2013, I installed Tor (we'll dive deeper into this shortly), purchased a single Bitcoin (worth about eighty-five dollars at the time), signed up for Silk Road, and bought what I judged to be mostly legal: a contact list with details for various hackers. I messaged one person or group and inquired if I could pay them to crash a website I disliked, by overwhelming their server with a flood of internet traffic. "Sure," the person replied. Such a DDoS (distributed denial of service) attack would cost me about one hundred dollars for a twenty-four-hour takedown. "How do I know that you are capable of doing this?" I asked. The hacker proposed taking it down for just a few minutes. Just as any respectable ice-cream shop gives a tiny scoop of its sweet delights to curious browsers, so did the hacker. (I declined the offer.)

Darknet trade, such as the hacker-by-hire service, is typically enabled by the combination of three tools—Tor, cryptocurrency, and a mix of manual and automatic encryption. Tor's utility is that it masks online traffic, by rerouting it through multiple globally dispersed and randomly selected hubs, without recording the trail. This makes it difficult for anyone, including the world's top intelligence agencies, to track down specific IP addresses. That is, if you use the Tor browser to access a particular website—for example, the *New York Times*—your internet service provider (ISP) cannot tell where you're headed, as your traffic first goes through a decoy server in the Tor network. And when you finally land on the *New York Times*, after multiple detours, the site's administrators cannot tell where your journey began, and therefore, *who* you are. Thanks to Tor, people can operate in cyberspace without revealing their real-world identities. Not even subpoenas will help law enforcement, because no one knows where you and your computer are located.

Payments on darknet markets are usually done in Bitcoin (but increasingly in the digital currency Monero). Early on, people thought of Bitcoin as anonymous, but it's actually designed to be traceable as it moves through the blockchain. It nonetheless remains useful in illegal markets as it can be shifted around online without going through banks and commercial payment processors. That means that people can buy Bitcoin with a fraudulent ID or no ID, and then use it to pay for banned goods and services, out of the hands of any regulatory force. Many people use manual encryption to protect their communication and verify their identities, on top of whatever encryption the markets offer (or claim to offer), which I did when I started interviewing drug dealers. The maker and seller of psychedelic chemistry, for example, said he was happy to answer my questions but demanded that we encrypted our electronic messages (he kindly walked me through the process).

Most people, I now know, use the program Pretty Good Privacy (PGP), which is actually *really* good. It's currently uncrackable, even for supercomputers—which is also why the US government tried (and failed) to limit access to it.[9] And encryption is not going anywhere, even in the time of AI: the inventor of PGP, Philip Zimmermann, told me in a phone call that there are ways to encrypt messages that even quantum computers are unlikely to crack.

Encryption works by rendering a given text unreadable to outsiders, which is important to users of darknet markets, in case someone—perhaps police or hackers—gains access to their computers and finds evidence of banned trade. Encryption can also be used to sign a message and thus to verify an online identity as people move across cyberspace, from market to market. Encryption—and the trust people had in it—enabled an openness and directness that is rare in markets for banned goods, where people have good reasons to be as discreet as possible.

Drug Trade Unshackled

In premodern markets, people assessed potential exchange partners based on social distance, where smaller was better (e.g., in kinship, clans, territory, and ethnicity), or formed coalitions to vet and monitor the conduct of strangers. Networks are still important in contemporary trade, as the risk of getting screwed remains, which is why buyers of preowned cars prefer to buy from people they know.[10] But rule of law has made market activity more predictable and conflicts easier to resolve, and today most exchanges are impersonal. Conventional (offline) drug market trade, however, still has premodern characteristics—exchanges go through personal networks, and external and internal constraints impede sophisticated development.[11]

Police operations often force buyers and sellers off the streets before they have the time to establish durable ties and role structures (e.g., understandings of who is selling what, to whom, and how reliably) that market order depends on. The *absence* of law enforcement is also a problem as it creates opportunities for crime between market actors: a robbed drug dealer is unlikely to call the cops. These challenges hamper offline drug markets' growth (unless they have support from powerful crime syndicates with military and political capital), as scale makes them obvious takedown targets.[12] To avoid this, market actors keep their exchange networks small. Although drug dealing on the TV screen often occurs on street corners, where buyers and sellers exchange goods and bills in handshakes, most drug transactions are done in private spaces and within personal networks, where participants know each other or are vetted by mutual connections. In other cases, the only way to build trust is through repeated interactions.[13]

With open secrecy, many of the constraints that have hitherto characterized illegal trade are stripped away.[14] The trust that people build up over time by buying and selling on markets like Silk Road is no longer dependent on people remembering past experiences and connections, but stored in digital data that have the semblance of objectivity. That is, with the tools of Tor, cryptocurrencies, and encryption, actors can participate in crowdsourced feedback systems, such as Amazon-like star ratings that build up as buyers and sellers trade and even write detailed consumer reports.[15] These reputation measures become tangible proxies for trust that can be publicly displayed (e.g., linked to in seller profiles) and even exported (more on this in the next chapter). In other research I've called such publicly available information for social credit "data": people's digital footprints, such as qualitative reviews and quantitative ratings serve as proxies for trustworthiness, status, and economic potential.[16]

Moreover, because darknet markets enable open and anonymous (or pseudonymous) communication, sellers can even advertise their goods—an impossibility in conventional illegal markets.[17] For instance, drug vendors can make claims about drug purity ("1g MDMA crystals purity 84%+"), origin ("0.2 g Uncut Quality Peruvian Cocaine"), pharmaceutical manufacturing ("Oxycontin 30 mg/10 tabs Teva"), and lab test results ("5 g Pure Crystal Happiness! Lab-Tested 80%+ Europe's Finest MDMA"). Buyers, meanwhile, can go window shopping and assess the worth of a good as a category (e.g., cannabis or cocaine) and in relation to other goods of the same type

(Yasmin's cocaine versus Jerry's cocaine). The marketing information in the darknet economy isn't backed by legal guarantees of course, and accusations of fraud—such as undelivered orders—are common. But risk is dramatically reduced compared to offline drug markets. Market operators can administrate economic activity much like states do: they can surveil and assess economic activity, sanction rulebreakers, mediate conflicts, and tax participation.

The New World

Open secrecy gave people the ability to build a new and different world, with legal worries sidelined, or at least dramatically reduced. It was a remarkable opportunity to do something different but also a challenging one. Legal constraints are more than practical obstacles: they sit deep and shape how people think and act.[18] Someone who has been helicopter-parented her entire upbringing might relish the freedom of adulthood but also find herself structuring her new life in familiar ways. To get a sense of how darknet market consumers frame their activities now that they could speak freely, openly—about what it is they're doing, and how they redefine the meaning of it—I analyzed thousands of consumer reports of cannabis and psychedelic drugs purchased in five early darknet markets, including Silk Road, during the 2011–2017 period.[19]

I found that both psychedelic and cannabis consumer reports tended to focus on professionalism and product quality, often in direct and business-like consumer language, rather than the countercultural ideas the drug is associated with, such as anticonsumerism.[20] A review of a cannabis product of the "Bubble Gum" strain, for instance, described its physiological and psychological effects in the tone and cool detail of someone describing a bottle of Pinot in a newspaper review: "Nice hybrid that leans on the sativa side of things. Fairly energetic while also a great stay at home smoke. If you are familiar with the Cherry Kush it isn't nearly as 'stoney' as that . . . the Cherry Kush packs a bit more of a punch in the indica department." The author, clearly a cannabis connoisseur, enjoyed the tasteful drug's uplifting and calming effects, which were more balanced than she has experienced from other strains. The readers are assumed to be familiar with the sedating and energizing effects of various cannabis types.

Surprisingly, to me at least, reviews of psychedelic drugs—which are much more powerful—were similar in tone and focus. In a report of LSD blotters, Shaman spends about half of a 350-word review on customer service dimensions. He wrote that the order arrived in the US Northeast after twenty calendar days and detailed the product obfuscation: "The package blends in very well with ordinary junk mail. . . . You can open it and touch it but you won't even know what's inside the package." But it wasn't perfect. "The package is smooth and flat and I cannot see the blotters when I hold it against my lamp . . . but if someone else opens my mail they would probably find it." The report notes that the seller answered questions within twenty-four hours. Shaman treated the order as if it were a conventional act of consumption, even though psychedelics like LSD are powerful drugs that can change mood, foster positive behavioral changes, improve life satisfaction, and affect attitudes about life and self (and also induce terrible trips).[21]

In another review of a cannabis product, a market actor named Dabs likewise focused on customer service:

VACUUM SEALED: YES. Decoy: YES. Handwriting: NO . . . Communication: 10+/10 . . . Kept me updated and replied to my questions very quickly. Stealth: 10++/10. Best stealth I've seen from any vendor. Multiple decoys, well-layered MBB, product was well persevered . . . It's great to see new concentrate vendors let alone someone with professionalism and a solid product.

Dabs's positive review, which is organized as if following a template even though no formal review guidelines exist, highlights impeccable shipping, product obfuscation, and communication. Dabs was particularly impressed with the "stealth," as the seller used a machine-written address label, several decoys, and placed the product inside moisture-barrier plastic bags—steps that are believed to reduce the risk of detection by sniffer dogs and postal workers. In an uncertain market good stealth signals thoughtfulness—as a customer said in another report: "without stealth . . . you have nothing so it all starts there . . . thanks for caring!"

Consumers in any market—legal or not—base their choices at least in part on moral judgments, as they have a sense of what's right and wrong for people like them.[22] For example, is it okay to buy a shirt made with cotton produced in Xinjiang, despite reports of widespread human rights abuses? Such considerations are imperative in drug markets, where goods and services are seen through contesting frames.[23] Actors in openly secret drug markets have, as noted, a new-found opportunity to talk openly about shadowy matters, present their perspectives, perhaps develop new ones, and justify their participation in legally banned darknet exchanges. What does this new world look like to them? The consumer reports I analyzed suggest that drug e-commerce does not promote countercultural ideas or new ways of living and being. Many report writers, particularly in cannabis reports, sideline how drugs make them feel, what the drug-taking experience is like, moral questions and justifications, legal concerns, and the social context of their consumption. Instead, the reports invoke mainstream consumer language, as if they are merely engaging in another kind of recreational consumption, in line with research on drug normalization.[24] There are exceptions in consumer reports of psychedelics, but they are rare.

Depending on one's perspective, this "new world" is reassuring or disappointing. The consumer reports suggest that legalization of drugs that are harmless when consumed in moderation and in safe settings, such as cannabis and psychedelics, will fit neatly into mainstream consumer societies that are of course used to dealing with drugs that can be sources of joy but also personally and socially destructive, such as sugar, nicotine, and alcohol. That is, the reports suggest that the status quo is unlikely to be affected much by improved access to drugs that are currently banned or controlled. Ironically, e-commerce might even have a tempering effect on the drugs. Why? Consider that drug-taking is a socially constructed practice that draws on available definitions and interpretations of physiological and psychological effects. For example, someone who consumes a drug for the first time needs some kind of assistance in interpreting and labeling the arousal and comfort he or she feels, because the effects can have multiple meanings that can both discourage or encourage further consumption.[25] "Munchies," for example, or a warped sense of time, are not inherently pleasant feelings, until they are recognized as such. The consumer reports strip away such interpretative guidance—they primarily treat the drugs as purchased products that are measured up against standards of capitalist market exchange, such as whether the product description was accurate.

For people who hope that widening access to drugs will promote alternative ways of living, this is potentially a disappointment: openly secret commerce may be, despite its connotations of radical newness, a project that reinforces the status quo. But it did build a global and highly capable community that is still active with no end in sight, fourteen years after Silk Road launched.

The Darknet Community

People who signed up for Silk Road, the first darknet market, entered a platform with an unprecedented variety of drugs on offer, detailed information about vendors and their products, vibrant consumer and dealer networks, and newfound opportunities to express their views through discussions and consumer reports. They also faced unique challenges. These circumstances, mixed with an apparent excitement about being part of a transformative project, laid the foundation for not just a functional darknet market but a community, a large group of people with common interests and shared values who interact and support one another.[26]

Practical problems brought people together. One example is how actors established a system for microlending of Bitcoin. Market actors who were a few dollars or cents short of an order—for instance, due to sudden jumps in the exchange rate—could borrow from other community members rather than start a conversion of minuscule dollar amounts, which was cumbersome in the early 2010s. In designated threads, people made unprompted offers of and requests for "spare coins." For instance:

> SIRMYSTERY: Gotta have the OSCT [official spare coins thread]. :) Sending good vibes tonight to all my homies.
> DOWNTILL: Got some pocket change if anyone's short.
> STARDUST: Evening fellow coiners. I am here to help if and when I can. Good to be here ;D
> BLUEJEANS: I need to borrow a tiny amount to get an order to go thru.
> ANTHONY: PM it to me :)
> BLUEJEANS: Thank you very kindly Anthony!
> ANTHONY: ฿0.01 sent to Bluejeans.
> BLUEJEANS: Well thank you again Anthony that actually worked! I took care of business and sent it back..should be back to you soon..thanks so much!!
> ANTHONY: And repaid :D Thanks, Bluejeans :)

The microloans show how spending money sometimes isn't just about obtaining stuff—how we decide to spend our funds can also be about creating, transforming, and differentiating social relations.[27] Darknet market users lent money and paid their debts to display trust in individuals and the community at large. By offering microloans to fellow participants, people supported a nascent community.

All collective projects depend on shared meanings and identities.[28] It's no surprise, then, that illegal markets often have distinct cultural characteristics that go beyond rational exchange and risk management. Darknet market participants are mostly concerned with finding good deals and often look for signs of professionalism in their exchange partners, as seen in the consumer reports quoted earlier. However, other discussions suggest that market participants also see darknet trade as a radical libertarian movement that contests legal definitions of what is right and wrong, echoing the sentiment in Ulbricht's early promotion of Silk Road. For example, after Ulbricht was arrested in 2013 (see more on this in chapter 4), many former Silk Road users framed him as a pioneer in a bigger fight for drug law reform.[29] ShannonAMPM said that people are "indebted to his efforts in establishing free markets for all." Cynic agreed. "[Ulbricht] opened new frontiers. Boldly went where no man had been before. We would not be here if it were not for him." Slingshot compared Ulbricht to Christopher Columbus: "He discovered America [and] yet he died broke, and virtually forgotten. . . . [Ulbricht] may have done something groundbreaking and revolutionary and I will give him credit for that."

People lauded Ulbricht's construction of the first darknet market because it invented, in the words of Astro, a way to "delete the harm" of "drug dealing" by getting rid of the "mafia" and "violence." With Silk Road "everyone had what the fuck he/she wanted" without any "harm." Another participant wrote: "I hope that one day not too far we will be all free [to be] doing drugs in a safe and well-informed environment." Vendor U_Tell_Me expressed a similar sentiment, writing that Silk Road "really has changed how drugs are sold" and that Ulbricht may "one day be a hero," because the war on drugs might end because of his actions and people "who run these sites, the vendors who sell products and the customers who purchase products." These market participants will "one day" be seen as part of "the chain of events that destroyed an unjust war on drugs." Markets like Silk Road, he wrote, "are the first step in taking back something that our governments never had a right to take—our freedom of choice." Market actors like U_Tell_Me used their newfound ability to speak openly about their involvement in banned trade to critique the law and appeal to higher ideas of personal liberty.

The talk about Ulbricht as a leader in a bigger fight against unjust drug laws suggests that he not only succeeded at constructing a functional e-commerce market but also a sense of community for market users who had more than instrumental motivations. The goal of building a community was a clearly formulated goal in Ulbricht's writing. For example, in early 2012, when Silk Road had just a few hundred vendors and trade was growing fast, Ulbricht drew on political rhetoric to unite market actors. He wrote in the market's discussion forum that "Silk Road give[s] people the option to choose freedom over tyranny [and] buy and sell just about anything without worrying about being attacked by gun toting men in uniforms." Further evidence of community building is found in other forum posts: from 2011 to 2013 he facilitated discussions about philosophy, drug law reform, and politics, organized a lottery, arranged movie nights, and hosted and actively maintained a book club. And in a "State of the Road" message posted in the forum in January 2012, less than a year after he started promoting the market, he wrote in first-person plural that Silk Road had become "a vibrant community full of interesting characters." Silk Road, he said, would not be what it is or possibly even exist without "our superstar vendors and ever helpful moderators" and the "truly awesome people . . . who has [sic] stepped up along the way to point out security flaws, contribute their ideas, and take this experiment on as their own and stand with us." This "community," Ulbricht wrote, made Silk Road work better.

Ulbricht drew on the same collective power in his efforts to keep the trade going in ways that would support his design vision—for instance, when he tried to get people to start using the escrow system described earlier in the chapter, using financial incentives. He explained in a forum post that instead of charging a flat commission (6.23 percent) on all trades, which makes trading out of escrow attractive for large orders, "we will charge a higher amount for low priced items and a lower amount for high priced items." The revised pricing would, he hoped, convince more people to use escrow, which would make trade safer and also generate income for the market (and Ulbricht). Even when talking about commission rates, Ulbricht framed Silk Road as a collaborative endeavor: "Together, we can beat the scammers and make the Silk Road market a place where you can buy with confidence and peace of mind." By cultivating sociability and attending to practical exchange issues, he mixed two worlds that some people say don't mesh: community and money.[30] It worked because many Silk Road users were activist-minded: some saw their market participation as contributions to a revolutionary fight against the war on drugs and had forged strong social ties that went far beyond practical issues. One dealer I interviewed even used the L-word to describe how he felt about his digital peers: "I love them, they are family to me." That spirit was tested by the crackdowns that were to come.

4 *Crackdowns and Adaptations in the Digital Underworld*

Western law enforcement agencies have spent big sums on reining in darknet e-commerce. And by some measures, they have been successful. They have arrested drug dealers and market operators, and shut down trading platforms like Silk Road. When presenting these accomplishments in press conferences and on social media, officials on both sides of the pond say that the darknet is not as anonymous as market users might think. A US federal prosecutor stated after a market shutdown that "criminals can no longer . . . hide in the shadows of the dark web," while the UK's National Crime Agency (NCA) said that "the hidden internet isn't hidden and your anonymous activity isn't anonymous. We know where you are, what you are doing, and we will catch you."[1] What they didn't say is that their professional wins were the result of traditional police work, not flaws in the technology that helps people hide their identities and thus underpins the darknet economy. For example, the Federal Bureau of Investigation (FBI) was able to locate Silk Road's operator Ross Ulbricht because he had used his full name in an old forum post. The darknet infrastructure still works and trade is thriving.[2]

Law enforcement efforts to rein in the darknet economy were a driving force in its transition from a niche pocket of activity to a large, decentralized, and vibrant world of constant movement of people and capital, between various markets and online communities. That is, by cracking down on darknet markets, initially Silk Road, the police inadvertently strengthened the larger realm. Viewing shocks as building blocks in an emerging economy may seem counterintuitive, given their destructive nature. The shutdown of Silk Road, for example, deleted seller profiles and aggregated reputation data, and threatened to cut ties between exchange partners who were suddenly unable to communicate in the marketplace's internal messaging system. But because the darknet community could cooperate and communicate in open secrecy, they could fight through their challenges and emerge stronger and more sophisticated.

The Library Crackdown

The catalyst for the darknet economy's transformation into a mature and stable space for banned commerce was the shutdown of Silk Road, which came about, like many other disruptive technology events, in the Golden State. On a Tuesday afternoon in early October 2013, Ross Ulbricht visited a library in his San Francisco neighborhood, where he shared an apartment with three friends. He found a place to sit, opened his laptop, connected to the wireless internet, and, using the Onion Router (Tor), logged on to Silk Road. As the site's administrator, Ulbricht had access to an overview of its statistics, and the figures told him that he was a rich man. People across the world had used the website he created to buy and sell drugs for more than two and a half years, and commissions had made him a millionaire. But at a quarter past three that day, that life ended. A woman who was sitting across from Ulbricht suddenly snatched his laptop away before he could log off the marketplace, and in tandem other FBI agents moved forward and quickly apprehended him. In Ulbricht's home law enforcement found computer servers loaded with additional information about his online activities, and later the same day, the marketplace was terminated. Thousands of users lost their money, but no one lost more than Ulbricht, whose 144,000 Bitcoins were confiscated. The value at the time was $28 million.

In addition to law enforcement operations like the library crackdown, the early darknet economy faced two sources of destabilization: exit scams and theft by hacking. Several darknet markets have been raided by digital intruders who stole millions of dollars' worth of Bitcoin from various markets. This is possible because payments are typically processed through the markets and are thus temporarily stored in them, often for many days if exchange partners use the market's escrow system. In an exit scam a market facilitates trade between buyers and sellers to earn their trust and then shuts down without notice. Examples of early exit scams include the market website Sheep, which stole $6 million in user funds in late 2013, and the market Evolution, which closed in March 2015 with $12 million in the bag.[3]

"Silk roaders unite!!!!"

Shocks, in particular the legal efforts to destroy the world the darknet community created, accentuated that world's moral meaning by bringing people together.[4] For example, Silk Road pivoted offline after the library crackdown, but its forum remained online for several months, likely because it was hosted on different servers. During that period thousands of participants expressed solidarity with the community and its other members. One Silk Road member, MRsneaky, who had spent "countless hours" on the market's discussion forum, said he wouldn't know what to do without it. "A piece of me has been taken," he said. "I never thought I'd feel so strongly about ppl I've never met . . . I really feel like this is my community . . . Long Live SR!!!!!"

A peer with the username Cloudboom expressed a similar sentiment: "I spent so many hours here, same with all of you, just reading everything, getting to know everyone and making money without dealing with punks." He called for the community to carry on ("I hope everybody regroups"), a spirit shared by many others, such as New_Lax: "Silk roaders unite!!!!" Other members spoke like leaders, attempting to transmute a moment of solidarity to concrete steps that might help the community survive. SSBB, who after the crackdown found himself "inextricably drawn back to the place that I love," said that "he cannot imagine my life without being a part of this community" and declared that he and everyone else who felt similarly about the loss needed to act: "We have a choice in front of us now, we need to regroup and find a new home."

Silk Road members mourned the sudden loss of their darknet market. But they spoke of their community in the present tense—suggesting that it extended beyond the e-commerce site that started it all—and many called for its members to find a new digital home. That was easier said than done for criminal activities that had just been hit by one of the world's most powerful law enforcement agencies. However, they did gather in a new forum and eventually moved to a new marketplace, which was created in part by former Silk Road staffers. The opening of that marketplace was affectionately celebrated:

SIR MEATLOAF: Brothers and sisters! Silkroad for me is not just a place to buy drugs, It's a community, It's home.
DOC: Welcome back and stay safe everyone.
JESSY: Great to see you Doc :)
DOC: You too Jessy :)
KINGSTON CANDY: Doc! Good to see you!
DOC: And the same goes to you my good man :)
CRESPO: Oh my fucking god. I just feel so . . . at home when logged in.
MUKULELE: My brothers and sisters, we are home again.

x: I'm home, thank you—strength and honor brothers and sisters.
MELLON: I must admit it feels much more exhilarating than I had
    expected it would . . . WELCOME HOME, WE LOVE YOU
    FAMILY.

Former users of Silk Road welcomed familiar usernames and spoke
of their community as "home," its members as "brothers and sisters," and the larger group as "family." Through their words, and by
signing up for the new forum and market, people expressed a strong
desire to be part of the darknet community's revival.

On another darknet forum called "the Hub," this one for users of
all markets, staff created an archive of Silk Road discussion threads,
which was "proudly" presented by its moderator, James. He was pro-
fusely thanked by a long list of Hub members for restoring parts of
the Silk Road community's treasured digital past. Soultroll, for one,
"got overwhelmed with joy" and "started to cry" upon reading "my
old vendor review threads . . . all the great feedback I had." The user
added: "Yes, I am a sensitive troll." The market crackdown risked
cutting off important social connections and taking away the validation and appreciation Soultroll got from working with and serving
customers of banned goods, which clearly wasn't just about money
for him. Other users were more measured in their responses, al-
though still appreciative, but strong emotions were common. BIG$$$
wrote: "This sure brought back some memories." Mama Bra re-
peated an expletive fourteen times, followed by "James, YOU ARE A
GOD!!!!" The person then asked for a Bitcoin address, "for those of
us" who wanted to cover or reduce the costs of hosting the "ABSO-
LUTELY amazing" archive. The response from James was that "do-
nations are not necessary but if you are so inclined . . . send them to
the address in the official donations post." His humble forum re-
ceived about twenty donations the following two months.[5] VC31 sug-
gested that James's archive preserved and momentarily revived a

collective history that held more significance than Silk Road users realized while the market was still accessible: "I never knew how much the Silk Road community meant to me and others."

Words and actions show how the crackdown on Silk Road solidified community ties. For many users Silk Road was more than an e-commerce site for the goods they desired, or new income streams— it was also a collective endeavor through which actors had formed meaningful social ties, to one another and the world that they had built and that was now under threat. In the aftermath of the Silk Road closure, actors denounced the state's efforts to curb drug use as excessive intrusions into people's lives. They expressed how darknet trade and the darknet community affected them personally:

DEPORTED: WE LOVE YOU . . . You guys have helped me more than any psychiatrist has.

HUNTERT: Through the use of hallucinogens procured from Silk Road, my wife and I have fallen back in love, I have faced and defeated many personal demons, I have mended many relationships in my life . . . I was awakened from my slumber and reminded that I was worried about all the wrong things. I love all of you and I pray that we will find a way to carry on this dream.

Between the lines of these statements and many others like them is the idea that there is something wrong with the status quo when drug-taking experiences that help treat mental health problems, mend broken relationships, and brighten lives are legally banned. The community activities that darknet markets like Silk Road enable were seen as part of a larger battle against structures that prevent people from living freely. Their hope was to "find a way to carry on this dream."

Libertas, who was involved in the creation of the new Silk Road market (often called Silk Road 2), described the library crackdown as an "infringement of our freedoms by government oppressors" and called for people to "stand on the shoulders of this tragedy that has befallen us and raise high what still remains—our sense of community, freedom and justice." Libertas was on track to profit from the rise of the replacement market he helped create, but even if his enthusiastic involvement was mere rhetoric, his spin had real consequences because it resonated with people, evidenced by how they used similar language. Undoubtedly some participants in the darknet economy—early adopters included, and possibly people like Libertas—cared mostly or perhaps even only about the drugs and the money, but even these people are political. By participating in the postcrackdown trade that was made possible by highly motivated actors, they challenge efforts to rein in openly secret commerce and thus undermine state power. Acts do not need to be political in intent to have political consequences.[6] Most likely, Libertas's efforts to support and protect a fragile online community, and his documented eagerness to take up profitable positions of responsibility, are not in contest. Economic sociologists dispute the common view that morals and money are like oil and water. Rather, they often intertwine in complex ways—for instance, in how people can do something out of genuine love but also appreciate and consider the money they make, or even in how loving relationships are also economic relationships.[7] In the case of the collective efforts to resurrect darknet trade after the Silk Road crackdown, actors like Ulbricht and Libertas are likely driven by a powerful mix of interests, which help carry on their digital underworld.

Political expressions were not limited to leadership figures. The crackdown response from SixEight, for example, sums up what many market users expressed. The community, the person said, "changed [my] and thousands of others' lives forever. We must all take responsibility and work towards creating a truly free society." To SixEight, Silk Road was a step toward that utopia. People like him who returned to darknet markets after the Silk Road crackdown were united by concrete practical challenges, a particular worldview that was reinforced by the police intervention, and out of the collectively experienced joy, loss, and hope grew solidarity and a fierce determination to protect their newfound agency in what they view as an overcontrolled environment. With that energy they set out to rebuild and innovate their way out of their problems.

Identity Verification before and after the Library Crackdown

One early problem in the darknet economy was identity verification. People discussed potential solutions long before the Silk Road crackdown, but there was no consensus on the best approach. This was in part because actors believed they could depend on Silk Road's market infrastructure—Ulbricht and his staff would be there to intervene and mediate when needed, for the foreseeable future. A case in point is a discussion from June 2011 suggesting that the market had no system in place for identity verification. In a discussion thread on the topic, Bungalow wondered, "What prevents a scammer/law enforcement to just make a new user with some already-established name?" To prevent this, Bungalow proposed "some form of verification."

K1ngkong "totally agreed," suggesting that they make the Silk Road forum invite-only. Asdf90 said he had observed numerous scamming attempts on BlackMarket during a Silk Road downtime, with people impersonating some of its vendors, and agreed ("100%") that some verification was warranted. Listentothemusic, who worked as a vendor, had experienced this: "Someone stole my name on BlackMarket to scam people . . . I just [linked to] my Silk Road profile." Dread said that people "could use [encryption] signatures," or, as Zen862 suggested, double-check vendor identities by sending them private messages on both sites. Egoa, meanwhile, said "some sort of code generated from Silk Road" would help verify accounts. In a sign of what was to come, G4bb3r posted an encryption signature and the following: "This message verifies that I am the true g4bb3r.

You can check this signature with my public key that's [on my] Silk Road profile." Ulbricht then chimed in: "If someone is impersonating you on the forums, just let us know on the [market] site and we'll do a password reset."

Silk Road members agreed that they needed a way to verify themselves. Two suggested using encryption signatures as a potential solution, but to other users, this complicated method was unnecessary because one could simply "ask the member on the other site" if they have the same username across multiple sites. Silk Road's founder agreed that adequate solutions existed, such as his own ability to delete imposters ("just let us know"). Other users requested the implementation of "some sort of verification" or "screening process" in the market website or "some sort of code generated from Silk Road." There was no system in place for identity verification. Encryption signing, which was to become the standard after the Silk Road crackdown, was at this stage just one of many options.

The idea that encryption should be used to verify identities was absent from similar discussions in the forum for BlackMarket, Silk Road's sole competitor at the time. For example, in a 2012 thread titled "Why do you need [encryption]?" a user named Dutchy said he didn't "get it." None other than the market's operator Backopy replied, saying that "encryption is used to encrypt sensitive data . . . so even if the server gets compromised and is seized your data remains safe." Dutchy responded: "Aaah alright now I get it!" Another member, oxy, added that "the main importance" of encryption is to obfuscate potentially incriminating information, such as "when you buy drugs and you send the seller a message containing the pick-up address along with the other details. If that's compromised, it can be used against you." These quotes and others like them show that even though market actors had sound reasons to promote encryption technology at the time, they had yet to adopt it as an identity verification tool. Even BlackMarket's operator stated that the purpose of encryption is to protect "sensitive" communication such as postal addresses, not verifying identities.

In another BlackMarket thread from 2012, several Silk Road sellers had temporarily moved to BlackMarket due to technical problems. As they introduced themselves, they attempted to verify their identities in various ways. Farmer1, who claimed to be within the "top 12% of vendors on the Silk Road" with more than two hundred completed transactions and "perfect feedback," included as evidence a link to his Silk Road forum review thread and an email address. Several other users made similar announcements, without using encryption to verify their identities:

> DELTABLUES: Switching from Silk Road to BlackMarket.
> KOLTBIZ: Looking forward to do great business here too!
> CINDELLE: I too have come from Silk Road . . . I have no stats on
> here. Guess I'll have to build them!

One relocating vendor, Koltbiz, attempted to verify his identity by posting an update on Silk Road's forum, "just to give you guys peace of mind that I'm the real Koltbiz," and included a link. Relocating vendors like these demonstrated the need to be mobile, and to avoid dependence on one market, but they were unsure about how to bring their identity and all the social capital and trust tied to it with them. Of dozens of posters in the same thread, several Silk Road sellers confirmed their identity by sharing email addresses and by updating their forum pages. Only one used encryption-signing. Like Silk Road, BlackMarket had no established system for identity verification. The impetus for change was the crackdown on Silk Road.

Immediately after the Silk Road closure, identity verification was one of several problems under discussion in the market's forum (which was hosted on different servers). One of the most active threads on the day of the shutdown was titled "Vendors post your contact info here," created by a buyer. Thirteen dealers shared their contact information in that thread on the same day, and eight of them used encryption to sign their messages. This suggests that market actors knew that they could verify their identities using encryption, but that they needed an impetus to start doing so. One of the signees was "Al Capone": "Well established vendor with 100% satisfaction . . . contact me through PM or [email redacted]. Long live Silk Road! [encryption signature redacted]." Al Capone stated that he is an experienced dealer with a track record of pleasing his customers. By posting his encryption signature, market actors could verify his identity and email address.

Similar verification practices helped sellers verify their accounts on the new market, Silk Road 2. A case in point is the vendor Technohippy, who, upon trying to sign up to the new market, found that his username was already taken or "stolen." The person instead registered as "Technohippy2.0" and put in a request for his Silk Road identity to be verified and retrieved. "As soon as we are [verified]," he wrote, "we will be back with even more products than before." The vendor also used the forum thread to squash rumors of their arrest ("we have just remained under the radar"). Members of Silk Road 2 were happy to see the return of a familiar seller:

> KNUCKLES: Welcome back! Glad to hear you didn't get busted!
> CHARLIESHEEN1080: Technohippy you motherfucking legend!!!!! So glad to see you back.
> ROCKNESSIE: I am SO FUCKING DELIGHTED you weren't busted.
> LEVELHEAD: Very happy to see you back Technohippy.
> ILTC: Welcome back. [Market staff], please let us know when he has been verified.
> MARKET STAFF: Verified. He decrypted the PGP message I sent him.

A member of the market staff responded with an encrypted message that was locked to Technohippy's public encryption key, which he had previously made available on the old Silk Road forum. This meant that the encrypted message could only be unlocked by the person who had Technohippy's private encryption key—presumably Technohippy himself. And indeed, he decrypted the message, told the market staffer what it said, and thus verified his identity. The verification process enabled Technohippy to reclaim the original username, disprove rumors, regain customer trust, and carry on his business operations. According to my calculations, Technohippy made at least $757,000 by continuing to sell in three other darknet markets with his original Silk Road username.[8]

In two forum threads Silk Road 2 staff conducted a similar but systematic encryption verification of all interested sellers from the original Silk Road, both titled "Accessing the vendor roundtable." One market staffer explained in an announcement that "former Silk Road vendors" would get free vendor accounts on the newly created marketplace, if they could verify themselves in the way Technohippy did. Applicants were instructed to message the staff directly or in the forum thread, signing with their encryption key, to be "fully reinstate[d]." "Sign using the same [encryption] key as published on the previous Silk Road forums," the instructions read, "as we will be using this to verify that you are who you claim to be for security purposes." More than 230 vendors replied to the announcement, more than the staff could handle. As one staff member wrote: "If you do not have access to the old Silk Road forums, or did not post your [encryption key] on the old forums, don't bother PMing me asking for verification. . . . We can not open the door to everybody." About 140 sellers from the original Silk Road market were verified in the two forum threads and most likely many more in private communications.

To document and measure the emergence of encryption signing in the darknet economy, I counted instances of the practice in five darknet market forums in the 2011–2016 period.[9] I found that encryption-signing surged after three types of shocks: police interventions, hacks, and scams (Figure 1). The increase was particularly sharp after the library crackdown and the closure of Silk Road in October 2013. A reversion to the mean rate of encryption-signing in the weeks and months following most of the shocks suggests that identity verification was used to remedy uncertainty in disruptive moments.

Encryption-signing for identity verification was introduced in the 1990s, so the point here is not that the technology was created after the Silk Road crackdown.[10] Innovation is not just about eureka moments in garages and basements—the moments when new ideas are conceived—but also about disseminating existing tricks and putting them to work in fresh and more meaningful ways.[11] In the darknet economy, the novel, systematic manner of verifying identities with encryption-signing did not converge with commerce until the FBI shut down Silk Road. A crisis of confidence in the survivability of the biggest market stimulated collaborative problem-solving. The solution of encryption-signing enabled darknet market actors to operate with consistent usernames in a digital underworld where everything else was in constant flux. The crackdown on Silk Road generated problems, unity, new thinking, and collaborative work, and the outcome was that people constructed new systems and practices that enabled market actors to remain hidden and protected while continuing to operate in public, in a decentralized economy.

Insider Knowledge for Everyone

A second crackdown-inspired innovation in the darknet economy was information hubs—independent websites that provide detailed assessments of available markets and related information. These hubs became essential to the darknet economy because they provide crucial information to all interested parties. In conventional illegal

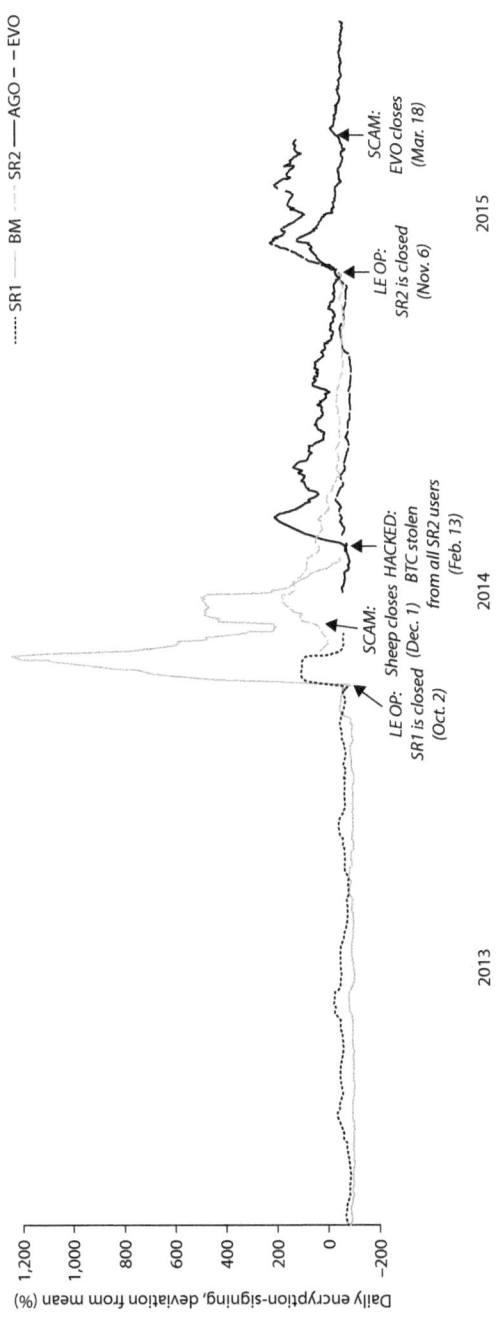

FIGURE 1. Encryption signing in response to market shocks in the darknet economy, 2011–2016.

trade, which is usually embedded in social networks, information scarcity makes it difficult for buyers and sellers to compete effectively. In the darknet economy, however, information hubs help actors to make informed decisions, which in turn enable orderly competition. For example, after the shutdown of Silk Road, actors could read up on alternative markets and make informed decisions about where to go. Information hubs also help the economy grow. Outsiders who might learn about the darknet economy from media coverage of the Ulbricht trial can, with a few keyword searches, locate market overviews and other practical guides.

To better understand the darknet economy, I wanted to measure activity on the information hubs people kept referring to in the markets and forums. Studying banned activities is notoriously difficult—data is difficult to obtain—but the easy and secure communication enabled by open secrecy made my task easier. For example, one day, while I mined data from an information hub, a pseudonymous moderator contacted me; he had noticed that I was unusually active on the site (data-mining often entails thousands of server requests per day). I explained that I was writing about darknet trade, to which this person replied: "Let me know if I can help in any way!" Other users were also surprisingly helpful. To measure the activity in information hubs (which operated more like newspapers and had no registered users or discussion posts to count), I contacted the site owners, who kindly agreed to share their visitor data with me. My interactions with these actors made me confident that open secrecy is an apt name for describing and explaining what is different about the darknet economy. From public conversations between market actors, it was clear that these people knew very well that law enforcement was chasing them, but they nonetheless responded gracefully to my inquiries for more information and provided elaborate details and answers to my questions.

The data I collected and analyzed on information hub activity—mostly from 2014 to 2017—show how information hubs are particularly important in the darknet economy after shocks. The blog DeepDotWeb, launched in 2013 "in the wake of our friend being arrested by local authorities," publicly stated that it aimed to make "the dark net safer"—for instance, by providing information about market reliability. The site produced thousands of articles and had more than 22,000 unique daily visitors. Another information hub, DNStats, which specialized in automated testing of market uptime, was formed because the founder "was always seeing people wanting to know when a site went down, how long has it been down and when did it come back up." DNStats had more than 5,500 daily visitors. Darknet markets also had a presence on Reddit, before the social media platform banned them in 2018.[12] The Silk Road and Silk Road 2 subreddits had more than 24,000 subscribers in total, who wrote more than 122,000 comments, mostly in 2013-2015. A subreddit for all darknet markets, created about two weeks after Silk Road was shut down, had nearly 160,000 subscribers and more than 1.1 million public comments. The subreddit maintained a FAQ and a frequently updated list of available markets.[13]

The Hub, the forum that published old Silk Road posts, came online a little more than three months after the library crackdown. "We've had it rough, and we've seen it all," the staff explained in their introduction to the site. In the same rhetorical style of Ulbricht and Libertas, Silk Road 2's moderator, the Hub staff added: "From falling victim to scams and dishonesty, to seeing our brothers arrested and our digital homes torn apart. With all of this happening, we felt the need to build something that would bring stability, continuity and guided decision-making to our community." Activity in the forum and all other examined information hubs surged after market shocks (Figure 2).

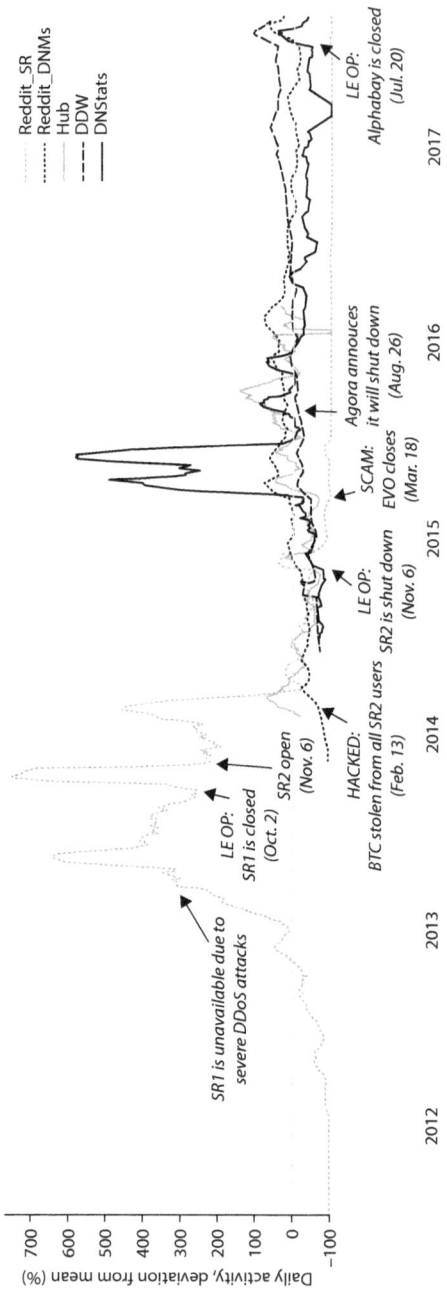

FIGURE 2. Information Hub activity after disruptive events in the darknet economy.

Information hubs helped people make informed decisions after disruptive events in the darknet economy. They could look up market lists, compare market features, and observe or partake in relevant forum discussions. With encryption-signing and access to information, actors could migrate—with intact pseudonyms—to the best darknet markets currently available. The clustering of established sellers enabled competition, and the emergence of new markets created order.

Dark Nomads

History tells us that communities have always been ready to hit the road when necessary. Truly nomadic communities first started to appear in Eurasia around 1000 BC, maybe even earlier. Some traveled without any fixed routes, while others followed the seasons and returned to an established winter refuge once a year. These wanderers relied on technology such as horse saddles and wheeled transport, which had been around for hundreds of years before external threats from regional civilizations gave people the impetus to start using these tools to create a new way of life.[14] Nomadic life in the darknet economy was enabled by external threats, which gave people the impetus to innovate, as they did by adopting encryption signatures for identity verification and making information hubs.

The darknet economy grew rapidly in its early nomadic years. Silk Road's monthly revenue was $1.22 million in 2012 and $7.48 million a year later, in a period of stability.[15] I estimate that in the fall of 2014, about a year after the FBI crackdown, combined seller revenue in Silk Road 2 was down to $6.37 million per month, but trade continued in two other markets, Evolution and Agora, where monthly seller revenue grew to $8.49 million and $10.45 million, respectively.[16] Most of the trade was driven by dealers who operated nomadically. Vendors who maintained profiles in both Evolution and Agora accounted for a majority of sales in the two markets and earned notably more than single-market sellers, even though there were fewer nomads than non-nomads (909 vs. 2,843).

Another measure of darknet nomadism is the movement of people and capital after the crackdown on the new Silk Road 2, about a year after the library crackdown.[17] I found that migrating Silk Road 2 sellers remained active for a mean of 105 days in the market Evolution, which closed in March 2015, and 167 days in Agora, which shut down voluntarily in the fall of the same year. The mean monthly revenue for each Silk Road 2 seller who continued in Evolution was $4,600, while Silk Road 2 sellers who continued in Agora earned $8,900 per month (in part because that market lasted longer, including several months after Evolution, when Agora dominated the darknet economy). In total, about a quarter of all Silk Road 2 sellers continued in Agora and Evolution, and likely many more under different usernames.

Shocks incur substantial costs for sellers, as pending payments are canceled and future earnings reduced as the dust settles. Recall that Technohippy decided to "lay low" for several weeks after the FBI shut down Silk Road, and thus lost income during that period. But because innovations enabled him and many other sellers to start operating nomadically, the darknet economy moved beyond the duopoly it was in the days of the first Silk Road market, when Black-Market was the sole alternative. The darknet economy has decentralized and is more resilient and able to outlive market shocks. Law enforcement has continued to disrupt trade but no longer poses an existential threat, as administrators, buyers, and sellers have adapted: diversification across multiple websites has diminished the state's ability to halt transactions entirely, rules of exchange are no longer dictated by a single marketplace, and novel identity verification systems enable dealers to hang on to their reputable usernames even if they have to relocate.

The decentralized exchange structure that grew out of the darknet's setbacks was fragmented but stable. State pressure was central to this decentralization because it united people and forced them to work together to solve pressing problems. Uncertainty generally impairs market trust and trade, but in some cases, it is also a powerful driver of productive change.[18] When outside shocks disrupt order, people will identify threats and other challenges, propose and test solutions, and organize new courses of action.[19] Understood this way, shocks are not mere destructive setbacks but events that foster innovation and community as people frantically evaluate existing arrangements and possible alternatives. In pressing moments, entrepreneurial actors often make new combinations of ideas that existed in their minds for which they lacked the impetus to realize, such as encryption and identity verification.[20] The darknet economy may still appear chaotic to outsiders, as popular markets rarely last longer than a year, but with novel solutions to common disruptions, buyers and sellers know that their trusted exchange partners will be able to participate in future transactions even as individual markets are closed. Darknet trade was fragile immediately after the FBI took down Silk Road and arrested Ulbricht, which is possibly part of the reason the responses of market actors were so emotional, but people figured out how they could cooperate and communicate from the shadows to make the darknet economy's organization more robust.

In 2017, following another market crackdown, the FBI's acting director Andrew McCabe stated that critics may be right to say that as we shut down one site another site emerges. But that is, he added, "the nature of criminal work. It never goes away. You have to constantly keep at it."[21] Law enforcement in late modernity no longer claims to be able to eradicate crime, as it once did, but makes claims about its effectiveness and indispensability.[22] And police pressure may indeed, under certain circumstances, lower crime incidence rates, push the targeted activities around the corner, and restrict the development of illegal markets or exchange networks. It has also been argued that illegal markets are shackled, because exchange partners operate in the shadows: it is difficult to establish product value because of information scarcity, deficient competition, and cooperation problems that inhibit efficient organization.[23]

Legal pressure undoubtedly affects trade in the darknet economy. Shocks burden market actors with liabilities of newness: structures are unstable, legitimacy is low, and better-known alternatives—for example, offline trade or social media exchanges—might seem more reliable and less complicated.[24] Moreover, sophisticated anonymization technology will not prevent the kind of human error that led to the library crackdown and similar law enforcement successes. But open secrecy has unsettled the long-standing whack-a-mole dynamic of crime and control McCabe alluded to. In the darknet economy individual buyers and sellers have learned to solve coordination problems at the expense of law enforcement and circumvented many of the obstacles common to illegal markets. The darknet economy transformed into a decentralized economy with effective information flows and nomadic actors—not *despite* legal pressure but *because* of it.

II *Fighting Censorship*

5 *Climbing the Great Firewall of China*

All modern states work toward progress, however they define it, by making the noisy social world legible, orderly, and easier to manage.[1] A central challenge in that endeavor is to find the right balance between liberty and control. It's a long-standing issue. Émile Durkheim wrote in the late nineteenth century that while some regulation of individual life is imperative, too much of it will limit human potential and stunt societal development.[2] More than 130 years later, the Chinese Communist Party (CCP) is testing Durkheim's theory, by continuing to pursue economic growth and material prosperity while tightening social control.

China's rise at the end of the 1900s and in the early 2000s came about due to effective industrialization and the work and entrepreneurship of its citizens.[3] Instead of bringing about personal liberties, as modernization theory and many Western commentators expected, state control of civil life tightened, in part because China's economic rise enabled the CCP to bankroll the largest, most capable surveillance system the world has ever seen.[4] Built up since Mao's time, but in particular in the decades following the Tiananmen Square military crackdown in 1989, the costly surveillance apparatus employs tens of thousands of workers who monitor a growing list of persons of interest, by visiting them, recruiting informants in the neighborhood, monitoring payment data and travel records, and in recent years, observing them through expansive video surveillance and facial recognition systems.[5]

The Chinese cyberspace was for a while seen as an enclave for public life without state interference, and people would openly discuss historical events, domestic and international affairs, and literary works, and also engage in contentious and unruly debates.[6] But that has changed. Online activities are now reviewed and filtered—for instance, by removing talk about matters deemed sensitive—and supplemented with generated content, such as comments that celebrate the country's leadership.[7] China's digital past is also fading into the night. He Jiayan, a tech writer, recently conducted a range of searches of various entertainment and cultural figures from the late 1990s through the mid-2000s and found that nearly 100 percent of the content from the first decade of China's internet is gone. "Chinese-language internet content predating the emergence of the mobile internet has almost entirely disappeared," He wrote.[8] His post was removed the following day, replaced with a 404 message that read: "This content violates regulations and cannot be viewed." Data on languages used across the internet supports these findings (Figure 3).[9]

Many Chinese people circumvent state censorship and connect to the open internet with virtual private networks (VPNs), but this has gotten harder. The CCP cracked down on VPNs in 2017—the IP addresses of the most popular ones were blocked, and Apple was forced to remove hundreds from its app store.[10] A few mainstream VPN services remain available, some get special permission to access the open internet, and alternative solutions—such as VPNs installed while a Chinese citizen is abroad or with the help of techy friends— are rarely punished while still being technically illegal. Why is some censorship circumvention permitted? Likely because a complete blackout would cause too much inconvenience and anger in the population. As a spokesperson for the popular Expressvpn said, "The

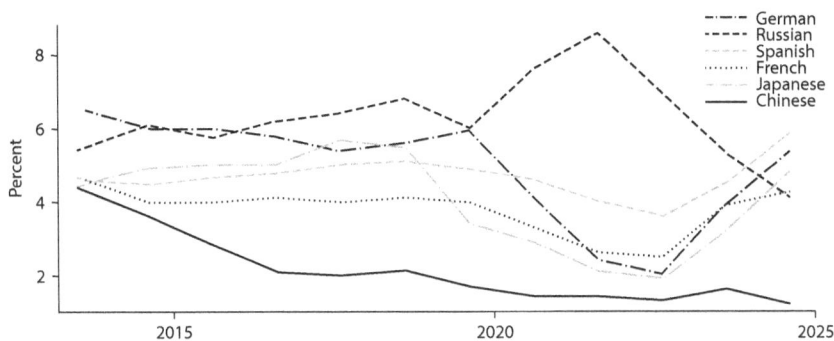

FIGURE 3. Percentage of global website content by language. *Note:* For a cleaner visualization I included only languages that were between 10% and 4% in 2013. Web Technology Surveys (2024).

Chinese government wants to have their cake and eat it too . . . they want to control [the internet], but also to exploit the range of economic possibilities that digital freedom offers."[11]

Some scholars argue that this halfway-censorship, or 75 percent-censorship, helps the state's vast but stretched surveillance system maintain social control.[12] By allowing some VPN traffic, those who really want to access the open internet despite the friction can get there. At the same time, frequent throttling of VPN connections—for instance, during sensitive periods such as political anniversaries—make local, legal, and speedier sites attractive. And finally, usage of mainstream VPN services is easy to detect, which gives the government another metric to include in their surveillance system. In a talk about China and information technology in 2000, the former US president Bill Clinton wished the CCP "good luck" in its efforts to control the internet when he spoke about its emancipatory potential, to giggles from the audience, but recent book titles on the matter suggest that the Party got the last laugh: *Censored, Surveillance State, The Sentinel State, The Perfect Police State, The Perfect Dictatorship.*[13] Even a monograph on resistance to the state's co-optation and control of Chinese culture and history has a black cover and a title that emphasizes darkness—*Sparks*.

Has the Communist Party found a new balance on Durkheim's scale? Has it found a way to maintain its own rule by controlling information flows and thus quelling dissent, while continuing to govern in a firm style that gets things done, such as by reducing poverty and improving material living standards? In general, does information technology primarily empower authoritarian states like China, in this case by enabling cost-efficient micro- and macro-surveillance, or is the technology, as social movement scholars have argued, first and foremost a source of liberation for the people, by supporting collective action and the ability to resist state control?

One answer lies in the struggles of a secretive community of software developers that few people have heard of. They have for more than fifteen years worked to cross the Great Firewall.

Circumventing Censorship through "Incremental Action"

In 2011 the pseudonymous developer Clowwindy created Shadowsocks, one of the first firewall ladders that helps people evade censorship without being detected or slowed down. Shadowsocks has since been improved and updated by a growing community of developers inside and outside China, and today millions use it to access the open internet. Shadowsocks makes VPN traffic look like random, unidentifiable internet activity. It's steganography, digital camouflage.

A few years later, in 2015, V2Ray was introduced; its goals were the same, but the program was more sophisticated. A prominent developer told me it was a "game changer." Netizens could use it to make their illegal VPN connections look like video calls, regular web browsing, or something else, making them difficult to discover. Its enhanced flexibility is beneficial for political dissidents who might need various encryption and obfuscation levels as well as for users who merely want anonymous access to streaming sites without compromising on video quality. The tool is also highly adaptable. If firewall technicians figure out how to block or detect certain obfuscation protocols, as they occasionally do, people can switch to another one and carry on.

Shadowsocks, V2Ray, and a few similar tools were the first generation of high-quality open-source solutions to help global netizens circumvent state censorship. Both Shadowsocks and V2Ray have remained functional since they were introduced to the public and are still in use—a remarkable fact considering the CCP's devotion to information control. Because a community of committed developers work faster than firewall technicians, and because they can communicate and collaborate effectively in open secrecy, not even the CCP can wholly control who has access to the open internet in China.

This dynamic is unusual, because in protracted struggles between movements and the state, the state has a major advantage. The state can use bureaucratic systems to demolish resistance at the pace of a turtle, one protestor at a time, over years, while social movements, which undoubtedly also work across complex timescales, often thrive on the emotional energy of the moment, when people are driven by outrage and hope as well as a sense of passionate urgency that makes legal risks and sacrifices like unemployment and street camping possible.[14] Gradual development of software or other tools that undermine state control is different. Iterative action, as I call it, transcends time and space: connected actors work together gradually, patiently, sporadically, although at times feverishly, such as when security holes are discovered.

States have surely been empowered by innovations in information technology, through powerful tools for surveillance and information manipulation, and by getting access to the granular data that surveillance capitalism generates on everyone. But information technology also enables anonymous and pseudonymous groups to communicate and collaborate in open secrecy. The ladder community—the people brought together by a common commitment to censorship circumvention—has since its genesis built, maintained, and disseminated highly technical solutions to collective problems, even in the face of great risk. On public sites and platforms, masked by pseudonyms, they partake in asynchronous development, where technical problems are dispassionately and patiently unpacked and fixed, steps at a time. Such incremental action is difficult to stop.

Data from the popular code-sharing platform GitHub—which enables collaborative software development—indicates that the ladder community is growing. In 2013 the number of active developers who worked on projects related to Shadowsocks or V2Ray was forty-five. In 2023 the tally was over one thousand. These measures are flawed, as some users have started over with new identities for security reasons. But it is clear that the projects have expanded. The total number of saved code changes—"commits" in GitHub parlance—has increased more than twentyfold since 2013, with notable jumps in early 2020, at the start of the COVID-19 pandemic, and in the first few months following the so-called blank paper protests in late 2022, when the CCP's Zero-COVID campaign had made people so exasperated that some protested it publicly. Several developers appeared only recently, but many have been active for years; the mean duration of activity is seven months.[15]

In total, more than forty-six hundred people have contributed to the Shadowsocks and V2Ray projects and related software. The ladder community now offers censorship-circumvention tools for all major operating systems. Figure 4 visualizes the distribution of labor. Most developers (the tiny dots in the figure) make only a few additions, but they add up and sporadic contributors occasionally become committed participants (larger, darker circles). For example, one person I talked to said she discovered "some bugs," suggested

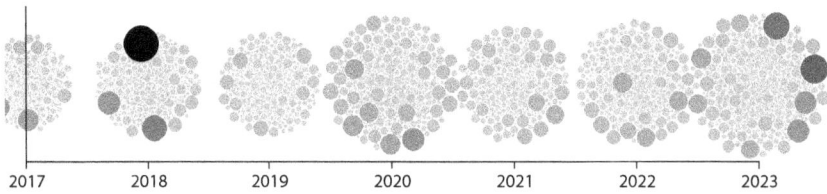

FIGURE 4. Ladder developer activity, 2018–2023. Each circle represents one developer; circle size reflects their number of commits to ladder-technology repositories on GitHub.

ways to fix them, later submitted "new features," and eventually became a "member of the community."

The measures of developer activity tell us that more work is getting done and that the community is growing, but merely looking at numbers misses important nuances. For instance, some developers make minor additions to a project, such as correcting typos, translating instructions, or editing a script's style, while others take more creative and complex steps, such as flagging and fixing vulnerabilities. These "designers," as one person called them, can shape the direction of future projects. Examples include Clowwindy and Victoria Raymond, the respective creators of Shadowsocks and V2Ray.

Designers and other developers discuss their work in private and public chat rooms and make decisions through deliberation. They often reach consensus quickly, as many of their problems have obvious solutions. When voting fails to settle disagreements, people sometimes split and pursue different paths, on their own or in small groups. One infamous case in the community is ShadowsocksR, which was introduced in early 2015. The developer Breakwa11, whose online persona is a "young female college student," copied the original Shadowsocks code to a new GitHub page, added new functions, and presented the result as a superior tool. "The original version," Breakwa11 claimed, was "difficult to use" and had "various problems."[16] (These claims were disputed.) In another case a prominent contributor to V2Ray called RPRX created Xray, "the best" V2Ray, according to its GitHub page.[17] This project has its own community of developers and maintainers who optimize speed, resolve bugs, fix security issues, and make other improvements that keep the code working.

Shadowsocks itself has a similar origin story, although it was not a copy of an existing tool. Clowwindy introduced Shadowsocks as an alternative to the pioneering ladder GoAgent in 2012 in a public discussion forum for developers. Clowwindy wrote that he had made a "simple" but "very stable" ladder. After having used it for "more than a year," he released it to the public and invited other developers to critique and/or join the project. Dozens of forum members—including GoAgent's lead developer—responded supportively in a rapidly expanding conversation about Shadowsocks's architecture, its utility, possible improvements, potential ports to different operating systems, and ideas for alternative versions.

Distributed Cognition

This nascent ladder community was and is empowered by open secrecy. Open secrecy enables members to maintain a public presence, with their masked identities intact. Pseudonymous ladder developers have for more than a decade conversed about controversial and legally risky technology in public and semipublic spaces, such as in chat groups and online discussion forums. They subscribe to an open-source spirit of code-sharing and have a digital platform on which they can edit and expand on one another's accomplishments, debate designs, and make collective decisions, all while accommodating idiosyncrasies, breakaway developments and developers, and experimental ideas. These characteristics make the ladder development network highly resilient. Because the communication flows through multiple websites, apps, and globally dispersed servers, they can reorganize when needed—for instance, if a prominent communication tool is shut down. Their contributions can be backed up and passed on, and collaboration will continue even after the loss of peers to law enforcement crackdowns and long after the emotional energy of new social movements has typically subsided.

The Great Firewall keeps improving, but the challenges it poses for the ladder community have thus far been surmountable. Problems are common, but in the words of one developer, they have never found themselves in a true crisis, where all their ways to connect to the open internet are suddenly blocked, and "nobody can describe what's happening and how to [solve] the issues." Nonetheless, the community is busy. Software functionality and reliability require debugging, performance improvements, and other fixes, just like Microsoft Windows requires updates. Some of the maintenance work is complex, but much of it is the kind of upkeep that "anyone" who is "quite nerdy" can do, as one developer explained. The low bar for making meaningful additions strengthens the community, as a large pool of occasional contributors spot problems faster than just a handful of dedicated developers would.

Ladder developers and users were often reluctant to speak with me, considering the risks of openly challenging autocratic states, but I could alleviate their concerns by verifying my identity with encryption signatures in the same way as they do, and as I did when I interviewed actors in the darknet economy: First, I made my public encryption key widely available—I posted it on my university staff website, social media, and on MIT's PGP Key Server. (The public encryption key is a bit like an email address—you want people to find it, and you want people to know it's yours. If it was shorter, one could have it on one's business card.) Next, I contacted developers directly, by email or in chat messages. To sign these messages—that is, to prove that they came from me—I generated a unique signature for the exact message I sent them, which was generated with my *private* encryption key, which only I have access to (or someone who has my password). To verify it all, the recipients could copy the message I sent them, and my public key (which they would get from a place I had posted it, like my university profile) into an encryption program, which would verify its authenticity. We usually talked in a digital space that enabled end-to-end encryption. At times, the interviewee would prefer that we encrypted all our communication manually— that is, not just once but every time we sent a message—to make the correspondence unreadable to outsiders (e.g., in case one of our computers was hacked).

As noted, developers work together on public code-sharing platforms like GitHub, which enable collective improvements of code and accounting of contributions. Git, the underlying software, makes it easy to publish code and invite alterations from specific collaborators or the larger developer community. All edits are recorded, which makes it easy to keep track of who has done what and keeps all previous versions backed up. In other words, Git supports distributed cognition: people can think about problems and propose and trial solutions together, over time and space.

In one example from July 2015, about three years after Shadowsocks was made public, Clowwindy and two other developers were trying to get the software to run on Apple phones and tablets:

CLOWWINDY: I have ShadowVPN fully working on an iPad. The next step is to add [a user interface], etc.

SHARPVISION: @LY has a working port of tun2socks on iOS. Maybe he can help.

CLOWWINDY: Good to see we can join forces on the tun2socks bridge! @LY I've added you to the team. You can push directly to the repo.

LY: Thanks!

In this exchange the developer SharpVision suggested on GitHub that one of their peers could help them work on a ladder for iOS, and Clowwindy granted editing access to the recommended person, LY. Their collaborative work eased access to the open internet for China's Apple users. A few days after the chat, Clowwindy successfully connected his experimental iOS tool to China Telecom's 4G network, but the line was blocked. A reset with a new IP address worked, but only momentarily, so Clowwindy returned to the lab: "I'm coming back to working on Shadowsocks again," he wrote on GitHub. Developers who later joined the discussion thread were familiar with and unfazed by the challenge, and together they solved it.

Solidarity Forks

But soon after the technical conversation about porting Shadowsocks to iOS, Clowwindy wrote on GitHub that the police had somehow tracked him down and ordered him "to stop working on [Shadowsocks]" and "to delete all the code from GitHub." He had "no choice but to obey," and added, "I hope one day I'll live in a country where I have freedom to write any code I like without fearing. I believe you guys will make great stuff." The community response was immediate. Here are some of the messages from the same day:

> Thank you so much for providing such great software.
> Love you!
> Thank you.
> Thanks, with all my heart.
> My first comment on GitHub. I just want to say, thank you.
> Thank you for giving me a way to know the great World Wide Web.
> Thank you for bringing us the real Internet!
> Thank you for the great work.

Today's a historical moment. Something will change. We'll see.

Great appreciation for your work! Can't live without it now.

This commit will be remembered as evidence of oppression and a monument of the fight against it. Never would've thought a commit could bear such weight.

Ideas are bulletproof.

I'm obliged to say, thank you for keeping the doors open!

Wish you the best. Stay out of trouble. Same problem in my country too.

Thank you for the outstanding work. Please take care of yourself. Delete anything if necessary; people have their backups to carry on.

People thanked Clowwindy for creating a path to the open internet, noted the gravity of his actions, and suggested that he was an important part of a bigger political struggle. Some people acknowledged his personal sacrifices and risks—which ranged from firm warnings to imprisonment—and stated that others would indeed carry on his work. The messages above are representative of the sentiments of the nearly five hundred others posted in the days after Clowwindy's announcement. Many more messages were written months and even years after. For example, in late 2018 one GitHub user wrote, "Great job for Chinese people, and for a better China," and in 2020 someone posted to "pay respect to the pioneer of anti-censorship!" The discussion page, which is still open for submissions, has become a place for sympathetic and grateful community members, and outsiders to salute the developer and commemorate his work.

It's unclear how the police found Clowwindy. There was no public trial and presentation of evidence, unlike in the case of the darknet markets discussed in chapters 3 and 4. Perhaps Clowwindy failed to encrypt his communication in a weak moment influenced by sleep deprivation, afternoon hunger, work pressure, heartbreak, or too many beers. It's difficult to always avoid mistakes when you live an alternative life online and work against the state. Ladder designers are particularly vulnerable because they experiment, as when Clowwindy worked on a new iOS ladder for China Telecom's 4G network: his unusual connection methods might have flagged the firm's cybersecurity personnel.

Days after Clowwindy posted his farewell message, the designer behind GoAgent was also contacted by the police and told to erase *his* work. And a few years later, in 2019, the key developer of the "game-changing" firewall ladder V2Ray vanished. Victoria Raymond has not been heard from since, either publicly or privately. It is unknown if she was told to never use her account again, if she was arrested, or if something worse happened. Or not. I've been told that on at least two occasions, for security reasons, prominent developers decided to start over with new online accounts. Some retire by choice. As one developer explained, "I have a day job, other hobbies, and life goals." Another said he was "tired of hiding." Someone also heard that Raymond disappeared because she got married. But most people I talked to about this believe Raymond vanished because of the intensifying government crackdown on internet access.

Despite the disquieting unknowns, ladder developers are stoic about personal risk and difficult to deter. One person told me that when "the news about the developers disappearing" broke, "I felt it was unfair for them, but since I'm always trying to be careful online anyway, I don't think I changed anything personally because of this news." Another interviewee felt the "need to protect myself well" but did not worry about other developers leaving ("doesn't affect me"). Others are more political in their resolve. One developer lamented the "sad but expected" loss of people "I personally know" but added that "none of the disappearances have affected my commitment to Internet freedom." Another developer was transformed by the legal threat to their activities: "When I learned that Clowwindy was threatened by the Chinese government, I realized that anti-censorship is a revolution. In the past, I didn't tell others how to break through censorship because I was afraid of being criminalized by the government. But since then, I started sharing anti-censorship software." Developers mourn the community's losses but are not surprised by them. They express defiance and echo the comments on the GitHub discussion page about Clowwindy (and similar salutes to GoAgent's developer).[18]

Despite the dramatic loss of key leaders, the number of contributions to ladder technology on GitHub is growing. Some existing members become more involved, and new recruits make the community more resilient. Law enforcement interventions undoubtedly deter some, and have perhaps slowed development in particular areas, but on the whole the community's continued activity suggests that conventional policing strategies will fail as long as there are more people who are so frustrated with online censorship that they want to fight it and can do so in open secrecy. In the words of one developer: "It's far easier to raise mosquitoes than killing them all." The community survives also because they operate in a decentralized ecosystem, like the darknet economy discussed in chapters 3 and 4. Developers and their supporters work together across numerous projects, platforms, and websites; they share "access to critical resources [so] there won't be a single point of failure," as one developer told me. Other interviewees expressed similar sentiments:

> Decentralization is very important to free speech.
>
> Decentralization is key . . . servers get banned.
>
> [We now] distribute . . . many different things . . . among different persons.

Much as the digital drug trade reorganized after law enforcement interventions, ladder development decentralized because of state

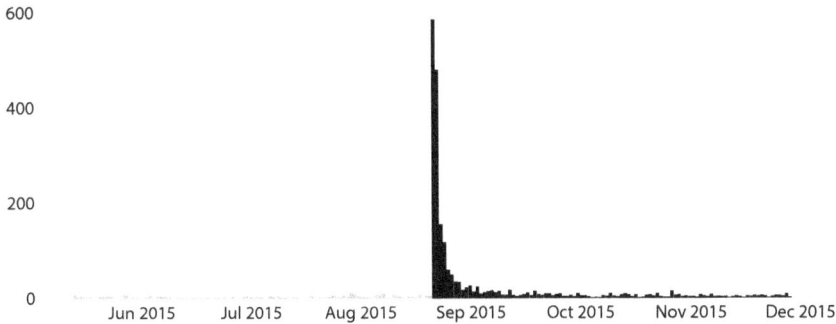

```
600

400

200

  0
        Jun 2015   Jul 2015   Aug 2015   Sep 2015   Oct 2015   Nov 2015   Dec 2015
```

FIGURE 5. Forks (copies) of Shadowsocks, after its original developer, Clowwindy, was tracked down by police and told to stop working on ladder technology.

pressure. One case in point is V2Ray. The program was originally tied to an account owned and controlled by its creator, Victoria Raymond. When she stopped responding to messages, her peers copied her code to a new project page and distributed editing access to several key figures, in case one or more of them were snatched away. Another example of decentralization in response to shocks is "solidarity forks," public backups of projects under threat. Shadowsocks's code was copied hundreds of times in the days after Clowwindy posted his farewell message (Figure 5), and V2Ray has been forked nearly ten thousand times to avoid centralized dependency. As developers can communicate in open secrecy, they can determine which copies to develop further.

Police crackdowns appear to stimulate community growth. Recall that one person came to see ladder development as "a revolution" only after a police intervention, and GitHub data show that at least four people who posted thank-you messages in response to Clowwindy's farewell statement later started contributing to ladder projects with the same usernames.[19] That's a small figure, but the work of Clowwindy and Victoria Raymond illustrates how important single individuals can be, and likely many others joined the community without posting in that commemorative thread, or picked different pseudonyms. Crackdowns also bring national and international attention to the censorship fight. A notice about the Clowwindy incident on Hacker News—a US site popular with tech entrepreneurs—generated more than five hundred comments:

> I was visiting China recently . . . I thought bypassing The Great Firewall was going to be [easy]. Oh boy, I was wrong. . . . The government does deep packet analysis. . . . You need to disguise your VPN traffic [with] tools that most Westerners have never heard of. . . . I have a lot of respect for all these Chinese hackers like clowwindy who try to escape censorship, as it takes more technical prowess than you think.
>
> I am in Iran, you cannot believe it, same here, they use deep packet inspection too.
>
> I suspect that they got the [deep packet inspection] technology from China. As a Chinese netizen I don't know if I should be proud that we have world-class advanced technology or be ashamed. Possibly ashamed.

The above conversation among people in the United States, Iran, and China was prompted by a story about Clowwindy's legal trouble. Sometimes such discussions lead to collaboration (more on this in chapter 6).

· · ·

Police interventions stopped Clowwindy from further refining Shadowsocks, at least under the same username, but dozens of developers have carried on his work. Clowwindy's core obfuscation protocol remains effective—more than fourteen years after it was created, and almost a decade after the police intervened. The disappearance of Raymond also failed to deter the community, and the project she created—V2Ray—has become a popular (some say superior) alternative to Shadowsocks. Statements of solidarity and gratitude, copies of code, continuing development, decentralization, community growth, and public commitments to the fight against censorship suggest that the Party has failed to halt ladder development.

But software development does not put products in people's hands—making something useful does not automatically translate into widespread adoption, especially if the tool is complicated and controversial. In the next chapter I explain how that job—dissemination—has been picked up by entrepreneurial black market vendors.

6 *Black Markets for Censorship Circumvention*

Firewall ladders like Shadowsocks and V2Ray are camouflage—they make unusual internet traffic, such as virtual private network (VPN) traffic, look normal—and thus allow people to evade censorship without being detected. Combining ladder technology (the camouflage) and proxy servers or VPNs is easy for tech-savvy folks. But it can be cumbersome for those who are not. That friction deters many from connecting to the open internet, but there's a workaround: buy a black-market solution. Just as Prohibition in the United States created an underground economy for alcohol in the 1920s and early 1930s—since most people who wanted to drink did not want to participate in illicit production of it—a market for firewall-climbing services has emerged in China. "Airports," so named because the Shadowsocks logo is a paper plane, are readymade combinations of ladder technology and proxy servers or VPNs that get the user all the way to the open internet.

Most airports are small and informally organized: someone has set up their own server, provides access to friends and acquaintances, and receives payments or thank-yous via messaging platforms such as WeChat.[1] But many airports operate on a large scale, with thousands and thousands of paying users. With such subscription figures, earnings add up, even if the individual rates are low. In April 2022 the average price of a monthly 100 GB subscription was 25 yuan, or about $4, about the price of a Chinese Big Mac, and hosting such a service costs far less.[2] One airport operator told me that he charged a "very affordable" 12 yuan a month per user, which still generated income. He spent two to three hours on the gig every day, mostly "teaching new clients how to use the service and [replacing] servers that are often blocked by the [Great Firewall]." His customer base grew through word of mouth.

How large is the "airport" market, and how many people in China use these ladder services to access the open internet? Until now, no one has had a good answer. To make a rough estimate, I collected data from ten popular airport review services, where one or more individuals, acting like citizen journalists, tried out airports and shared measures of connection speed and often their compatibility with Western video-streaming platforms and other popular websites. These testing services covered almost four thousand distinct airports in the years 2020–24. It's hard to know how many users each airport has because the operators don't share that information. But we can look at something public: most airports run a Telegram channel where subscribers get updates on pricing, technical details, and other relevant issues.

The mean number of subscribers for the 91 Telegram channels I examined was 1,595. Since joining these channels is optional—and potentially risky for users—this count likely underestimates the total user base for a typical airport. A 2023 data leak that included the full user count for four airports confirmed this. I looked up their Telegram channel subscribers and found that for these the ratio of paying users to channel subscribers was about fifteen to one. Using that ratio and my total airport count mentioned above, I could calculate an estimate of the full airport market. The result: between 2020 and 2024 there were almost ninety million airport users in China.[3] The estimate is highly, highly conservative, because my list of known airports includes only services that were either popular enough to be tested or requested testing by the testing services I examined, and only in the 2020–23 period.

Smartphone apps should also be included in the tally. The Apple App Store and Google Play list numerous free and commercial apps with ladder technology, with and without built-in proxies. These apps are banned in China, but descriptions, functionality, and reviewer comments suggest that the products cater to Chinese users, who download them from abroad or from a foreign version of the app stores, accessed by borrowing someone's airport logins or by buying a foreign account on the e-commerce site Taobao (e.g., a foreign Apple account gives access to foreign versions of the Apple App Store).

In 2024, Android apps that use Chinese ladder technology had been downloaded more than thirty-five million times from Google Play. Apple does not provide download data from its App Store, but a third-party company estimates that the most popular iOS ladder app, Shadowrocket, has been purchased more than seven hundred thousand times.[4] Considering that people replace their phones every two years or so, these numbers do not represent unique users. But, despite the uncertainties, the data illuminate a thriving shadowy market for Chinese ladder technology.

In some ways the airport black market is a conventional market. Providers gain customers by offering reliable, well-functioning, and reasonably priced services, and users assess quality through personal experience, online and offline discussions, and reviews that evaluate reliability, speed, and compatibility with bandwidth-heavy services, such as video-streaming sites. But the airport market has unique challenges, due to its legal status. Some airports stop working—for instance, because the provider is apprehended, runs off with subscription payments, or gets too busy and opts to retire. And users risk more than inconvenience. If an airport fails to use up-to-date ladder technology, important security fixes that protect user identities may be neglected. The state's absence as a market guardian allows for opportunistic and illegal behaviors, such as when airport operators launch DDoS attacks on their competitors—intentional flooding of traffic to make a website or service unavailable—or hack them and threaten to expose user identities. Another concern is that some airport providers might work *with* the state. Several airports hedge their legal risks by prohibiting political activities, engaging in censorship themselves, even collecting visitor data. In one case an airport provider shared user data with a police investigation into "darknet transactions," possibly a commercial operation like the markets discussed in chapter 3 and 4—some fentanyl products sold on the darknet originate from China. It's also possible that the police operate an airport, much like the Dutch police operated an online drug market to collect information on buyers and sellers (see chapter 11).

Ladder developers have the know-how and reputation to do well in the airport market, but the ones I spoke to have no interest in selling airports. Some are too busy, juggling a job alongside ladder development, while others simply prefer to focus on obfuscation protocols. In the words of one developer, their time is "better spent on more critical aspects." Several developers said that it's safer to avoid mixing ladder development and money:

> Most developers believe that if they don't involve money, they will only receive a warning if discovered. Although the authorities in China don't always follow the law.
>
> In theory, we can benefit [from airports] . . . but we should keep a low profile. . . . Censorship resistance is resistance. . . . Keeping it free can reduce our risk.
>
> I don't think it's a good idea to make money by helping people bypass the [Great Firewall]. . . . This may constitute a crime.

Their concerns are warranted. Several ladder developers have been punished for selling firewall-circumventing services, and big earners face the stiffest terms. In 2017 a man from Jiangsu who made $165 from selling firewall-circumvention services was held by police for three days, while a Dongguan-based man who made $2,000 for a similar service was sentenced to nine months, and a man from Pingnan who pocketed $76,000 was given a five-and-a-half-year prison term.[5] One person I talked to, who provided internet access to at most two thousand people, was in prison for three years.

That airport providers profit from open-source ladder technology made by unpaid volunteers does not bother any of the developers I spoke to. The community permits commercialization, and as two participants put it, airport providers create "easy-to-use [and] cost-effective ways" to "help more people cross" the Great Firewall. Enabling users to access the open internet on a consistent basis, at scale, is a major logistical undertaking that a voluntaristic community is poorly equipped to handle, but a for-profit market with sufficient supply gets the job done. New markets sometimes emerge in response to pressing social problems.[6] The airport trade, which is built on the work of activists, sustained by businesspeople, and caters to a large consumer base, suggests that black markets can drive social change—in this case by providing a nationwide shadow infrastructure that helps people get the information they want and need.

Global Adoption

As the Iranian developer said in the previous chapter, Chinese censorship tools and know-how—for instance, for VPN detection—have been exported to other autocracies.[7] In turn, the global interest in ladder technology has also increased. It's quite a twist: the Chinese Communist Party (CCP) has, by attempting to tighten information control, globalized anticensorship technology. One developer told me that people who struggled to understand instructions written in English and Chinese reached out to the ladder community, which then called for translators. A person who rewrote the entire Shadow-socks user interface in Russian said he wanted to help people circumvent website blockades put up by Russia's mass-media governing body Roskomnadzor in 2012. In South Korea, where Chinese and Korean ladders are used to bypass local firewalls (e.g., at universities), a developer translated Shadowsocks to give his peers "a better experience": "[The internet] is generally censored [on Korean university campuses], and [this] has even prevented me from accessing Source-Forge and a few other development-related sites. . . . Internet censorship does some good things, like banning illegal porn, [but the government] is doing too much. It forces Internet service providers to [monitor traffic,] which is expensive and degrades network performance, [and] they should not log or know what I do online." By making ladder technology more accessible for his compatriots, the Korean developer pushed back against what he saw as excessive government interference into personal affairs that also had the annoying practical consequences of adulterating and degrading connectivity.

The increasingly global relevance of ladder technology was evident in Iran in 2020, when protests raged and the government tightened internet control. Iran's firewall is starting to resemble China's in that it's getting harder and harder for citizens to connect to the open internet with VPNs, and a growing number of Iranians have therefore turned to Chinese ladder technology, sometimes with technical assistance from outside the country. A case in point is this conversation from GitHub:

[pseudonyms added]

IRANDEV1: Somehow, the Iranian firewall validates the TLS packets and drops them if they are invalid. . . . Right now, I do not have any work-around for this issue.

CHINADEV1: Thanks for the update. This is sad. Just out of curiosity, technically how does the Iran firewall find out it's Cloak and not regular HTTPS?

EURODEV: If Iran's firewall is indeed able to differentiate between Cloak and real HTTPS, you can try simple-tls. This encrypts your Shadowsocks traffic with real TLS1.3, so theoretically there's no way to differentiate.

IRANDEV1: Is the speed and stability good?

IRANDEV2: Thanks for your advice.

EURODEV: I have been using it for a month now, and have not noticed a significant difference compared to Shadowsocks.

IRANDEV1: Cool, thanks!

Iranian developers used Shadowsocks and the obfuscation code Cloak to make their VPN traffic look like regular internet traffic, but Iran's firewall detected them. The solution, proposed by a European developer, was to use a protocol developed by a Chinese developer.

An Iranian man I spoke to, who initially used Google Translate to understand Chinese ladder technology, said that the problem discussed above was solved, but only temporarily: "The situation has worsened . . . The censorship system is becoming more complicated and limited every day." In his view the contest between censors and circumventors was a costly and time-consuming game with no winners as censorship isn't just a concern for activists but also affects the Iranian economy: "We spend a lot of time daily passing censorship. . . . I am a programmer. I worked in the IT field for many years. Access to tutorials, documents, resources, and large projects is vital for us." Another Iranian developer said that his (Iranian) employer gave him and his colleagues access to foreign Shadowsocks servers for "overcoming restrictions." This is one of many examples of how rules that make sense to the state are sometimes out of touch with people's needs and capabilities, thus resulting in widespread disobedience that delegitimize the leadership.[8] The same developer said that censorship in Iran was now "so vast" that you "rarely find a smartphone . . . with no VPN and/or proxy set up on it."

Iranians I talked to operate airports and share access to them with trusted parties. But unlike the thriving Chinese community, Iranian developers and airport operators who used ladder technology typically worked on their own or in small groups. Why is there no openly secret community of censorship-circumventing developers as in China? One possible explanation is that Iran's information control isn't yet as sophisticated as it is in China, and therefore that it's easier to circumvent censorship with conventional and widely available VPNs.[9] An Iranian airport market might also struggle with business logistics because Iran lacks widely used online payment systems, such as China's WeChat and Alipay, which might make it harder to organize large-scale trade of banned digital services. But most important, people there have not needed to build ladders from scratch, a formidable challenge that created a community in China.[10] Like in the darknet economy, the need for people to get together and collaborate strengthened community ties. An Iranian market might emerge, as the Iranian government appeared to intensify its crackdown on internet access in 2024, by criminalizing VPNs. The trajectory of one Iranian developer is illustrative of how people respond to such challenges by adopting more sophisticated censorship circumvention solutions:

> Many years ago I subscribed to [Iran-focused] VPNs, [but] they were either unreliable because the government actively tried to block them, or they worked well, which made them suspicious. . . . I used international services for a while, but . . . they can't be trusted either, [so] I started looking into [cloud servers]. A lot of hosting options were blocked, and many are too well-known, [so] there is a high

chance that the government would intercept their IP addresses. . . . I [then] came across [an airport] which utilizes Shadowsocks at its core. It was incredibly easy to set up and use, fast and reliable.

Ladder technology appeals to Iranian developers because mainstream VPNs are seen as potential surveillance and censorship targets, as their operators might prioritize profits over user safety—for instance, by collaborating with the government—or harm users in other ways, such as by cutting support. A case in point is the global VPN provider Surfshark, which announced in 2021 that it would end its Shadowsocks compatibility because this function had low demand in democratic countries, where the company makes most of its money. Iranian users protested the decision on social media:

> We in Iran use Shadowsocks a lot. If you disconnect, our communication will also fail. Please don't do this @surfshark.
>
> The Shadowsocks protocol is second to none in terms of user experience imho. It's exceptionally fast, light on resources and easy to use. . . . Hope you @surfshark reconsider and don't ditch it any time soon.
>
> Please @surfshark, we love your services.
>
> We have experienced one of the best secure Internet and web browsing servers with you. Please do not delete shadowsocks. We really need it in Iran.

Despite pleas from its Iranian users, Surfshark proceeded with the unplug.

When pathways to the open internet are blocked, as when Surfshark discontinued its Shadowsocks support, knowledgeable volunteers guide netizens to alternative options, like traffic controllers at an actual airport. One Iranian developer told me that he first learned about ladder technology from such a traffic controller shortly after the government banned the social media site Twitter: Vpnclub, as he goes by, provides information about censorship evasion strategies in Farsi and sometimes even pays for servers and passes them on for free. Vpnclub told me in 2022 that he had updated his main communication portal—a Telegram channel—on a near-daily basis for seven years. In August 2022 the channel had almost 130,000 subscribers, and in June 2023, after a year of protests, the tally was close to 300,000.

Vpnclub's influence goes far beyond these figures. Nonsubscribers can also access the posted content, and some pass on what they learn. For example, two Iranian developers I spoke with, whom I contacted separately and who have no known ties to each other, said that they have shared info from Vpnclub in their personal networks. Both developers called the channel administrator a "hero." Because Vpnclub can communicate openly and safely to masses of people with a secure and recognizable pseudonym, he can single-handedly help hundreds of thousands of users, perhaps millions, climb state firewalls.

Institutional Support

Western technology companies have complicated and morally ambiguous relationships with autocratic states. For instance in China they helped people connect to the internet in the 1990s, and thus helped bring about a thriving digital public sphere in the 2000s and 2010s where people could learn about the world and themselves, and in some ways live richer lives.[11] But the same companies sometimes kowtow to the states in which they hope to operate, at the people's expense. Cisco was famously involved in the creation of China's Great Firewall, and Yahoo!'s China division shared a dissident's private communication with the state (which proceeded to arrest him).[12]

Microsoft's China office threatened people who used its cloud service for airports. Its notice, posted in both Mandarin and English, said that "no company or individual can provide hosting service for illegal 'over the wall' proxy sites [or] VPN service." But the next sentence, set in boldface, is the most chilling: "**In order to avoid unnecessary risks and losses, we recommend that you conduct self-examination and rectification immediately.** [You] **assume all the consequences of such violation.**"[13] Microsoft's warning suggests that the company was ready to hand over information about its users to Chinese law enforcement, just like Yahoo! did. Technology companies will often neglect people's privacy concerns, even trample on them, if it means they might benefit from better relationships with the government.[14]

But Big Tech's presence has also benefited the Chinese ladder community. For example, although Microsoft is no ally of airport users, its 2018 acquisition of GitHub bolstered the code-sharing platform's ability to withstand cyberattacks (such as a massive state-sponsored DDoS the same year).[15] This allowed it to continue to serve as a dependable base for ladder development and software distribution. Yet there's no safe haven. US sanctions made parts of GitHub unavailable in Iran until Microsoft received an exemption in 2021, and ladder technology that depends on American services has become increasingly unreliable there.[16] For instance, US sanctions might force Microsoft to ban a Shadowsocks airport that uses its cloud services, if it detects traffic from Iran coming through. Similar sanctions on China may disrupt ladder traffic, at least until the community figures out a workaround.

Google is another complicated case. The company's downfall in China started when it was told to censor its search results there. The firm complied with the demand but informed users whenever their queries were filtered, information that the Chinese government soon ordered them to remove. Eric Schmidt, then Google's CEO, wanted to give in to the demands, arguing that the market was too important to ignore, but due to political pressure in the United States, protests from its own staff, and resistance from cofounder Sergey Brin (and eventually his founding partner, Larry Page), the company refused. In the face of an equally unrelenting Chinese government, Google left China in 2010.[17] Likely because the company now has little to lose in China, the company supports censorship evasion tools that help people climb the Great Firewall. In 2018 the Google unit Jigsaw, which "explores threats to open societies," launched Outline, a software tool that makes it "easy to create a VPN server, giving anyone access to the free and open internet."[18] The key technology in Outline is Shadowsocks.

Regardless of whether the ladder community cares about the status boost of its code being picked up by Google, it benefits from the company's resources. In 2018, Jigsaw hired the German IT firm Cure53 to audit the security of its Shadowsocks-based products. (The firm found four vulnerabilities, which were promptly fixed).[19] And some of Google's talented developers are now solving issues and creating new functionalities that volunteer developers might not have the time or interest to work on. For example, while ladder developers tend to focus on optimizing and securing obfuscation protocols, Outline staff have created a slick and user-friendly tool that makes it easy to set up an airport. Google also helps disseminate ladder technology: in October 2022, as protests were ongoing in Iran, a link to Outline was placed on the Farsi version of Google's front page.

Censorship circumvention technology also receives indirect support from nation-states, and some of it may end up supporting Chinese ladder developers. The Tor Project, which aims to provide anonymous access to the open internet by making and maintaining censorship circumvention tools, received about $2 million a year (from 2016 to 2020) from various US government sources and a similar amount from mostly American private organizations—the lion's share of its funding—as well as a steady but smaller line of support from the Swedish government.[20] This may aid further ladder technology development because Tor recently recognized the high quality of Chinese ladder technology, just like Google did, and in June 2020, reached out to the developer community to learn from it. In a "forum for public discussion about Internet censorship circumvention," a Tor employee initiated a conversation about V2Ray, on behalf of the organization's "team reading group." They wanted to "broaden our understanding" of ladder technology, he said.

A key figure in the ladder community, who has actively contributed to V2Ray development for years, offered to provide information and answer questions. He explained that V2Ray is "designed to be a platform in which users can design their own protocol stack to suit their needs." V2Ray's flexibility "cover[s] them all." The conversation was soon joined by Vinicius Fortuna, who leads the team that created Google's Outline VPN. "I consider [using] other protocols [like V2Ray]," he said, "even though our flavor of Shadowsocks is working . . . in Iran, Turkmenistan and somewhat in China." One challenge for Outline was to find a protocol that supports User Datagram Protocol, which can quickly transfer large volumes of data and is thus useful for video feeds. "Does V2Ray support this protocol?" The same ladder developer said V2Ray's support for UDP is "limited" because "Chinese [internet service providers] always try to sabotage UDP traffic . . . What kind of UDP usage would you advise V2Ray to support?" Fortuna replied that they see "significant UDP traffic in Outline servers . . . I imagine the main use for UDP is video calls and watching videos (e.g., YouTube). Gaming is probably relevant too." This conversation connected Tor, members of the Chinese ladder community, and one of the creators of Google's Outline. The Tor team were impressed with the ladder technology and later invited several ladder developers to an online meeting focused on V2Ray and eventually hired one of them for a full-time job. In 2022 the conversation turned to whether Tor should integrate V2Ray in its own tools.

Travel Destinations

Where do people go after they've climbed the Great Firewall? Some clues can be found in Google Trends data—measures of its popular search terms. As noted, Google is unavailable in China, unless you have privileged access or use a mainstream VPN or airport.[21] Such re-routing typically obfuscates your location, but because Google collects data from the cellular network towers or internet connection points that you're using, as well as your device's GPS coordinates, many China-based users of its services are correctly geolocated and included in Google Trends. This data is limited because many ladder and airport users will avoid Google, and people who really want to hide their tracks can do so—for instance, by disabling GPS or by subscribing to an airport that is designed to trick geolocation services. But despite these drawbacks, Google Trends data offer insights into an area that is difficult to study.

The most popular search words for China-based Google users in 2011–2024 were, as in the United States and many other countries, the names of common websites like Baidu and Facebook as well as generic terms like "weather." Because the top results are so mundane, Google Trends also measures rising queries that have "the biggest increase in search frequency since the last time period."[22] These data suggest that firewall-climbing netizens in China mostly look up sports ("world cup", "Paris Olympics"), technology trends ("chat gpt," "stable diffusion"), current affairs ("US election"), political figures (Sun Zhengcai and Wang Qishan, and in 2022, Hu Jintao and Jiang Zemin, and in 2024, Donald Trump and Kamala Harris), popular movies and TV shows, and influencers such as Li Jiaqi. In some years "sensitive" topics appear in the list of rising keywords.

The Nobel laureate Liu Xiaobo was a popular subject in 2012, interest in "Hong Kong news" surged in 2019, and in 2020 the top rising queries included "coronavirus" and "Wuhan pneumonia," while 2024 included "Ukraine" and "Lebanon." Shadowsocks was a trending topic in 2015, the year the police contacted Clowwindy, and V2Ray trended in both 2017 and 2018, a period in which the CCP intensified its crackdown on conventional VPNs. These trending queries show that China-based users of Google search for uncensored information about what's going on in the world, look up things they like (such as TV series), and in general examine ways to gain digital autonomy.

The appearance of Shadowsocks and V2Ray in Google's lists of trending search terms suggests that by tightening internet control, the CCP boosted activity and recruitment in the ladder community, or at least indirectly stimulated interest in their technology. Like in the darknet, crackdowns on openly secret domains backfired. Ladders transitioned from being niche technology discussed in hacker forums to mainstream tools. This is a familiar dynamic as governments struggle to control the liberatory forces of information technology across the world. In chapter 3 and 4, I explained that police crackdowns on digital drug markets forced their participants to reorganize and thus spurred innovation and decentralization. The outcome was a more sophisticated and resilient darknet economy. The same pattern has played out with internet censorship in China. Excessive information control frustrated netizens, stimulated interest in anticensorship tools, and provided the impetus for action, and with open secrecy, pseudonymous and anonymous actors could build software solutions to their problems, disseminate the work across semipublic channels for encrypted communications, and publish it on open platforms. Through development, discussion, debugging, and distribution in open secrecy, people created a resilient, self-sustaining community. Today their work helps millions of users climb the Great Firewall (Figure 6).

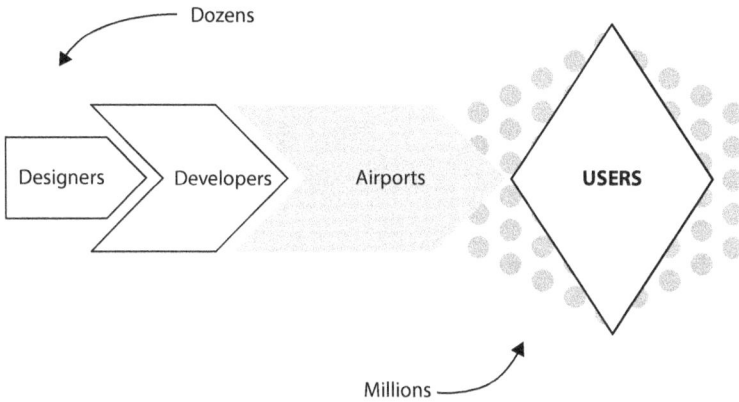

FIGURE 6. Dozens of designers and a larger pool of developers create and maintain ladder technology, which is used in commercial airports that ultimately help millions of Chinese internet users climb the Great Firewall.

It's a Social Nonmovement

Does newfound access to the open internet stimulate interest in politics? Google Trends data can't answer that question—we don't know if the people who searched for information about Liu Xiaobo and the Hong Kong protests were apolitical before they got connected, or if they're just curious about stuff they've seen on WeChat. But a 2019 experiment offers some valuable insights.[23] The study found that nine hundred university students in Beijing who were provided with censorship-circumvention software generally stuck with local websites, in support of the argument that Chinese netizens are content with what they get within the walled garden that is China's internet.[24] Those who ventured over the firewall spent most of their time consuming entertainment, in line with the Google Trends data, and pornography (adult search terms are removed from Google Trends). But people who were offered financial incentives to read the Chinese-language version of the *New York Times* continued to consume foreign news sites after the study period, even when they had to pay out of their own pockets. These people also read more Wikipedia pages. The study's findings suggest that censorship circumventors mostly want to access familiar stuff they like but learn to appreciate unfiltered, credible information after being exposed to it. Such learning moments can come about due to external guidance, as in the study, or, as data from Google Trends suggest, after regulatory interventions and crises create the need for accurate information, such as when popular websites are blocked, VPNs are removed from app stores, Hong Kongers rise, or a mysterious pneumonia starts killing people in Wuhan.

Politics are rarely discussed by ladder developers and airport providers, at least in public. When I browsed discussion groups for ladder technology and airports on a daily basis in the summer of 2022, I anticipated that the usual talk about technical challenges would change on June 4, the day of the Tiananmen Square protests and massacre. I expected members of the ladder community to use their liberty to speak the unspeakable, but the conversations on that day were no different than on any other June day. This is partly because many chat groups for ladder technology and airport services discourage or even prohibit talk about politics. The developers I spoke to, who are actively building tools that undermine state control, said they avoid sensitive issues in their conversations:

> Many of us dislike the government's policies in regards to the blocking and censorship. But I'm not an activist. . . . Software development is my interest. Also, I found the online services outside of the Great Firewall have better quality than their alternative in China. I am a hardcore movie and TV show fan, and the streaming services in China are bad. Sometimes you can't even see the complete movies or TV shows because of the censorship. So I do all my media consumption on Netflix, Disney+, etc. Once I've tried them I really can't go

back. The same thing applies to my choice of music streaming services, cloud storage services, instant messages, etc. . . . I'm just trying to improve my quality of life.

I believe in the open-source spirit: one for all, all for one. Therefore, I make sure that each piece of software that I design helps as many people as possible. I am not politically motivated. I don't believe I can change anything with my capability. I do hope free speech and free expression is a thing in every country, but I don't plan to do anything politically.

As long as you don't publish serious political statements or conduct criminal activities (drugs, gambling), which I don't, I don't feel I'm taking too much risk. It's definitely about rights; I'm just trying not to be too political.

Developers believe in free speech for themselves and their peers and compatriots at large. But they do not critique the government that limits that free speech. They support open-source development, which embraces collaboration, the sharing of ideas, decentralized power, and independent thinking, and they use open secrecy to reclaim the information access that the state withholds. But they don't conceptualize their own tenets and actions as "political," articulate collective goals or demands, or link their efforts to construct and maintain a censorship-circumvention infrastructure to bigger ideas about state governance and legitimacy. For my interviewees, the apolitical framing of what they do helps them keep going. They are, they claim, simply tech-savvy people living their digital, transgressive lives—they are neither monetizing their inventions nor calling for reform—and that narrative helps them avoid undue risk, and neutralizes related concerns. It might also make outsiders more likely to join them.

Keeping community discussions focused on technical matters also avoids ideological splits. People might hate or love the Chinese

Communist Party and still be on the same page regarding the need for freer speech, or at least best coding practices, and the potential of new ladder designs. In the words of one developer: "[Our ladder is] inclusive of all people, regardless of their political views." As noted, some airport operators go a step further and ban political activity on their networks, and the people who test and review airports appear disinterested in helping dissidents or the politically curious find the right connection: that is, they often note whether the airports they test work well for video streaming but say nothing about whether the services allow browsing of "sensitive" issues or monitor user data.

Even though people in this underworld avoid talking about politics, their acts *are* political. Even if they merely want to get online for their own independent reasons, write code because they like contributing to open-source projects, or sell airport access to make some extra money, or a lot of money, because in aggregate, their actions undermine state control of information. Regardless of individual motivations, and despite the absence of an articulated collective goal, their work pushes for social change. It is what has been called a social "non-movement."[25]

Disenfranchised people sometimes try to reclaim their rights and resources in gradual, nonconfrontational forms of resistance that improve their independent lives directly—for instance, as people break out of a censorship bubble to obtain the content they desire, or the information they need to do something. These acts, even if they are minor and driven by independent rather than collective motivations, add up.[26] Such quiet encroachment is particularly powerful on openly secret platforms, because the individual acts are recorded and can be built upon, in the way ladder developers work iteratively, often to improve and extend the work of others. This iterative action helps the openly secret community outlive its key designers, like Clowwindy and Victoria Raymond, whose code still brings millions over the Great Firewall.

Odd Coalitions

The Chinese Communist Party worries about people finding solidarity in projects outside of its control. The Party targets feminist and LGBTQIA+ networks, infiltrates civil society, regulates religion, controls labor unions, and tells curated stories from the past that they hope will bring stability and unity to a fast-changing society.[27] Keenly aware of the variegated sources of identity formation in late modernity, the Party attempts to influence people's cultural ideals and academic aspirations and guide their making of meaning. It has banned musical "idol" competitions; ordered broadcasters to promote masculinity and cut portrayals of effeminate men; blocked access to K-pop fan groups; required tech companies to remove video games that promote "money worship," "sissy" culture, and other "incorrect values"; ordered the removal of the popular language-learning program Duolingo from app stores; discouraged the teaching of "Western ideas" in universities; restricted access to video game platforms; and shut down popular influencers like Li Jiaqi, who included a tank-shaped cake on his show before June 4.[28]

These efforts to control what people care about and how they live their lives may have unforeseen consequences, as they unite citizens who differ in many ways but now share a desire for more autonomy. That is, through excessive social control, the Party unites feminists, gamers, democracy activists, students and their parents, Netflix binge-watchers, students of German philosophy, BTS fans, LGBTQIA+ people, Catholics, and consumers of pornography. This is a potentially dangerous mix for the Party. Huge numbers of people who are united in a fight that is widely deemed worthy have, thanks to the ladder community, reliable platforms on which to act. These are all key ingredients in successful social movements.[29] Conventional nationwide protests in the form of rallies for political reform are unlikely to materialize in today's China, but people tend to find safe ways to express their discontent.[30]

The Party should consider more cost-effective means of social control. Studies have found that people are broadly content with its leadership, and will likely remain so, if they feel that their lives materially improve, but excessive censorship might change that.[31] That is, the leadership's worries about public discontent might become a self-fulfilling prophecy, as the perceived need for stringent information control sows unifying resentment in a swath of people who otherwise have little in common. Freeing speech, on the contrary, will not only ease an overworked surveillance system and cut its costs, but might also strengthen the Party's legitimacy, as any major reform here can be framed as a case of the Party responding and adapting to the people's needs and wants. An insistence on continued censorship would be atrophy—a key ingredient in the fall of the Soviet Union, the source of the CCP's worst nightmares.[32]

The Party's decision to export its censorship tools to its autocratic peers might also work against its rule, by further globalizing the anticensorship struggle. Development of ladder technology is already directly or indirectly supported by foreign open-internet advocates, such as the Tor organization, states like Sweden and the United States, companies like Google and Microsoft, and on the microlevel, developers in autocracies like Iran and Russia use Chinese ladder technology, which is increasingly available in English, to further spread the scripts. If the Chinese Communist Party elects to crack down even harder on censorship evasion, this growing global community will surely return the favor.

An example of such a boomerang effect is how many active members of the ladder community have for a variety of reasons left China but still contribute to ladder technology from their diasporas. The transnational transformation of the censorship fight fits CCP propaganda messaging, which often warns of foreign powers that aim to damage China, but ladder technology is homegrown, and its increasingly global spread is the Party's own doing.[33]

Has the Party found a new balance on Durkheim's scale? Has it found a way to maintain social order, by quelling dissent, while continuing to rule effectively, in a way that gets things done and materially improves people's lives? The accomplishments of the openly secret ladder community and its growing capacities for action suggest not. Instead, the Party will likely need to adapt to the growing call for autonomy. A rhetorical cliché here would be to invoke the image of a ticking time bomb, or perhaps bring back Clinton's smug prediction that the energy and activity of an uncontrollable internet will help bring about political reform. Perhaps he was right, after all? My judgment is that he really was wrong. Access to the open internet will not translate into democratization. (In the next three chapters I will demonstrate that it might even undermine it.) But the cat is out of the bag, and aiming for maximalist control of it is risky.

The CCP has proven time and time again that it's supremely adaptable, and it will likely be able to manage a freer internet.[34] The Party's pragmatism is evident in how it responds to localized protests about social and economic issues—which are common—by meeting the people's demands in a manner that is highly selective and self-serving, and thus a serious challenge to its rule is avoided.[35] More liberal internet rules can likewise be to the Party's interest: by meeting the people's digital needs and wants, the CCP may slow ladder development, undermine the odd coalitions of disgruntled netizens, and gain legitimacy in the people's eyes. A blackout will backfire.

III   *The Digital Far Right*

7 Deplatforming the Digital Far Right

In 1956, William Shockley and two colleagues won the Nobel Prize in Physics for their work on semiconductors, the tiny pieces that help transmit electricity inside computers. Shockley, who had violent tantrums as a child and was homeschooled because his parents distrusted public education, later used his status as a physicist and inventor to promote the false idea that the accomplishments of European and North American scientists, explorers, and artists were due to their genetic composition.[1] He warned against the mixing of races and promoted policies that would have been welcome in the Third Reich, such as a "voluntary sterilization bonus plan" for low-IQ mothers. Shockley's eugenics were roundly denounced by many, including scholars who had the biological expertise he lacked.

Shockley is not alone in the camp of mechanically adept people who have drawn absurd conclusions about social matters. Consider that engineers are overrepresented in the Islamic State, perhaps because some of them prefer to avoid ambiguity, are drawn to the notion of "order," and seek simple solutions to complex problems.[2] Refactoring might aid engineers in their technical work but is no help in navigating intricate social and personal issues, such as how to live well as a human being or how to make a community better. In search of silver bullets, some people think that societies will improve if their populations are based on a singular principle or marker that makes people feel kinship with one another, as citizens of an imagined community.[3] The determination of who should be included or excluded in such an imagined community can be based on such arbitrary factors as religious faith, skin color, eye color, absence or presence of facial moles, penis length, ability to reach a high vocal pitch, or, as the Nazi Party set as a criterion for citizenship in 1935, whether one is of "German blood."[4] These characteristics acquire significance when people with power use them as filters, to determine what belongs and what is out of place, and as people use them to define their own identities, which are constructed in relation to others, through difference and distinction.[5]

Extremists' affinity for mechanical logic might explain why members of the far right were early and eager adopters of information technology.[6] They were communicating over computer networks in the 1980s, before the World Wide Web, and a prominent member of the Ku Klux Klan (and friend of Shockley), David Duke, was active online from the mid-1990s.[7] Around that time another KKK figure, Don Black, launched the website Stormfront, which he introduced as a "resource for those courageous men and women fighting to preserve their White Western culture." Stormfront is still available, almost three decades later, which is a rare feat for any internet community. Since its founding, the digital far right has grown into a sprawling jungle of countless sites and multiple social media platforms for globally dispersed activists and sympathizers.[8] Three sites that stand out (which I will return to later in this chapter and the next two) are the pioneering Stormfront, the high-traffic news blog the Daily Stormer, and the ambitious far-right social media platform Gab.

Stormfront has remained characterized by its KKK association since it launched in the 1990s. Many of its members have been active in the community for years, some more than a decade. Stormfront has cut out swastikas and other Nazi signage, but it remains vile and tactless, and its aesthetics have barely changed since the turn of the millennium. A prominent far-right scholar once called it "the Chevy of the far-right." The Daily Stormer, a prolific site for news commentary, uses memes, aggressive rhetoric, shock value, and a Gawker-like writing style to attract young readers.[9] The social network Gab is more mainstream in tone and appearance. Its marketing language avoids profanity and vulgarity and embodies the futurist "doer" energy of Palo Alto, California, where its founder and CEO Andrew Torba once worked (a point he often makes in his newsletters). Torba presents Gab as an alternative to "woke" Silicon Valley that is up to date on current tech trends—for instance, by offering AI tools—while promoting "Christian culture" (code for whiteness) and permitting racist, misogynistic, and antisemitic posts from its members, in the name of "free speech." This contemporary far-right triad is a sobering force of influence. Each site promotes variations of the same idea, that white people in the United States and Europe are under threat because of their shrinking demographic majority. All have been frequented by murderers.

Wolves

Dylann Roof, who had a Stormfront account and read the Daily Stormer, entered the Emanuel African Methodist Episcopal Church in Charleston, South Carolina, on a June evening in 2015.[10] The skinny twenty-one-year-old carried a fanny pack with a gun and eight magazines of bullets. He was nervous and worried that it showed, but a member of that night's Bible study group handed him a worksheet for the lesson, and for fifteen minutes Roof sat silently among the congregants. He hesitated, considered walking out. "But then I just . . . I finally decided that I had to do it."[11] He drew the gun, quickly, and started firing. He shot ten people; nine died.[12] Three years later, on a Saturday morning in late October, Robert Bowers, a middle-aged man who likes Hooters and builds his own computers as a hobby, walked into the Tree of Life Synagogue in Pittsburgh. Earlier that day Bowers had posted on Gab: "I can't sit by and watch my people get slaughtered. Screw your optics, I'm going in." He killed eleven people and wounded seven more.[13] After his arrest Bowers told a SWAT officer: "They're committing genocide to my people. I just want to kill Jews."[14] It was the deadliest attack on the US Jewish community ever.

Roof and Bowers—described as quiet by people around them—are examples of why the far right is now widely recognized as the most acute terrorist risk in the United States. According to a 2017 joint intelligence bulletin from the FBI and the Department of Homeland Security, "white supremacist extremism poses [a] persistent threat of lethal violence."[15] Since September 11, 2001, the United States has faced more attacks and higher fatalities from far-right extremists compared to Islamist extremists, even though the latter get far more attention in mass media and presidential speeches.[16] People with far-right views are also overrepresented in murder cases. In a comparison of far right–motivated and far left–motivated murder cases in the 2010–20 period, 84 percent of all homicides were carried out by people motivated by right-wing ideology.[17]

Countering radicalization is made more difficult by the emergence of open secrecy, because far-right actors no longer need to hide in hoods and robes. In full or partial anonymity, far-righters meet in public online spaces, with recognizable and verifiable usernames, and speak openly to one another and to onlookers. They discuss tactics, raise capital, and organize meetups, transportation to rallies, and movement between websites. Talk that was formerly confined to dark nooks of society is today nurtured in plain sight and broadcasted to the masses.

Their presence has made their potential value as supporters, voters, and consumers notable. That might explain why Elon Musk has on social media written about dangerous illegal immigrants, racism against white people, conspiracy theories about the intentions of the Jewish investor George Soros, and reposted a message claiming that Jewish communities push "dialectical hatred against whites."[18] It might also explain why Tucker Carlson repeated far-right ideas on his popular Fox News show (and now independent show), why Donald Trump refused to criticize attendants at the far-right rally in Charlottesville, and why the most popular podcaster in the United States, Joe Rogan, endorsed Trump for president and thus helped him win the bro vote and possibly the 2024 election.[19] Regardless of what these white men actually believe, they have expressed and supported ideas that are attuned with the far right and have thus gained the support of many of them.

The tech-enabled ability to spread dangerous ideas and mobilize support for them is a serious threat to social order, in the United States and anywhere else where large groups with antisocial goals can connect, communicate, and collaborate in open secrecy. The most sobering case in point is the radicalization of people like Roof. His mind-set is, like everyone else's, socially constructed through millions of minor and major encounters and experiences, offline and online, and at times people learn to see the world in ways that transmute into harmful action. For example, people who come to see the racial and ethnic Other as a threat will act on that, unconsciously and consciously, with dating discrimination, backbiting, snubs in the office hallway, by reposting conspiratorial ideas, making racist memes, joining neo-Nazi marches, orchestrating online trolling, and firing bullets that pierce through skin, crush cells, rupture blood vessels, and tear apart organs, lives, families, and communities. The radicalization of Roof came up when FBI agents interrogated him shortly after the Charleston shooting.[20]

FBI AGENT: We want to know . . . was this just Dylann? Did Dylann just come up with this all on his own . . . or is there somebody else there that's recruiting, training, getting paid, and saying, hey, let's go do this?

ROOF: No, I mean, it's pretty much just, you know, it sounds lame, you know, I don't really like to say it, but it's pretty much just the Internet, you know? All the information is there for you.

Roof and Bowers acted alone, when they walked into the Charleston church and the Pittsburgh synagogue—they did not act on orders from a team leader or plan in a group. But they knew that what they were about to do will make sense to many others out there. And these ideas that drive Roof and Bowers to kill and justify their actions are collective products. Even if the information is just "there" on the internet, as Roof said, that obscure website has been compiled or created, and shared, by people in search of scapegoats for their grievances and anxieties, and/or people who work strategically to build support for the far right. People who kill in the name of misguided beliefs about race and ethnicity are not lone wolves, *they are wolves*.

The digital far right might push people like Roof and Bowers over the edge but also mobilizes collective action, which is made easier by the variety of far-right expressions. In our late-modern time of high individualization, social movements are more likely to succeed if they give people the space to express their idiosyncratic grievances, which broad messages with wide support enable.[21] For example, a movement built around economic injustice is more likely to succeed if it can appeal to both a Brooklyn hipster and a Texan mother of five. For the far right, a case in point of such diverse mobilization is the 2017 Charlottesville rally, which was heavily promoted on the Daily Stormer by its founder and lead writer, Andrew Anglin. The groups and ideas that came together there were eclectic but coalesced under the banner "Unite the Right." Hundreds of white supremacists marched with lit torches, shouting recycled slogans (e.g., "Blood and soil," "Jews will not replace us"). The following afternoon, James Alex Fields Jr., an admirer of Adolf Hitler, demonstrated again how dark movements can translate into individual atrocities by driving his car at full speed into a crowd of counterprotestors. He killed one person and injured dozens. A police officer later said the car was splattered with blood and flesh. A pair of blue sunglasses was stuck in its rear.[22]

Regulatory Attempts

US-based websites are protected by generous free speech laws, but they're regulated indirectly, "softly."[23] State entities, nongovernmental organizations, firms, civil servants, politicians, and academics often discuss issues such as content moderation and ways to mitigate the harms of hate speech, which influence company behavior, for instance, as they seek to preempt public and political critique and ward off costly legislation.[24] For example, per Section 230 of the Communications Decency Act, Meta is not legally liable for what Facebook and Instagram users write, but the law's scope and potential amendments have been debated in heated public congressional hearings. In 2023 the Surgeon General Dr. Vivek Murthy issued an advisory in which he said that "social media use is associated with harm to young people's mental health" and called for policymakers and tech companies to act.[25] While some politicians are more willing to put pressure on large corporations than others, even those who typically favor small government advocate for some form of regulation.[26]

In the case of the digital far right, these regulatory forces have translated into de facto crackdowns, as companies don't want to be seen supporting or enabling social harm, particularly when media attention is hot. Apps have been removed, data jettisoned from commercial servers, domains canceled, and payment processes cut. After the Charlottesville rally, for example, GoDaddy and Google stopped hosting the Daily Stormer, which had celebrated the murder of the counterprotester Heather Heyer. Stormfront was dropped by its server provider and shut down. Discord, an online service that allows groups to set up their own communication hubs, shut down accounts associated with the far right, and Apple and Google removed the Gab app from their platforms, for policy violations. Parler, another far-right sympathetic social media platform, was dropped by its server providers and the same two app stores after the attack on the January 6, 2021, attack on the US Capitol.[27]

Some of the sites are gone. But, as in the case of darknet markets and ladder developers, the digital far right adapts. When the domain provider GoDaddy said after the Charlottesville Unite the Right rally that it would no longer host the Daily Stormer's URL, Anglin typed up a message to its readers, seemingly in a rush, with no time for capitalization: "we're having an outage. it'll be a minute. for the time being, those that know how please come chat on IRC." He added a link to IRC, shared details for how to access the Daily Stormer's "men's social club" on the platform Discord, and called for donations. "Consider helping us with financial assistance right now, money gives us resources to manage outages better." He included a Bitcoin address and, for "cash or check," a postal address.

The Daily Stormer's followers were given instructions on how they could stay connected with other readers on various communication platforms. The site later announced on Twitter that a backup version would be set up in the darknet, which is accessible only with The Onion Router (Tor), the same anonymization software used by the drug markets discussed in chapters 3 and 4. The Daily Stormer (likely Anglin) told VICE News that "we should have a real domain online within 24 hours. If it gets shut down again, people will know we are on the black web."[28] Because nobody wants to host the Daily Stormer, and because Anglin wants it to be available without Tor, the site has moved through a growing list of domain names on the so-called clearweb (the non-darknet), including Dailystormer.at, Dailystormer.net, Dailystormer.wang, Dailystormer.ru, Dailystormer.lol, Punishedstormer. com, Dailystormer.eu, Dailystormer.al, and Dailystormer.in.

Don Black, who has run Stormfront since he founded it in the late 1990s, has repeatedly complained about the costs needed to keep the community online, partly due to the need to deflect malicious attacks. In a 2015 call for donations "to support increasing pro-White activism," Black said that Stormfront would move to new and more secure servers, in part to protect and expand his "daily, two-hour radio show . . . which also came under sustained denial-of-service attacks recently." According to Black's own posts, at least $38,000 in donations were sent to him in a six-month period that year. A modest annual income perhaps, but sufficient for him to remain online, despite considerable practical challenges.

As noted, after Charlottesville the app version of Gab was removed from both Google Play and Apple's App Store, as it had been used for logistical support, and its regular website was forced offline after Bowers attacked the Tree of Life synagogue in 2018 (Bowers was a member and talked about his motives on Gab). Torba wrote that he is undaunted by the crackdown on Gab. "It doesn't matter" what journalists write, he said. "We have plenty of options, resources, and support. We will exercise every possible avenue to keep Gab online." Speaking to his vaguely defined enemies, he added: "You have all just made Gab a nationally recognized brand. . . . You can't stop an idea."[29] People on the Silk Road drug market and in the ladder community said the same thing when their digital realms faced regulatory pressure ("You can't kill an idea,"[30] "Ideas are bulletproof"[31]).

The challenge of hosting a contested platform appeared to energize Torba. He wrote many Gab posts and newsletters about his efforts to overcome his obstacles, and the high number of reposts and upvotes suggest that the external pressure, and the sense that they are in a winnable fight, makes users determined to follow Torba's lead. Anglin exploits similar tendencies among his readers. He frequently co-opts the Daily Stormer's disrepute and opposition in its branding—the homepage banner sometimes reads "The Most Censored Publication in History." Legal and moral condemnation can make crime seductive, and some people break rules and norms not because they are in the way of instrumental gain, but because they are there, because they taunt, and because obedience is boring and restricting.[32] In Charlottesville the grins and shiny eyes seen in the torch march suggest that these participants, like Torba and Anglin, enjoyed raging against the mainstream.

Stormfront users proudly welcomed new members after Facebook banned posts on white supremacism in 2019.[33] On Stormfront, they wrote:

> Being proud to be White is now "hate" to Facebook. [If you] need a place where you can be proud of your heritage, and work with others with common goals, then we welcome you to Stormfront.

> Thank you guys for accepting me. . . . Facebook limits free speech, but what should we expect from a Jewish owner?

> Thank you for the welcome. . . . Facebook is anti white . . . We as a race of people need to boycott Facebook.

> Hi all the newbies! *beer toasting emoji*

> Goodbye Facebook, hello storefront [sic], finally I can be proud of my people *beer toasting emoji*

> From the Appalachian Mountains in the proud, beautiful, Dixie-Confederate South-lands, greetings.

Stormfronters relished the sense of being a white supremacist haven in a contested environment. The Daily Stormer has had a less stable presence. It had to hop between URLs, and its leader, Anglin, has been on the run since he lost a lawsuit in 2018 for having encouraged his readers to verbally attack a Jewish woman and her family.[34]

But these challenges have failed to dent the site's output. From April 2013 through September 2023 the Daily Stormer published more than fifty-five thousand articles, with a daily mean and median of fourteen. The pieces are signed by Anglin, thirty-two other pseudonymous contributors, and "Daily Stormer," likely a byline for new or occasional writers. The figures tell us that the Daily Stormer is not a mere blog for far-right news commentary, as I first thought, or a sick joke, as someone who stumbles upon the site might think. Rather, the Daily Stormer must be taken seriously, as a prolific propaganda outlet. According to traffic data from spring 2024, the Daily Stormer had 250,000 unique monthly visitors. That is less than the social network Gab (760,000) but far more than Stormfront (70,000).[35]

Adaptive Innovations

A recurring theme in this book has been that crackdowns on groups that operate in open secrecy sometimes produce the opposite of the intended effect. In the case of the digital far right, both Stormfront and the Daily Stormer have become more resilient by learning to adapt to deplatforming efforts. Gab's reinvention, which in Torba's words came about because of crackdowns, deserves particular scrutiny. In July 2019, Gab switched its software infrastructure to a fork (copy) of the social network Mastodon, which is open source and can thus be used by anyone, much like no one can control how people use math. Mastodon opposed the move, correctly calling Gab a place for thinly veiled white supremacism, but said they were indeed unable to stop it.[36] Torba said that the purpose of the shift was to make Gab less vulnerable to interference. "Gab is now unstoppable and can never again be taken down," he said in an interview.[37] The shift might make the platform more enduring, as the software behind it is freely available on GitHub and can be easily tweaked and improved upon, not just by Gab's inhouse developers but also techy outside supporters, not unlike how the ladder community discussed in chapter 5 and 6 benefit from many helping hands. Torba has also cut the network's dependence on online hosters. Around the same time as the switch to Mastodon code, Torba wrote on Gab.com that after "over a year of work," Gab "finally" moved to its own in-house servers. "We have been banned from multiple cloud hosting providers and were told that if we didn't like it we should 'build our own.' So, that's exactly what we did."

Gab's descent from the cloud and adoption of open-source software made the platform more able to stand on its own, without support from technology companies. Evidence suggests that it worked. After the siege of the US Capitol on January 6, 2021, another social network that catered to the far right, Parler, was taken down, as Amazon Web Services canceled its hosting, but Gab remained online. Sign-ups increased dramatically. Torba sensed an opportunity to gloat, promote the platform's independence, and reinforce what he often called a community. He wrote in numerous Gab posts that the site experienced a huge influx of users and increased server demands. He also took the opportunity to signal his view of the Capitol attack. Thousands of people sent their support in messages and reposts:

Jan 11th 2021: 600,000 new Gabbers today *eyeballs emoji*
2.4k replies 2.1k reposts 107 quotes

Jan 17th 2021: I don't want to hear another word about Jan 6th until someone starts talking about all of 2020 with BLM/Antifa burning this country to the ground.
1.7k replies 9.0k reposts 382 quotes

Jan 17th 2021: We will be setting up an additional five servers [and] are also working on expanding our engineering team . . . Please consider supporting us. [Link redacted.]
1.1k replies 2.2k reposts 82 quotes

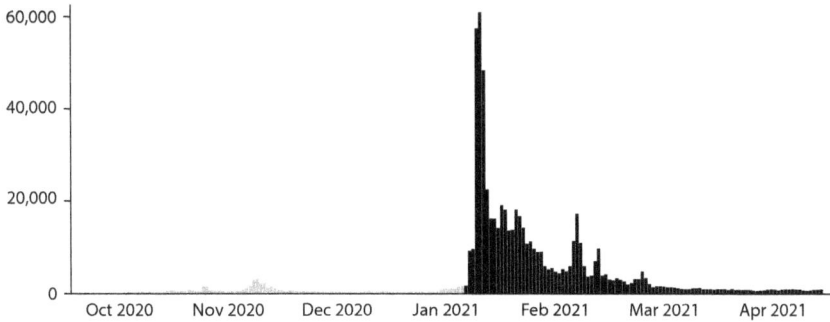

FIGURE 7. Tally of unique daily Gab posters, before and after the January 6, 2021, siege of the US Capitol.

The attack on the Capitol was for many a wake-up call about the internal threat to national security. For Torba, it was a recruitment opportunity.

Torba aims to build an alternative realm for "Christians," one in which efforts to overturn an election outcome is equated with protests against racist police brutality. That endeavor, which requires not just technological infrastructure but also people, was given a huge boost by the events of January 6 and the deplatforming of Parler. Torba's self-reported figures might be inflated—one study suggests that the record daily registration was 450,000—but activity after January 6 unquestionably increased.[38] I counted the number of unique active posters per day in the four weeks before and first week after the siege on the Capitol and found a sharp uptick in first-time posters (Figure 7).[39]

In 2021, nearly a month after the Capitol siege, when Gab activity was at an all-time high, Torba claimed again that the platform's challenges have been a source of energy and focused development for him and his team. "We've been deplatformed by 25+ service providers including both app stores, PayPal, dozens of payment processors, hosting providers, email services, and more," he said in a message to Gab users. "When this happens, I rejoice and praise God because I know that He is working to separate the wheat from the chaff." In Torba's words, the challenge he and Gab faced at the time was strengthening the platform. "Deplatforming," his preferred term for being shunned by technology firms, "reforms" Gab into "an even more resilient community, business, and platform . . . We aren't victims, we are builders."

As discussed earlier in this book, crackdowns on resourceful, highly motivated collectives stimulate creative adaptation of better technology, as people figure out how they can solve problems, such as dependence on proprietary software and commercial cloud hosting. Some users might be put off by the need to rebuild a digital network in a new place and learn how things work there, not the least of which is how to find that new network. Such practical challenges appear to have helped the digital far right grow more robust and adopt new practices.

Cloaked Money Flows

Far-right sites and platforms rely on donations, but struggled to find payment-processing services that are willing to work with them. Stormfront, for example, complained in 2012 that PayPal had canceled its accounts, and credit card companies later followed suit, after the Unite the Right rally in 2017 in Charlottesville.[40] Stormfront was therefore quick to embrace cryptocurrencies, which can be bought, sold, and transferred without going through banks or commercial money transfer services, and are therefore difficult to regulate. Cryptocurrencies can also be made anonymous—the same exact reasons that they appeal to people in darknet drug markets. Bitcoin has been an optional donation method on Stormfront since at least August 2014 and became "preferred" in late 2016. The Daily Stormer also started accepting Bitcoin donations in 2014, in response to a PayPal ban.

The adaptation is not without challenges, however. When several payment processors cut support to Stormfront in 2017, Don Black tried to raise funds by other means. In the thread's more than fifteen hundred responses, many users talk about Bitcoin, some with frustration:

Still no way to donate using PayPal or credit card? I can't figure out Bitcoin (trust me I've tried).

Just did my first Bitcoin purchase and attempted transfer to Don.

I'd like to donate. . . . I would consider snail mail as an absolute last resort. I'm not too familiar with Bitcoin—it sounds like something you'd use at a casino!

Sending cash or Bitcoin is the best way or perhaps the only way at the moment.

I used [Bitcoin] for convenience. everything was done by pressing the send button.

I cannot figure out Bitcoin, what it does, how to use it.

If Bitcoin becomes the only option available, I will unfortunately no longer donate to Stormfront.

I'd like to donate via paypal, can I do it? I do not have Bitcoin, just debit and credit card or help me please.

I don't understand Bitcoin. Why is it the preferred method? You can't buy groceries with it. :confused:

Bitcoin [can] circumvent the banking industry. Think about that. Our main enemy controls and owns banking.
Research Bitcoin. Bitcoin is the best.

The comments above and many others like them suggest that the transition from PayPal and credit cards to cryptocurrencies was not without pain and likely cost Stormfront money. But some members had already figured out how Bitcoin works, or were looking into it, or were educating others on its merits. Extremist fund-raising predates Bitcoin, of course, and envelopes of cash are also anonymous. But the cloaked character of cryptocurrencies will expedite the flow of money to shadowy groups, as they get increasingly easy to trade. When I bought my first (and so far only) Bitcoin in 2013, I had to transfer money to an Eastern European bank and pay a hefty commission. Today, Bitcoin can be bought using conventional payment services such as Venmo. Convenience matters because people are much more likely to do something if it's easy.[41]

People sometimes spend money to express love—such as when immigrants slice up their paychecks and send remittances overseas, or when people in pandemic lockdowns donated to charity.[42] But global money transfers can also express misguided despair. One example is from December 8, 2020, less than a month before the January 6 attack on the Capitol, when a thirty-five-year-old French programmer distributed more than $500,000 worth of Bitcoin to two-dozen cryptocurrency accounts associated with right-wing groups and individuals, before killing himself the following day. In an apparent suicide note, posted on his blog, the programmer wrote that he'd bequeathed his "modest wealth" to "certain causes and people," citing "the decline of Western civilization."[43] This Bitcoin transfer demonstrates how cryptocurrencies make it easy to funnel *large* anonymous contributions, which is trickier with cash. Shadowy movement of substantial sums has long been a major concern for states—seen, for instance, in the European Central Bank's decision in 2016 to permanently stop printing the €500 note. With cryptocurrencies, sending five million bucks is just as easy as sending five.

Evidence suggests that sizable transfers are indeed happening. A week after the Charlottesville rally, Anglin received a donation of 14.88 Bitcoin. The amount was symbolic: "14" refers to "the Fourteen Words," a white supremacist slogan ("We must secure the existence of our people and a future for white children"), while "88" stands for "Heil Hitler," as H is the eighth letter of the alphabet. The transfer was possibly a show of support from one affluent extremist to another, as the Daily Stormer was cut off by service providers after Charlottesville. But the benefactor could also have been a foreign state that seeks to sow discord in the United States.[44] The donation traveled through a complex web of Bitcoin wallets—more than two dozen of them—and the originating account had millions of dollars' worth of Bitcoins.

Identities are obscured in Bitcoin transfers, if the initial conversation from a regular currency is anonymous—for instance, if it is bought with a prepaid debit card that was bought with cash. But Bitcoin transfers are traceable as they move through the blockchain. This might not matter much to the average Stormfront donor, for example, but someone who receives lots of Bitcoin will be notable on the ledger and might struggle to cash out secretly. Some far-right actors therefore go a step further and request donations in monero, another cryptocurrency that is designed to be anonymous. Recently the Daily Stormer published its own guide for monero donations. An excerpt: "spies from the various 'woke' anti-freedom organizations have unlimited resources to try to link [Bitcoin] transactions to real names. With monero, the transactions are all hidden." Anglin prefers donations to be in monero because they offer additional layers of secrecy. Other actors in the far right, and the darknet markets discussed earlier in the book, are following suit.

The far right's affinity for cryptocurrency is partially ideological. One of the Stormfront donors quoted earlier in this chapter alluded to this, repeating the antisemitic trope that Jews ("the enemy") control the finance system, which Bitcoin has "the ability to circumvent." Electronic currencies can in theory undermine state-backed money, but the idea that the far right can somehow trigger a cascade that ultimately results in some kind of banking collapse is fanciful. The biggest consequence of far-righters' adoption of cryptocurrency is that in a strange turn of events, paranoia has gotten many of them rich.

Bitcoin was worthless when it emerged in the early 2010s. Its utility was first demonstrated in darknet markets such as Silk Road in 2011 through 2013, and years later, when they were increasingly seen as investment products and hyped to oblivion by retail investors and financial speculators. The valuation surge has benefited early adopters. When Stormfront started soliciting donations of Bitcoin in the summer of 2014, the price for one was around $400, and it has since passed $100,000. It is unclear when far-right recipients and early investors cashed out their cryptocurrency holdings, and perfect market timing is difficult, but the dates of publicly known donations suggest that some people have made lots of money. At least one hundred prominent far-right individuals have one or more active cryptocurrency accounts, and they have received and purchased Bitcoin, with a value that has since grown to tens of millions of dollars.[45]

Far-Right Economics

It is unsettling to learn about the cryptocurrency enrichment of hateful, dangerous actors, especially as it came about due to a mix of luck and paranoia. But this isn't merely a story about life's unfairness. Shadowy money flows help far-right actors maintain their projects and provide the resources to start new ones. If the donations keep coming Stormfront can carry on for another decade or more, and Anglin's propaganda machine can continue, even as its founder is abroad. Gab, which also accepts donations in Bitcoin, can keep its self-owned servers running and perhaps do more. Torba is now attempting to construct a "parallel economy," an e-commerce market for people "who share your values and want to support your business." If Torba's new market succeeds, he will have the means to expand his dark world even further. As of June 2024, "Gab Market-place" had more than twenty-two hundred active business pages.

Gab's own marketing materials present its marketplace with pictures of a white, masculine man wearing a "Christian Nationalist" T-shirt and white women with baby carriers, alluding to white supremacist fantasies of life in a homogenous homeland with conservative gender roles and full-blood white babies. In the market a "White Christian Man [with] Old School Values" sells T-shirts, including one printed with "Trump 2024" and on another one with "DRILL BABY DRILL." Even if dumb T-shirts dominate the Gab marketplace now, it does offer some conventional services and might expand. One example is a man in Phoenix, Arizona, who claims to have more than twenty-five years of experience in IT support and offers "direct on-screen [computer] assistance via secure, encrypted connection" for seventy-nine dollars an hour. Another is far-right coffee. "Hunter's Blend" sells "PREMIUM COFFEE FOR FREEDOM LOVING PATRIOTS," which "bypasses Left Coast importers & their agendas." Consumers can pay for these products and services with Bitcoin or sign up for GabPay, which gives users their own bank accounts, routing numbers, and even a payment card called Parallel. "By showcasing the card," the GabPay website reads, "you contribute to our ongoing stand against the woke mob." It also helps Torba raise funds: a filing with the Securities and Exchange Commission from 2013 states that the service collects 1.9 percent plus fifteen cents per transaction.[46]

Far-right trade might drive people further apart. As noted earlier, extremists often dream of making a separatist world based on whatever kind of "purity" they care about, or claim to care about, not unlike Torba's idea of an alternative economy for "Christians." One reason to think that the Gab market might succeed is that I've found in an earlier research project—on the sharing economy—that many people long for alternative ways of trading that are embedded in personal relations and local communities, because they dislike the faceless exchanges that dominate in our time, for instance, at large, over-lit malls.[47] Gab is trying to construct a dark version of such an economy. The Gab marketplace, even if it takes off, will never be able to compete with major conglomerates on price and offerings or replace global supply chains, but buyers there might be willing to accept a markup for things they need or want—for example, paying a premium for "patriotic" coffee in the way people pay for fair-traded arabica.

This far-right economy may grow into a meaningful supplement to the mainstream markets that foster new ties and thus reinforce the far-right community while generating funds for hateful projects. The potential consequences are particularly sobering because people already spend too much time on their own and an alternative far-right market that supplements impersonal transactions in the mainstream economy might reduce intergroup interaction, one of the few interventions we have that are known to reduce prejudice.[48] Markets also have a powerful normalizing effect on controversial consumption. As I've discussed earlier in this book, banned goods and services that are made to appear ordinary, even mundane, are increasingly treated as such.[49] Far-right branded coffee, tech support, and merch might have similar effects on white supremacist ideas.

· · ·

What is new about the digital far right is that open secrecy gives its members unprecedented capacities for action. The means to communicate and collaborate publicly enables widespread far-right messaging, which is sometimes penned by named actors like Anglin and usually consumed by people who refrain from using their real identities. The same public-cloaked dimensions enable solicitation of financial support, marketing of website relocations and novel services, distribution of guidelines and calls to action—all of which help a growing number of anonymous, pseudonymous, and onymous far-righters move in concert, through crackdowns and into novel spaces such as the darknet or Gab's alternative economy. These developments tell us that the current regulatory system is unable to rein in the digital far right. Like the darknet markets and censorship circumventors discussed earlier in this book, these shadowy groups appear uncontrollable.

Some sites that were shut down by Big Tech's deplatforming efforts did not reappear—but the evidence presented in this chapter suggests that groups with resourceful and motivated far-right actors will absorb many of those who relocate, adapt to problems, and continue in more solidified forms. Ultimately they are unlikely to be stopped by domain bans, canceled hosting, or terminated payment services. The pushback from technology companies has failed to stop the digital far right. In the next chapter I explain what its antisocial forces look like.

8   *The Digital Far Right's "Hate Focus"*

The digital far right generates lots of data that we can learn from, to better understand how its adherents talk about the world, to what degree people change over time, what keeps them engaged, and what inspires them to carry on, despite normative opposition from mainstream society and practical hurdles from technology companies that refuse to work with them. In this chapter and the next, I examine the three largest far-right sites: Stormfront, the Daily Stormer, and Gab.

Stormfront is a particularly good data source because it has served as a hub for white supremacists since the 1990s. The community has about 140,000 members who have posted at least once and a larger number of lurkers, who browse without participating. Many of its users have been engaged for years and posted thousands of times. Stormfront was originally for members and supporters of the Ku Klux Klan (KKK) but now welcomes far-righters of various kinds with the slogan "White pride, worldwide." The rotating homepage banner notes that "*every* month is White history month" (emphasis in the original). Highlights include European and American architecture, the Wright brothers' first flight in 1903, Leif Erikson's journey to the North American coast, the first transcontinental railroad in the United States, the airship inventor Ferdinand von Zeppelin, and the USS *Liberty* incident in 1967 (when Israeli forces mistakenly attacked an American warship), which Stormfronters present as evidence of Jewish hostility toward the United States. The most popular discussions on the site are about current events such as election outcomes and violent atrocities like terrorist attacks, all of which members connect to race and ethnicity or use to validate their concerns in threads with such titles as "Non-white on White crime report" and "Jews Are Dangerous." Stormfronters talk far more about Black people and in particular Jews than Muslims, Asians, and Hispanics (Figure 8).[1]

How do openly secret communities like Stormfront and Gab engage with external events? To find out I examined recruitment and rhetoric after terrorist incidents with four or more fatalities in the United States, 2002–21. Little is known about how such attacks affect the digital far right.[2] The data on terrorist incidents were obtained from the University of Maryland's Global Terrorism Database, which defines terrorism as "the threatened or actual use of illegal force and violence by a non-state actor to attain a political, economic, religious, or social goal through fear, coercion, or intimidation." For both Stormfront and Gab, I compared the mean daily activity in the four weeks before and first week after each terrorist attack. I find that on Stormfront, terrorism sharpens the hate focus on the racial or ethnic group that was targeted (in eleven of twelve analyzed events) and boost the number of new posters by a median of 11 percent. Gab was only available during three of the analyzed terror attacks. But for those three, the number of first-time posters increased by a median of 41 percent.[3] And like on Stormfront, terror aimed at particular racial and ethnic groups boosted hateful talk about the same groups.

For example, the week after Robert Bowers's deadly attack at the Tree of Life synagogue in Pittsburgh in 2018, antisemitic talk increased by 81 percent on Stormfront and the number of new posters increased by 4 percent. Gab is more complicated. As noted in chapter 7, Bowers posted on Gab before his atrocities, and the platform's owner, Andrew Torba, took the site down temporarily, as

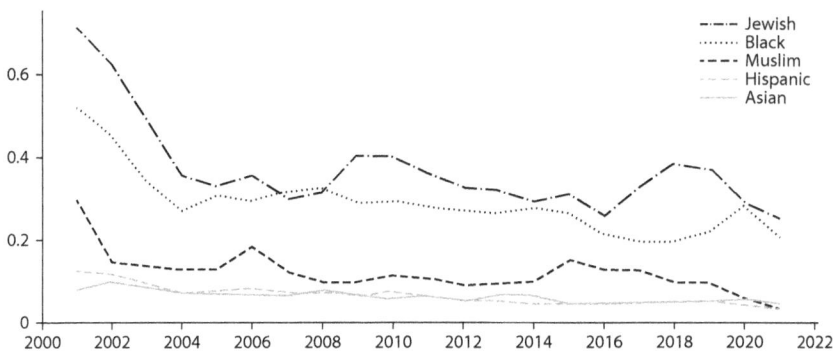

FIGURE 8. The hate focus on Stormfront, 2001–2021. The y axis is the mean number of topic keywords per post. *Note:* I found the keywords for each racial and ethnic category by using inductive-deductive topic modeling (IDTM), a method for computational text analysis that I recently developed with Annika Rieger. IDTM has four steps:

1. *Seed word discovery.* First I immersed myself in the content—I read hundreds of Stormfront threads, Daily Stormer articles, and Gab posts—to get a sense of how members talk about racial and ethnic groups. I then drafted dictionaries of keywords. For example, the dictionary for Black people included words like "Black," "Blacks," and various derogatory terms that I won't reprint in this book.

2. *Computational induction.* With the topic dictionaries drafted, I used the algorithm word-2vec to convert the Stormfront, Daily Stormer, and Gab data collected (about ninety-two million English-language texts) into a vector space, where keywords are mapped based on their co-occurrence and their semantic neighborhood. For instance, the words "Black" and "Blacks" were located near each other in the vector space, as they were used in similar ways.

3. *Qualitative refinement.* To ensure that each word's meaning aligns with its topic, I created and reviewed concordances—text snippets with keywords in context. This helped me decide on ambiguous words. For example, while the word "Black" often refers to Black people, it could also be a reference to Don Black, the founder of Stormfront. To determine that the word most often refers to Black people, I read three hundred randomly drawn cases of its usage. To eliminate such false positives, I replaced the phrases with bigrams (e.g., "Don Black" is replaced with "Don_Black"). After this step "Don_Black" is treated as one word, distinct from the word "Black."

4. *Quantitative deduction.* Next I counted finalized dictionary words for every text within the dataset. The results are visualized above.

several tech companies said they would stop working with the platform, for instance, by canceling its domain and data hosting.[4] But the two days before he did, including the day of the attack on the synagogue, first-time posters on Gab nearly tripled. The specific numbers are telling. The week before the attack, each day had on average 321 first-time posters. The day after the attack that number was 1,400. When Gab returned from its brief time offline (the fifth day after the attack), 1,550 users posted for the first time. In the same period Gab talk about Jewish people increased by 106 percent. Gab wasn't available when Dylann Roof murdered churchgoers in Charleston, but on Stormfront (the platform on which Roof was a member), the terror attack boosted talk about Black people by 37 percent and daily newbies by 74 percent.[5]

Does the emotional intensity fizzle out, or fester? I find that on average the heightened levels fall back. For instance, while talk about Muslims increased after an incident of Islamist terrorism, that chatter eventually dropped down to where it was before those atrocities. This finding suggests that many far-right people use sites like Stormfront and Gab to process and express raw thoughts and feelings about media-covered world events. Surrounded by like-minded peers, these users vent to a receptive audience. And then they cool down. But some of the post-shock energy appears to transform into commitment and/or attract dedicated far-righters. Stormfronters who signed up after a violent event tied to race and ethnicity—like a terrorist attack or police killing of a Black person—stay active for longer than people who join the site during quiet periods.

How long do new Stormfront members stay active? It depends on when they signed up.[6] The research shows:

When it's calm: ⟶ 271 days
After violence: ⟶ 301 days

The Obsession with Black People

Roof said in his interrogation after the murders that he "had to" do what he did because "Black people are killing white people every day."[7] Roof and many other Stormfronters frame African Americans as dangerous and "out to get" white people. But these far-righters misread (or don't read) statistics. Of the twelve terrorist attacks I examined, only one was classified as anti-white. Furthermore, data from the FBI show that most hate-crime perpetrators are white, and most victims of hate crimes are Black. Concretely, from 2011 to 2021, 30 percent of all hate crime cases were anti-Black, and only 11 percent were anti-white. Most hate-crime offenders were white (73 percent). These figures are not adjusted for population size—there are of course more white people than Black people in the United States—nor are they adjusted for socioeconomic differences, living conditions, institutional racism, and so on. Nonetheless, the figures undermine the far-right trope that Black-on-white crime is omnipresent. Roof, for example, said about Black people in his interrogation: "What I did [in Charleston] is so minuscule to what they're doing to white people every day, all the time." This is false.

In discussions of violent incidents on Stormfront, Stormfronters often refuse to acknowledge Black victims and instead foreground perceived or anticipated threats to white people, sometimes based on anecdotes or imagined data. One example is the initial reactions to Roof's attack in Charleston. Consider the following discussion posts:

> A White guy going on a mass shooting is made such a big event because it happens so rarely. Blacks commit mass shootings everyday in every major US city.

> The media and the left will use this to support their narrative that whites are slaughtering blacks. It will not matter what the truth is.

Well . . . They can't blame the police for this one!! But, worse, the White residents of Charleston may have to tread carefully.

I pray for all the whites in that area and elsewhere that will be killed and raped using this as an excuse.

Condolences to the families of the dead. A church full of christian black people is most likely NOT our enemy. There are definitely going to be retaliatory hate crimes against innocent whites.

Watch the propaganda show begin now. We all know it's about the agenda to enrage black people against whitey. This will be a 24/7 discussion on CNN and MSNBC, where black-on-white crime is never mentioned.

With one notable exception, these Stormfront posters ignored the real pain and suffering of the murdered churchgoers and their families while lamenting the hypothetical pain of imagined revenge victims. The attack was also expected to be used as propaganda by elites (common far-right code for Jewish people), to disarm white people amid the threat of "enraged" Black people.

Black Lives Matter?

How did Stormfronters and Gab users view the incidents (including graphic video evidence) of police brutality against Black people that sparked national outrage in 2020 and widespread debate about racism and law enforcement misconduct? Far-righters oppose the state's monopoly of violence, and some research has found that some white supremacists are turned away from extremism by vivid moments of brutality, such as eye contact with their own bloody victims, perhaps when they grasp the horror of their actions.[8] A similar effect might be generated by the high-resolution footage of a white police officer kneeling on the neck of George Floyd, a Black man, for nearly nine minutes until he died. Instead, I found more evidence of far-righters refusing to recognize Black people as victims. The posts below, from a thread created a few days after Floyd was murdered in 2020, is representative of the Stormfront narrative:

> 6-foot-6? Armed robbery record? Bouncer? No wonder the White cop had his knee on Floyd's neck. Also, the cops thought Floyd was intoxicated, apparently, and he resisted the cops. Why must Blacks always, always, always resist the cops?

> The Jew owned and controlled media will NEVER tell you the truth.

> Look, I don't shed tears over dead negroes. Especially dead criminal negroes. But the cops literally committed manslaughter by being negligent idiots . . . That being said, one less future prisoner to deal with.

> Cops don't kill people for no reason. But as said above, I do not shed tears over a dead negro. This is just being used as an excuse for them to burn and loot.

Here, yet again, Stormfronters seem to be indifferent to the loss of Black life. They excuse and even justify police misconduct and say that there are bigger issues to worry about, such as crime by Black people and Jewish media control. Floyd is characterized as a "criminal" who "resisted the cops"; racist biases in policing are denied.

Just like terror attacks, high-profile cases of police brutality shifted the site's hate focus and boosted new account creations.[9] On Stormfront, talk about Black people increased by 38 percent, and new users increased by 21 percent. In the most notable incident of police brutality, the murder of Floyd, Stormfront recruitment increased by 57 percent and talk about Black people jumped by 70 percent. Gab was only active during two of the examined police killings. One, the murder of Breonna Taylor, had a negligible effect on the community. The other, the murder of George Floyd, was followed by a 223 percent increase in new posters, and a 144 percent increase in talk about Black people.

White Fears of Black Male Power

Barack Obama's 2008 presidential victory triggered an unprecedented boost in Stormfront memberships and community activity, far surpassing all other measured events. Obama's election win reinforced the view that white (male) supremacy is diminishing, and Stormfronters saw the outcome as a wake-up call to strengthen white "racial unity."[10] Research suggests that gender has long been central to the far right's discontent with social change. For instance, KKK members in the early 1900s touted the need to "protect" white women from "aggressive and dangerous" Black men, and did so by terrorizing Black men though sexual torture and by violating "their" women. Some contemporary white boys and men who feel emasculated also join white supremacist movements to feel empowered.[11] The Daily Stormer is a case in point. The site is full of misogynistic language, and Stormfronters and Gab users exhibit particular vitriol toward white women who have relationships with Black men, using derogatory terms like "mud sharks" and "coal burners." They rarely deploy derogatory language against white women who sleep with Hispanic, Asian, Muslim, or Jewish people.

In a Stormfront thread titled "Race Traitors," which has more than twelve hundred submissions and has remained active for more than ten years, the vast majority of the complaints are about white women and Black men. (A distant second is white men who partner up with Asian women.) In the thread on Stormfront, posters portray Black men as violent, hypersexual, and aggressive, share cherrypicked news articles of white women supposedly killed by men of color, and frequently blame the women for their victimization—at times with schadenfreude. In the same thread, and others like it,

Stormfronters also blame mass media and state institutions for promoting multiculturalism and interracial relationships, which shrinks the pool of available white women for white men like themselves. As one person wrote: "I personally have always had a hard time trying to attract white women. . . . If you aren't extremely good looking with high status and loads of money, you won't get any attention. Add in the effects of [mass media] on white women and it is game over for your average white guy."

It's a vicious cycle. Defeatism, paranoia, misogyny, and racism are not going to help these men find partners and might in fact lead them further into the dark—sexual frustration and perceived emasculation have long been known to dangerously influence behavior.[12] One telling study, which I sometimes talk about in my classes, had men taking a rigged masculinity test that told half of the participants they were more feminine than the average man. In follow-up surveys this group expressed homophobic attitudes, support for war, and interest in buying an SUV.[13] Another study found that men with breadwinner wives clean less at home and are more likely to be violent toward their partners.[14] Most alarmingly, the Global Terrorism Database now has included a separate threat category: young men who are "involuntary celibate." There have been at least five such incel attacks in the past twenty years that have killed three or more people.[15] The same dangerous energy of perceived emasculation is evident in the far right's past and present hatred of Black men and female "race mixers."

The Jewish Obsession

How can far-righters get it all so wrong? Part of the answer is found in the conspiratorial cloud that embeds their second obsession, Jewish people. Stormfronters say that the Western world is controlled by a Jewish elite that directs government policy, state institutions like the public education system, many of the country's wealthiest corporations, and mainstream media. This elite, according to Stormfronters, does whatever it takes to maintain and expand its power, which they believe mostly comes at the expense of white people. If the Jewish "overlords" maintain their control of the state and continue to foster immigration, integration, and diversity, Stormfronters say, demographic changes in the United States will gradually reduce white majority. This is, in their mistaken parlance, white genocide.[16]

Antisemitism pervades Stormfront and sometimes appears in surprising places. One example is found in Stormfront's early days, after its discussion section was opened in fall 2001, when much talk was devoted to the 9/11 attacks. Stormfronters framed the atrocities as "evidence" that Islam is a dangerous religion and stressed that the terrorists were Muslim, but in some cases the 9/11 attacks were seen as "a wake-up call" to recognize the harmful consequences of Jewish power and Israel's "occupation" of the United States. For example, consider these posts:

> To those White Americans feeling absolute rage and anger, redirect it to where the blame really belongs. . . . I have no love of Arabs or Islam by any means, and I certainly don't believe that we should cower in fear from them. But . . . we need to keep our priorities straight.

> We should not expect to stay clean while we do Israel's dirty work throughout the world.

> As a White Nationalist, I declare neutrality in this "war." . . . This is a war between Arabs and Jews. . . White America should step back and let them fight it out.

> Israel . . . set the whole thing up to regain worldwide sympathy. May seem a bit far out. But look who we are talking about here. They are butchers of women and children already. Whether it's here or there makes no diff. to them.

On September 11, 2001 the USA became the USI [United States of Israel]. The media has declared all who defy the USI as terrorists.

These Stormfronters said that any anger or rage in response to 9/11 should be directed at "the Jewish occupiers" of the United States, who were responsible for the September atrocities, as they brought their conflict with the Muslim world to the United States. The victims of this world order, in their view, were ordinary white Americans who were losing control of "their" land to an anti-white Jewish conspiracy.

The Stormfront chatter was similarly paranoid after Robert Bowers attacked the Tree of Life synagogue in 2018, killing eleven congregants. One user said "his motive"—stopping white genocide—was "spot-on." Here are other representative excerpts from the discussion's first one hundred posts:

Who will be blamed?

Well, regardless of who actually did it, white males will be blamed one way or the other.

Jewish leadership [is] planning . . . our Genocide.

I listened to MSNBC for about 2 minutes and they said all the buzzwords. AR rifle, handgun, Trump rhetoric, antisemitism. We must really be crushing it in the midterms.[17]

[The] liars who manufacture the zeitgeist will all endure. . . . Here's my take: so a bunch of Jews died? I don't care. They don't care about our victims of multicultural "enrichment." [Emphasis in the original]

ISIS

ISIS has only killed muslims and Christians but never jews or suni muslims as ISIS gets financed by Israel and Saudi Arabia and supplied with American weapons!

This [is a] false flag on the part of the Jews . . . we have invasion forces of Muslims, Asians and Squatamalans marching into our land and a relentless effort to overturn the Constitution using this election cycle. This is no coincidence.

I'd say this event was planned and was seeded into public consciousness.

Imagine how fierce the calls for gun control will be after these Jews have been the targets of a shooting.

I call the ability to keep and bear arms a victory for Whites.

Some Stormfronters claimed the Pittsburgh synagogue attack was staged (i.e., "a false flag" operation) to extend Jewish power by taking away the guns white people need to defend themselves. People who acknowledged that real lives were lost also said that the murders were a justified response to Jewish rule, which they blamed for the demographic changes in the United States that are "slaughtering" white people. Not even the most absurd ideas were questioned—for instance, that ISIS, which has claimed responsibility for numerous terrorist attacks in Europe and the United States, is secretly supported by an Israeli-Saudi-American alliance. Stormfronters are in this sense open-minded and inclusive: they tolerate different views, if these in some way support (or at least do not dispute) the narrative that Jewish power is omnipresent and working against the "white race."

Conspiracies also abound in Stormfront conversations about the Holocaust. One might think that the endless evidence of concentration camp horrors—more than fifty-five thousand oral histories have been painstakingly collected—would make it hard to support, but Stormfronters say that the overwhelming documentation just proves that Jewish people have organized a systemic, large-scale, and enormously costly scheme to vilify Nazis, garner sympathy, and distract white people from their diminishing supremacy. Some Stormfronters seem to enjoy deconstructing oral histories from the Holocaust. In one such text the Holocaust survivor Bill Lowenberg explains over fifteen transcribed pages how he fled from an increasingly antisemitic Germany in the 1930s to the Netherlands, where he faced persecution yet again after the Nazi occupation. Lowenberg was arrested and transferred to Auschwitz and then to the Polish capital of Warsaw for forced labor. In a thread titled "Tales of the Holocaust," Stormfronters identify Lowenberg's "lies," as in this comment:

> [He claims,] "There were schools going all day long—during the day for the children like us." That's wonderful! Little jew schools for little jew boys, where they could be trained to grow up to be good little jews. . . . Then, a few paragraphs later . . . "It was a Catholic school." . . . He goes from a small JEW school to a large CATHOLIC school.

The Stormfront member suggests in a condescending tone that Jewish schools indoctrinate children "to grow up to be good little jews," then points out a potential contradiction in the account—Lowenberg's mention of attending a Catholic, not a Jewish, school—which is used to undermine his credibility.

Remarkably, a Helsinki-based historian has taken it upon himself to support stories like Lowenberg's within the Stormfront thread:

> Where does he say he went to a small Jewish school? . . . The highlighted text [might] simply mean Jews were allowed into the Catholic school? Can you explain why it could not mean that?

The response:

> When a jew says, "There were schools going all day long—during the day for the children like us," he is most certainly making reference to a jew school.

To the Stormfronter, "like us" can refer only to Jewishness, as opposed to age or any other identity marker. And he is adamant that the unclear characterization of Lowenberg's childhood school proves that Lowenberg's personal experience as a Holocaust survivor is made up. Over hundreds of forum pages, Stormfront members search accounts like Lowenberg's for trivial mistakes or unclear references. In another oral history imprecise wording makes it difficult to tell if a survivor grew up with or without a radio, which is taken as evidence that his entire life story is a lie. Stormfronters say that there is further evidence of falsehood in the repetitive nature of Holocaust survival stories, but this is difficult to avoid, as survivors faced similar challenges.

Do Stormfronters believe what they say in their posts? The man who tried to undermine Lowenberg's story posted dozens of times in the Holocaust thread from 2007 through 2010, which suggests that he was either obsessed about the Holocaust or worked strategically to promote the lie that it was a hoax. It might not matter, because the outcome is the same. Falsehoods are repeated, made familiar, and might start to make sense to readers, because the more you hear something the truer it seems, and again, real victims are rejected at the expense of imagined ones.[18] Just as the murder of Black people becomes stories about white victims among these far-righters, evidence of Jewish persecution becomes evidence of Jewish power and "white genocide."

Ways of Seeing

If you believe that most authoritative and objective sources of information are controlled by a shadowy elite that has nearly unlimited resources at its disposal, how do you verify or falsify claims that you are unsure about? Newspapers like the *New York Times* might say that they strive to be fair and accurate in their reporting, but isn't that exactly what *they* would say? If I draw on research to debunk far-right conspiracies in my college classes, isn't that what *they* would do—enlist people like me to brainwash the youth? I teach and do my research in good faith, but this only makes me more useful to *their* goals. According to the digital far right: I'm an unknowing, delusional stooge. In this belief system my editor, the press that publishes and promotes this book, the people who review it, and the university that employs me are likely controlled by the same elite.

People who think this way will find it hard to trust hate crime statistics from the FBI, studies of race and ethnicity in the United States, or serious writing about the far right. The reality shown in mass media is always going to be a limited, curated representation of what's happening out there, as the front page has finite real estate and reporters hook their stories onto trending themes. As a former journalist I can assure you of that. But the mainstream press generally covers what seems important and definitely isn't a perception-management machine that works for a Jewish conspiracy. If journalism has a bias, it is sensationalism or, less crudely, ideas about what people will find interesting—not the furthering of "white genocide." It is also true that authoritative data sources, such as FBI statistics on hate crimes, are flawed, as all data collection efforts and analyses include mistakes and biases. But responsible people do what they can to minimize these mistakes and biases, and the results are generally more credible than dinner-table conversations and social media posts.

To deal with the perceived absence of objective sources of information, people "do their own research." This works only if people look at valid data and know how to read it. One example can be found in Roof's manifesto, where he writes that he was "truly awakened" by the way the media portrayed the killing of Trayvon Martin: "I kept hearing and seeing his name, and eventually I decided to look him up. I read the Wikipedia article and right away I was unable to understand what the big deal was."[19] Roof decided to "do his own research." He typed the words "black on White crime" into Google and, as he wrote in his manifesto, "[I] have never been the same since that day."

Compiled by a white supremacist organization euphemistically named the Council of Conservative Citizens, a list of so-called Black-on-white crimes radicalized Roof: "There were pages upon pages of these brutal black on White murders. I was in disbelief. At this moment I realized that something was very wrong. How could the news be blowing up the Trayvon Martin case while hundreds of these black on White murders got ignored?" He eventually came to see Black people as violent pawns in a Jewish-led campaign against white people.

Roof revealed preexisting far-right beliefs in his choice of Google keywords and by saying that he was "unable to understand what the big deal was" in Martin's death. Roof's story about his "awakening" might be just a performance, its details selected to convince the world that he is in fact a concerned, curious, and informed individual. Or he was unable to critically evaluate the content he found online.

Roof's radicalization, the misreading of hate crime statistics, and the wayward investigations of Holocaust survivor stories show that the digital far right fosters a particular kind of confirmation bias—the tendency to favor information that agrees with one's existing beliefs and ignores what doesn't—that undermines credible sources, foregrounds alternatives, and thus makes it increasingly difficult to determine what's real and invites the consideration of false ideas (Figure 9). This loop is reinforced by critiques of "the mainstream media" and state institutions such as the public education system, where children learn that some sources of information are more credible than others. Information distrust involves not only searching for

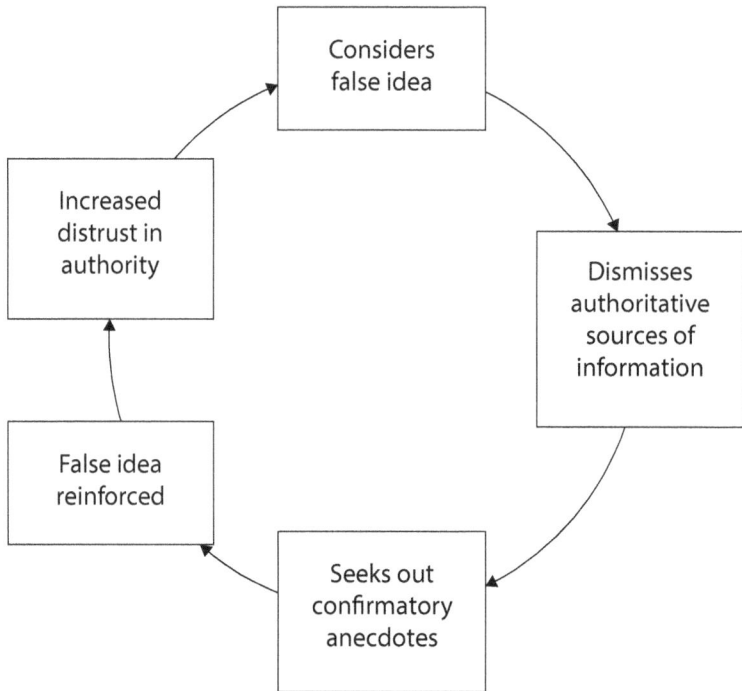

FIGURE 9. Information distrust. A person encounters a false idea (e.g., "the president is a puppet"). The person dismisses credible sources as "untrustworthy" and seeks out stories that support it (keyword search: "the president is a puppet"), thereby reinforcing the false belief. Ultimately the person develops an even deeper mistrust of authoritative sources.

supportive evidence of an existing claim (for example, the president is a puppet, put in place by a secretive elite) but also rejecting credible, objective sources of information. Furthermore, it is driven by actors who seek to undermine trust in more objective, authoritative sources (such as serious newspapers and academic works), including by the world's richest man, Elon Musk, who uses his social media presence to steer people away from conventional news sources and instead rely on anecdotes.[20]

White Victims

Stormfronters say that white supremacy is not about hate for the Other but love for their own kind.[21] They present the status quo as a crisis for white people. They are, they say, threatened by violent non-whites, in particular by Black people, while a Jewish elite works to reduce the number of whites, by promoting immigration and multi-culturalism, leveraging its control of the state, mass media, business, writers like myself, and a public that has been brainwashed to embrace diversity. The same forces, far-righters say, prevent white people from identifying as a racial group with common interests.

Many far-righters miss the crucial point that races are categories of political identity that are under perpetual construction. For example, in the United States, Irish, Polish, and Italian people were once seen as nonwhite.[22] More recently, millions of Americans revised their racial identity from their 2000 to 2010 census forms, suggesting that many racially mixed people came to see themselves and were treated as "belonging" to different racial categories.[23] But Stormfronters see whiteness as fixed, based on pseudoscience about European genes.[24] Similar sentiments are expressed on Gab and the Daily Stormer—the latter even has a countdown to the estimated moment when whites will drop below 50 percent of the US population. White supremacists across this digital landscape claim to be in a race against time, fighting the "extinction" of their people.

The framing of white people as victims is a recurring motif on Stormfront. One post introduces newcomers to the "pro-white movement" and includes a telling quote from Sam Dickson, an outspoken white supremacist and former lawyer for the KKK: "What is it that we want? What is it that we want that is so horrifying to the establishment of this country? What we want, at a minimal level, is merely the survival of our people."[25] It's true that demographics change. But the victim narrative is as narcissistic as it's absurdly entitled; if the fears of people like Dickson are real, they are based on a logic that does not belong in any society. Consider this analogy: A thirty-year-old man who prides himself on being the accomplished young adult of his family—perhaps even the pride of his local community—sees his younger sisters as a status threat and actively undercuts their efforts to do well at whatever they're doing. He recruits his friends to the fight against what he calls a secret alliance of feminists who plot the demise of his kind, such as the local Jane Austen book club, colleges that offer scholarships for women from low-income families, and so on. What is it that he wants that is so horrifying? In his view, he merely wants to protect his dignity and bring pride to his children. At a minimum, he wants the survival of the world his forefathers created.

In the discussions that followed Dickson's quote, Stormfronters argue that members of the "white race" have a moral imperative to preserve their genetic purity, which they say is the source material for Western Civilization and various achievements, such as those presented on the Stormfront banner mentioned above. In the words of the prominent KKK figure David Duke, a friend of Don Black and William Shockley, and occasional contributor to the Daily Stormer: "Nations rise or fall based on their genes." Another Stormfronter called Ford claims, providing zero evidence, that "as much as 90 percent of a person's intelligence and character is set by DNA before birth. . . . This is why Blacks, as a group, do the things they do." He contends that the greatness of a society is determined by the presence of white DNA, which he considers more critical than its sociopolitical system. This Stormfronter's example is that Switzerland, which in his view has an inferior "socialist" system, is "a better place to live . . . than Nigeria, even though [it's] capitalist."

Stormfronters aim to awaken whites to the reality of white victimization, so that they can band together and create a homogenous, "racially aware" collective that can defend or regain white people's rightful place as society's dominant group. If need be, they aim to start over and build a white nation that is racially segregated and can prosper in peace, riding off of their perceived superior DNA. To build this utopia, Stormfronters call for white reproduction, homeschooling, and a transformed state that will steer society toward becoming a white ethnostate. They intend to achieve this by banning nonwhite immigration, implementing mass deportations, and other means of "restoring" white control of land and resources.

Expressions of even more radical ideas on how to handle racial and ethnic minorities who already live in the lands these far-righters seek to reclaim are rare, as incitement of lawless action currently violates US law. (All three sites analyzed in these chapters on the far right claim to oppose violence.) But the link between violence and their worldview is strong. This is evident in how far-righters respond to atrocities committed by people like Roof and Bowers. As noted, I found that terror events that target specific groups are matched by shifts in the hate focus. Stormfronters and Gab users also talk more about white people after terror events. Like I did in the previous chapter, I compared the daily mean in the first four weeks to the daily mean in the week following the incident of interest. I found that on average, the twelve examined terror attacks were followed by a 12 percent increase in talk about the "white race"—their perceived victimization, their heroes (1488, Hitler), their state-building aspirations (ethnostate, white_nation), and common self-identifiers (christian, european). The increase in talk about white people was particularly sharp after the shootings in the Emanuel African Methodist Episcopal Church in Charleston (+18 percent) and the Tree of Life synagogue in Pittsburgh (+22 percent). On Gab, talk about white people increased by 16 percent after the five terror events that took place while the site was available. Talk about white people also increased after the same high-profile cases of deadly police brutality examined earlier in this chapter—by 6 percent on Stormfront and 32 percent on Gab. Talk about the "white race" got the most attention after the killing of George Floyd: up 21 percent on Stormfront and 80 percent on Gab.

Stormfronters see their movement as a civilizational struggle based on evolutionary principles. They claim that if nothing is done, future generations will inherit a desolate and dysfunctional society in which white people are a despised minority and Western civilization has crumbled. The remedy, according to them, is to preserve white dominance and genetic purity by getting rid of the Other. Expulsion is purification. Destruction is preservation. Hate is love. In the next chapter I explain how this mix as well as different rhetorical and aesthetic styles have helped the digital far right expand and reach a wider audience.

9 Hyggelig *Hate and the Mainstreaming of the Digital Far Right*

Far-righters talk a lot about weapons, so I wanted to see if gun shows include references to white supremacy. At such a gathering in Virginia, the attendees were, as expected, overwhelmingly white and male, and there was plenty of evidence of political conservatism (Trump flags and T-shirts), victim rhetoric ("Real Armor for Real World Situations"), nostalgia about the glorious past (paintings of caped white soldiers riding horses through romantic landscapes, led by someone who looked like the Confederate general Robert E. Lee), and apocalyptic paranoia ("emergency food supply" packages, "survival" bags). I did not see any clear-cut expressions of support for the "white race" or "white nationalism," but just a few minutes after I entered the gun show with my friend, a biracial Malaysian scholar, she said, "I'm getting so many hostile stares." I realized that I was receiving a fair share myself, presumably as a "race traitor."

When we found refuge in an Indian restaurant in the same building, which served us poori and sweet, gingery chai in oversize paper cups, we reflected that the gun show also included patient and friendly people who in good faith offered us shooting training (lean forward, weight on your toes), discounted books, and instructions on how to install magazine extensions on our semiautomatic rifles. The mix of cordial commerce, racist hate, chai, paranoid marketing slogans, and genuine smiles shows how the ordinary and the extreme are sometimes found in the same place. The digital far right displays a similar mix: evil isn't just normalized or made trivial there, as in Adolf Eichmann's claim that he was merely doing his job. Rather, evil is presented alongside talk about family life, folksy pleasures, and innocent eccentricities—even domesticated, made homey and neighborly.

The Stormfront community is in many ways *hyggelig*. The Danish and Norwegian word *hygge*—contentment through everyday pleasures such as drinking coffee in the morning or warming one's cold toes in front of a fireplace—gained global attention in 2016, when six books on the concept were published (*The New Yorker* called it "the Year of Hygge"). One example of Stormfront hygge is conversations about what to put on the dinner table. In one such thread, which are among Stormfront's most popular, a member shared his plan for the evening: "Baked rigatoni. It's sort of like lasagna."

> Sounds yummy! Mind if I join you? *rolling laughter emoji*
>
> Sure you could still join me! I always make enough that there's several nights worth of left-overs. *big grin emoji*
>
> I do that too, but then I eat it for breakfast and lunch the next day. *rolling laughter emoji*
>
> I took the easy way out tonight. Frozen pizza. *nervous smile emoji*
>
> Anyone ever had Nutella? . . . I just made a peanut butter and Nutella sandwich. . . . I like it.
>
> Mushroom tortellini w/ garlic bread. *beer toasting emoji.*

Far-righters are like the rest of us at times in that they enjoy pizza on lazy days. But the same pseudonymous people quoted above also say, in other threads, that their "righteous hatred of [Black] people grows more everyday," that nonwhite lawbreakers should be executed "cheap[ly] and effectively" with "a bullet to the head," and that they refuse to be friends "with anyone who isn't a [white nationalist]." The person who baked the rigatoni posted elsewhere on Stormfront that the United States is controlled by Jews and added about Muslims: "I hate every last one of them. *mad emoji*"

The danger of *hyggelig* hate is that it not only normalizes extreme views, as cooking and killing are discussed in adjacent threads, but that it also fuses extreme views with a wide range of commonplace experiences, practices, and events. In this way *hyggelig* hate produces a worldview in which everything "fits" the far right's deep-seated delusions about the "white race" being under threat. Andrew Anglin, the Daily Stormer founder, intentionally links the far-right messaging on his site to pop culture nostalgia. In a leaked guide for new contributors, Anglin encourages writers to get personal: "Stuff from childhood is always endearing, throughout an adult's life. . . . I personally remember Star Wars, David Cronenberg, Legos, Final Fantasy, Starcraft, Marvel comics, Dragonball, and so on, and I'd imagine these memories are shared by many if not most readers."

New pop culture is also deemed useful by Anglin. For example, in a Daily Stormer article from December 2023, he wrote about the sixth installment of the hugely popular video game franchise *Grand Theft Auto* (*GTA*). The game, Anglin claimed, is out of place in a "woke" society, because it allows players to go on "mass shooting sprees, to have sex with hookers and then kill them and take your money back, to run over Orthodox Jews in your race car." These sources of "fun" are being taken away from boys and men by "the Western ninnying morality police," who "hate the idea of boys and men being able to let off steam by engaging in violent fantasies." For this reason, Anglin explains, the new *GTA* has a Mexican woman as its lead. "And it's a love story, so you're going to be playing as a woman having sex with a man."

Anglin claims that the video game designers' choice of a female, Hispanic protagonist represents excessive political correctness. Although male leads are indeed overrepresented in pop culture, Anglin ignores a near endless list of dramatized, canonized entertainment with central nonwhite characters, such as *Scarface* and *The Wire*.[1] What's more, increasingly inclusive film and TV productions—with superhero films like *Black Panther* and *Shang-Chi*—are more about the profit potential of making stuff that appeals to broad audiences than about political correctness.

Anglin says he does not want to give up the ability to enact misogynistic violence through an avatar that looks like him. The vulgar commentary is distasteful but clever in how it taps into widespread discontent with perceived political correctness and a trending topic (the *GTA* trailer was widely shared on social media platforms by the time the post was published). Writers at the Daily Stormer follow Anglin by connecting far-right ideas to the cultural zeitgeist, and thus brings its young male readers into the far right's aggrieved sense of entitlement.[2]

Stormfronters sometimes connect white supremacism to bigger personal issues, even life's milestones. In a thread titled "Ladies, What Have You Done to Contribute [to] the White Race?," which has more than sixteen hundred posts, a majority of the participants list child-rearing. Some examples:

> I married a white guy, had two very white kids. I keep my kids out of public school so they're not brainwashed. I donated to this site recently to help spread the message.
>
> I have one white kid and hopefully there will be more soon.
>
> [I] drive older folks to medical appointments, try to set up young white women who are having babies with baby gear and find the resources to go to university.
>
> Four children and 18 grandchildren! :) Worked for two boards and churches which teach the preservation of the white race.

I am 40 and have no kids so [I] contribute nothing . . . Still, at least I haven't produced any non white kids.

I am married with one son, hopefully we will have more children. We will raise him to be [racially] aware.

I've had 5 beautiful racially aware white children with my husband.

You ladies and the others like you have given the White Race the greatest gift.

Two smart, attractive white children, two clever, amazing grand babies. I'm starting my own business, offering services to the people I choose.

Bearing and raising children are framed as bringing new members into the "white race," dating decisions become expressions of solidarity or betrayal, and homeschooling prevents "brainwashing." Some posters support white supremacy through donations, volunteering, and discrimination against nonwhites. Daily Stormer articles and Stormfront discussions train the far-right eye, offering people ways of seeing their environment and in minor and major ways live for "the cause."

Gab differs from Stormfront and the Daily Stormer. It's contemporary, like the latter, but rather than vulgar, Gab is slick and familiar for the generations that admire the tech industry and its evangelized founders. Andrew Torba, Gab's CEO and public face, embodies the confident, entrepreneurial California cool and is proud of Gab's startup asceticism ("Facebook has 44,942 full-time employees. Gab has 6"), although that hasn't stopped him from idolizing Elon Musk. For instance, shortly after Trump was reelected in 2024, he wrote: "I have to thank Elon Musk for mainstreaming the free speech movement and normalizing sites like Gab. [He has] acted as a giant shield for us for the past two years . . . the enemies we faced for the past eight years have largely shifted their attention to him and off of us. . . . Very grateful."

Torba's newsletters, sent out every three to four days, are spell-checked, serious, and uplifting in tone. In them he often references the wonders of open-source development, blockchain technology, and artificial intelligence—all buzzwords from the world of tech—but Torba still presents his platform as a hard-right alternative to liberal Silicon Valley. It's a mix with appeal. Gab is provocative, "disruptive," and antagonistic to established power structures in a Trumpian style, and yet it is familiar to young people who grew up with social media and are emotionally and habitually dependent on digital connection and attracted to convenience and technological progress.

Gab readers are often encouraged to think of themselves as part of a homogenous community. "We must surround ourselves with like-minded individuals who share our values, goals, and vision for the future," he writes in a newsletter. Elsewhere, Torba says that "Jews killed Jesus," that "Christ Is King and I Don't Care If That Makes Me Antisemitic," compliments Apple for releasing a "wholesome" ad with a "white family," often shares nostalgic far-right imagery such as white knights, and once reposted a graphic illustration of the "Biblical Order of the Family" which has the "husband" at the top, as the leader and protector of the family, and the "wife" as a subservient source of nurture and comfort. This regressive social order is presented as a vision for the future that can be "rebuilt."

Torba talks openly about his plan: to exacerbate political polarization. He writes that states in the South and Midwest are now "conservative strongholds," while the Northeast and West Coast are "liberal bastions," and claims that segregation between them is "inevitable." Torba here reveals his faith in the far-right trope that multiculturalism doesn't work and that diverse communities are ticking time bombs. And that trajectory is for Torba an opportunity for statecraft. He tells his followers that by seeking out and connecting with "their tribe," they can help move the United States away from the melting-pot society that characterizes it, first to gradual balkani-

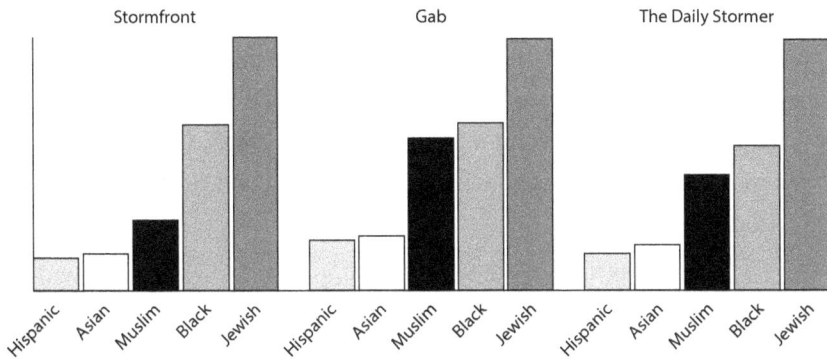

FIGURE 10. The ranked hate focus on Stormfront, Gab, and the Daily Stormer, 2017–2021. *Note:* I examined all English content from the five-year period, years for which I have near complete data for all three sites (although the Stormfront data is missing December 2021). I counted words associated with each racial and ethnic group, divided them by the number of posts, and ranked the results. For details on how I selected the topic words, see notes for inductive-deductive topic modeling (IDTM), chapter 8.

zation with sharply blue and red states and then ultimately to building something that sounds a lot like a white land within the nation.

"By investing in our own institutions and networks," he writes, "we can create a strong and self-sufficient base from which to launch our broader efforts." A critical aspect of that plan is to make babies—yet another recurring far-right obsession. As Torba puts it: "We have a duty to ensure the future of our people by raising strong, patriotic, and God-fearing children who will carry our torch for generations to come." Torba invokes common far-right ideas without the foul slurs and Hitler-homages of Stormfront, or the juvenile vulgarity of the Daily Stormer, usually without mentioning race or ethnicity at all, although he makes frequent exceptions for attacks on Jewish people.

The digital far right's aesthetic and rhetorical differences speak to different moods and audiences and might also promote different targeting. To find out which racial and ethnic groups get the most attention on Gab, Stormfront, and the Daily Stormer, I ranked the hate focus from 2017 through 2021, the five years for which I had complete data from all three platforms (Figure 10). I found that across the sites, despite rhetorical and aesthetic differences, the digital far right's largest homes are uniform in their hate focus. People talk the most about Jewish people, followed by Black people, and then Muslims, Asians, and Hispanics.[3]

The Far Right's Appeal

Why do people join the far right in the first place? Studies suggest that a central driver in the United States is that many white people feel like strangers in their own land. Life has always had lemons for everyone, of course, regardless of race, class, or gender, but historically white people (and in particular white men) have had it less difficult, as they have been protected by legal and social privileges, be it segregation, redlining, the denial of rights to other groups, or preferential treatment by teachers, employers, cops, juries, and judges. All of this ensured that although white people (especially men) would surely face problems in their lives, they were unlikely to end up "last"—a feeling that people are particularly averse to.[4] That status-based safety net—white privilege—is starting to unravel, especially for white men without a college degree.[5] Losing something valuable hurts, and this is happening after neoliberal policy shifts have, since the early 1980s, exacerbated economic inequality, made jobs increasingly precarious, and reduced welfare benefits.[6]

The causes, effects, and potential remedies here are complex matters, but in the far right's explanatory models they are clear and concrete—the blame is on the nonwhites. This articulation offers far-righters a sense of agency, as a challenging world is made plain and simple, with clear solutions and prescribed courses of action—get rid of the Other and things will get better. Those who subscribe to this fallacious perspective can channel their discontent and anger about the social world into action and work to "take the country back"—for instance, by supporting politicians and activists who call for halting or reversing liberal views and restoring the premodern cultural centrality of religion, family, national identity, and local community life. These sources of meaning used to offer guidance in life and were often invoked to justify existing hierarchies, with white men at the top, but they've become half-dead "zombie" institutions in our time of late modernity.[7]

In the words of Salman Rushdie, people have a God-shaped hole that they need to fill. Art is the plug for the secular novelist; for many others it's some mix of human relationships, work, hobbies, a dash of hedonism, and if they're lucky, a sense of purpose, which might be found in a career, gardening, one's backhand swing, and so on.[8] In this context an opportunity to be part of a bigger story is appealing. Andrew Anglin is a case in point. He was once a quiet, insecure high-school student with reddish dreadlocks and a "Fuck racism" patch on his hoodie. He found meaning in veganism, animal rights, and other progressive causes before taking up an interest in gonzo writing, drugs, and conspiracy theories in his young adulthood. He later back-packed in Southeast Asia, where he once had a Filipina girlfriend and became critical of colonialism. As he once said in a podcast: "You see the way white people—and it is white people—went around the whole world . . . and fucked everybody . . . I think the white race should be bred out." He moved to a small village on the southern Philippine island of Mindanao and spent weeks living among the indigenous T'boli people, trying out an off-grid life. But he began feeling depressed and lonely and eventually flew back to the United States, where he found meaning in another project: white supremacy.[9]

As noted in chapter 7, the Daily Stormer is more than a compilation of Anglin's observations and musings—it's a propaganda operation that calls for the construction of a new world, not in the Philippine jungle but in the United States and other white-majority nations. Its main directive is to recruit supporters through "entertaining" antisemitic commentary on "fresh" current events. Keeping the message clear and simple, Anglin writes, will avoid making people "confused and disheartened . . . all enemies should be combined into one enemy, which is the Jews . . . So no blaming Enlightenment thought, pathological altruism, technology/urbanization, etc. Just blame Jews for everything."

The propaganda of the Daily Stormer simplifies complex issues by blaming one ethnic group for all problems, and by packaging the message in pop-culture references, the site normalizes hate by making it entertaining and familiar. When I first read the Daily Stormer, it reminded me of how ISIS used videotaped executions and the aesthetic of first-person-shooter video games in their recruitment films, a jarring mix of heinous human acts and recognizable imagery and dramatic styles.[10] It works because provocative content embedded in timely themes gets more attention than general calls to action, and by challenging mainstream norms, the far right offers its followers a sense of power, which is attractive for the many young white men who feel emasculated and angry.[11]

Neutralizing Emotions

I suspect that the appeal of "humorous" far-right messaging is also about boredom. We live in a mundane and yet oversaturated pop-cultural landscape that serves up an endless, algorithmically controlled loop of material that is always the same: Superhero action films, politically correct morning shows, angry social media posts, and well-lit influencers. Even the disruptor-in-chief, Donald Trump, is a rerun—still dangerous but at the same time less interesting. People increasingly express themselves with bites from this flattened culture.[12] Excitement, for instance, is now shown with a GIF of fans at a Taylor Swift concert.

In this cultural landscape young people turned to YouTube to find other things than what was on television. The video platform's algorithms, which once favored content that racked up views regardless of its nature, generated unexpected hits, such as the goofy Swede Felix "PewDiePie" Kjellberg, who filmed himself playing video games. Memes appeal to the same sensibilities, as absurd, quirky, and fun pieces of content that are sometimes meaningful because they communicate camaraderie among those who get it. For example, when people gathered to express "Sub 2 PewDiePie" to boost the subscriber count of Kjellberg's channel, be it in the crowd at the Super Bowl or in a march in Tallinn, Estonia, they laugh together and relish the joke that they are making a big deal of something dumb and pointless, while also contributing to a memorable fad.

When intensified competition lowered PewDiePie's audience he mixed in edgelord behavior in his work. He upped profanity in his recordings and, in what was (hopefully) a sequence of poor judgement, hired a pair of South Asian men to film themselves holding up a banner that read "DEATH TO ALL JEWS." Kjellberg later said, "I'm not anti-Semitic or whatever it's called. . . . It was a funny meme."[13]

Young members of the digital far-right are fluent in this language and speak it with purpose. The Daily Stormer, for example, mixes memes and serious hate to "spread the message of [white] nationalism and anti-Semitism to people who are just becoming aware of this type of thinking," such as when they branded the same Taylor Swift an "Aryan goddess" and white supremacy icon.[14] Anglin encourages his writers to be hyperbolic, "even when it's totally ridiculous," because it is "fun" for readers and writers alike. He offers an instructive example: "Refer to teenagers who get arrested for racist [social media] posts as 'eternally noble warriors bravely fighting for divine war to protect the blood heritage of our sacred ancestors.'"

Dedicated, hardened far-righters also engage in carnivalesque practices. In the 1800s, Ku Klux Klan members dressed up for terror in festive regalia, colorful women's dresses, scarlet stockings, inverted suits, tassels, horns, and pointy hats, their faces hidden by fake beards and squirrel-skin masks.[15] A more contemporary example of the mixing of absurd humor and ghastly atrocities is the live video feed of twenty-eight-year-old Brenton Harrison Tarrant, who in 2019 walked into a mosque in Christchurch, New Zealand, with weapons. Just before he started shooting, he said to the GoPro camera on his helmet, which was sending live video to Facebook: "Remember, lads, subscribe to PewDiePie." He killed fifty-one and wounded another forty.[16] Another mention of PewDiePie appeared a few weeks later, this time in a manifesto that was released shortly before its author murdered one and injured three at a synagogue in Poway, California. "I had the help of a man named Felix Arvid Ulf Kjellberg," he wrote. "He was kind enough to plan and fund this whole operation—the sly bastard."[17]

In addition to signaling in-group status, humor can reduce physical pain, like morbid jokes can lighten things up following a surgery, and ameliorate stressful experiences. Did humor made it easier for Tarrant and his California peer to take human lives? It can't be ruled out. When I first heard about the Christchurch shooting, I felt shock, disgust, grief, and despair about the world and what people do to one another. When I read that the killing of worshippers was preceded by a joke about some Swedish gamer on YouTube, my initial feelings, raw and crystal-clear empathy, shifted into a kind of absurd horror, mixed with and perhaps tempered by confusion, puzzlement, astonishment. I wondered, *Is this real?*

The characterization of the digital far right as a site of strategic mobilization are in line with the scholarship on conservative and right-wing movements.[18] But the three sites I've analyzed suggest that open secrecy are also important for how they enable people to express and engage with emotional currents. It has been argued that people who join the far right do so in part because they feel shame about their perceived or actual inability to live up to what they think others expect of them, such as becoming dependable breadwinners, which transmutes to anger at scapegoats (e.g., job-stealing immigrants, welfare-freeriders, and globalist policymakers). Open secrecy brings a wider range of emotions to the fore. In the aftermath of terrorist attacks, people go to Stormfront and Gab to vent. Many of them stay for the hygge. On the Daily Stormer, Anglin says that he has been able to recruit readers by crafting stories that mix hyperbolic jokes way out of line with the comfort of familiar memes and pop cultural references. Gab's Torba, meanwhile, has turned deplatforming efforts into narratives about survival, the little guy against Big Tech, which members support by reposting them thousands of times. His tales of success—for instance, Gab's ability to get off cloud hosting, proprietary software, and mainstream payment processors—invoke hope (about being able to carry on) and excitement (about the new future they're building).

Do People Who Join the Digital Far Right Get Worse?

Does the strategic storytelling and emotional energy of the digital far right change people who join it? Do members of Stormfront and Gab express more hatred in their posts over time, or are they mellowed by hygge, memes, and the liberatory ability to express misguided frustrations through anger and laugh about horrors?

Measures of what people write do not capture what they think and feel, as language is an incomplete representation of how we engage with each other, and talking is performative.[19] For example, far-righters sometimes tone down their hate speech and Stormfront did remove swastikas from its site not because they disagree with what the symbols represent but to avoid repelling curious outsiders.[20] But a review of how members of Stormfront and Gab write over time might illuminate patterns—be it trending interests, perceptual shifts, developing communication strategies, or emotional currents—that can help us understand them and counter their messages.

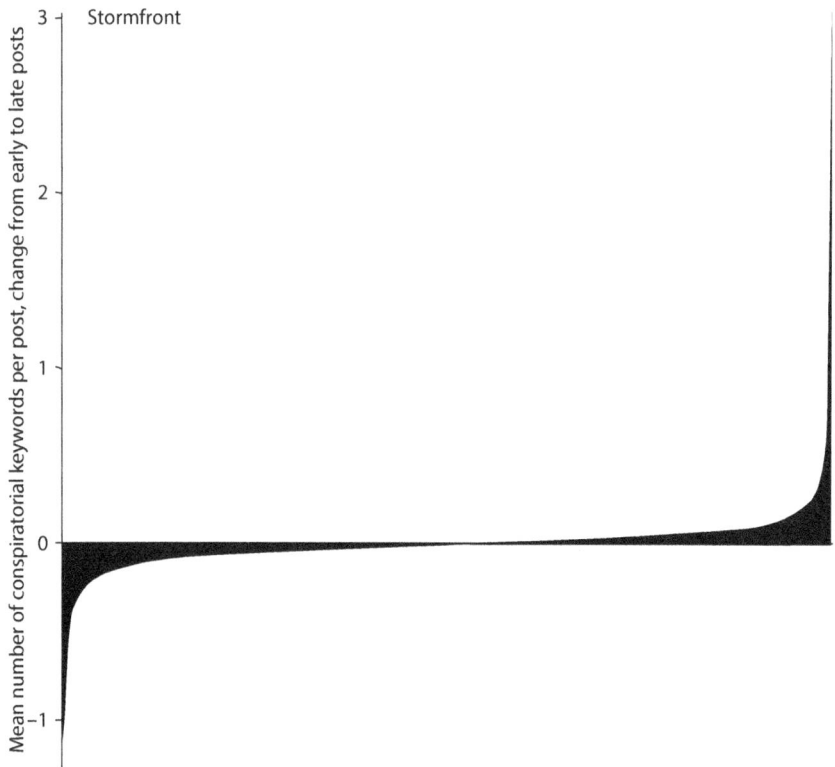

FIGURE 11. Changes in conspiratorial keywords per post (*y* axis) of highly active members of Stormfront (*this page*) and Gab (*next page*). The upward-pointing lines represent people who talk more about conspiracies in the last 25 percent of their posts than in the first 25 percent.

To measure individual changes, I identified members of Stormfront and Gab who had posted at least one thousand times. This ensured enough content for a chronological comparison. I then juxtaposed counts of topic words in their early (first 25 percent) and later (last 25 percent) posts. I found that on Stormfront, talk about Black and Jewish people decreased by a median of 23 percent and 17 percent, respectively, and talk about the "white race" dropped by 19 percent. Talk about conspiracies did not change. They

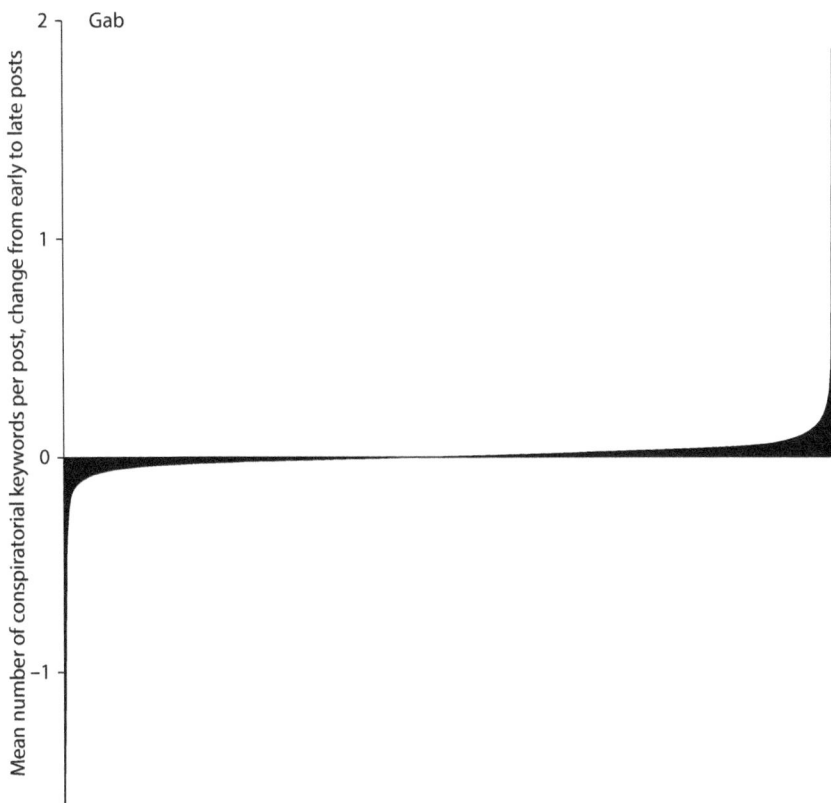

increased their participation in hygge threads by 15 percent.[21] These findings suggest that although the racist hate of Stormfronters becomes less expressive over time, the conspiratorial perspective that underpins it festers. That is, they talked less about race and ethnicity and more about how the world is rigged against them. They also posted more in communal threads about everyday issues. In the five years of Gab data I had access to, members changed less: talk about Jewish people decreased modestly (–5 percent), while the amount of conspiratorial language and talk about Blacks and whites was stable.

One problem with measuring extremity with averages is that people who increase and decrease on some variables cancel each other out (Figure 11). This problem misses that there is a great deal of variety. Many frequent posters increased their talk about far-right topics by more than 50 percent (!) from their early to their later posts. Talk about conspiracies is a good example of how a closer look at individual-level data is needed. Recall that the overall median change in conspiratorial talk was stable on Stormfront and Gab. But on both platforms there's a substantial number of actors on each end of the scale.

Even though Gab users on average changed less over time, a *larger* proportion of them became extreme over time. "Extreme" is measured by at least a 50 percent increase in talk about race and ethnicity. On Stormfront, 26 percent of its high-frequency posters talked this much more about conspiracies from their early to later posts (13 percent about Blacks and whites, respectively, and 25 percent about Jews). On Gab, 23 percent talked this much more about conspiracies (36 percent about Blacks, 41 percent about Jews, and 30 percent about whites). What explains the difference between Stormfront and Gab? According to my measures, Gab had a more diverse user base compared to Stormfront. The Gab data also covers five years, while the Stormfront data covers two decades, meaning that even though people in both datasets posted at least one thousand times each, Gab users posted more in a shorter amount of time. Gab's contemporary functionality and softer marketing language likely attracts a younger crowd than Stormfront. Stormfronters might also be more extreme as the site has always catered to people who define themselves as "white nationalists"—that is, people with extreme views, who are highly motivated in their reasoning and are even less likely to change their minds than the general population, and, as seen in the figures above, many Gab users.[22]

Some people who leave the far right are drawn back to it because they miss the identity and meaning of being part of a collective project of existential gravitas.[23] How common is this? I found that of the Stormfronters who posted one thousand or more times, nearly a quarter left for at least one year, only to return and start posting again.[24] (I excluded Gab from this section because it is a relatively new platform and my data only covers the 2017-21 period.) Are Stormfront returnees affected by their hiatus? To find out, I examined returnees who posted at least one hundred times both before and after a break of one or more consecutive years.[25] These returnees appear to be less extreme after their time away (but also here there is a lot of variance). Their conspiracy talk decreased by 3 percent, while their postbreak talk about Jewish, Black, and the "white race" is down much more, by about 25 percent, 19 percent, and 26 percent, respectively. While it might seem obvious that spending time away from the far right is healthy, it's worth considering why. One possible explanation is that we are so immersed in the milieu in which we live that we fail to see how our perspective is shaped, be it company culture, our friend group, or the online community we are part of. Introspection, including the ability to see what is wrong in our lives, is in this sense overrated—we struggle to observe the mental models that we use to make sense of the world, because they are always on— much like we didn't realize that we had a teenage perspective on things while we were teenagers.[26]

Leaving the far right can be difficult. Skinhead gangs, for example, use intimidation and violence to deter people from exiting, and people who joined the far right because they felt marginalized might worry about the prospect of returning to that lonely place and might stay even if they've started doubting their involvement. The digital far right appears to be easy to leave, perhaps in part because not posting does not equal real disengagement—actors might still be involved offline—and in part because the digital far right is more like a sprawling village than a tight-knit gang with deep personal relations, where someone's absence is less felt. I read the first post of the returnees and people's responses. A few announced their comeback and explained their absence (e.g., "Hello Stormfront members! I'm back after about four years of not posting. I have browsed the forums consistently . . . just lurking and not commenting. I was a little paranoid about my (now former) employer finding me out"). Some reconnected with other users ("Did anyone miss me? *Smiley face with sunglasses emoji*," "Yes, you were missed. :) Welcome back." "Thanks. *Beer toasting emoji* I missed you, too. Things are okay. I got side-tracked . . . Kept listening to Stormfront radio, however. Anyway, I am glad to be back"). But most returnees simply posted in threads they found interesting, as if they never left, and no questions were asked by other members, who were likely oblivious to their absence.

The ease of departing and reentering the digital far right may entrench antisocial perspectives. Spaced repetition is key to making ideas stick, and personal or organized deradicalization attempts, which are often based on a clean break, may be hampered by convenient access to a place that makes participants feel at home. Far-righters who start feeling out of place are more likely to leave—for instance, as they get too old for skinhead gangs.[27] This might happen less to members of the digital far right, whose universe of meaning mixes ideology, activist strategy, misogyny, sexual frustration, status anxiety, and racism with talk about video games, dating, college, software development, futurism, mothering, large-language models, menopause, and finally in memoriam threads for those who pass on.

.   .   .

The digital far right could have been as fragmented and peripheral as their ideas are. Movements struggle to gain support if they lack people's respect and seem undeserving of attention and support, in particular if participation violates norms and might lead to social ostracization, job loss risk, even unwanted attention from the police. And organization is made even harder by crackdowns from technology companies, which are wary of public and political eyes on how their products and services mediate hate. But open secrecy has made it much easier for the digital far right to organize, and reorganize, following website takedowns and service disruptions. Anonymous, pseudonymous, and onymous actors can raise funds, solve practical problems like domain bans, recruit followers, mass-communicate carefully crafted messages, and broadcast how they feel about current events and the status quo.

These might include events such as when terrorists like Roof and Bowers kill racial and ethnic minorities, far-right sites are suddenly shut down, or when they find comfort in hygge or fun in crude jokes and hyperbolic writing. Shadowy groups have always been able to work together and typically find ways to carry on, but with open secrecy their voices are louder and reach farther, permeating the everyday and seeping deep into life's private, transformative moments and the stories people tell themselves and others to make sense of their struggles and what's happening in the world.

Outro

10   *Resisting Social Change*

States are modernity's protagonists. They transformed social life in Europe when they harnessed science, technology, administrative capabilities, legal monopoly of violence, and military manpower to control their territories and effectively tax their people.[1] With their newfound powers, states could look ahead and plan for the future like no other entity had. They could set concrete goals and work toward them, not with prayers but with data-driven decisions on demographic management, human development, and resource allocation. For example, European states could, through incentives and coercion, enforce industrial capitalism and global trade on the world.[2]

As people adapted to the modern currents of human life—their opportunities, needs, and pressures—they left their villages and towns, superstitions and traditions, and became increasingly urban, rational, secular, and perhaps most of all, individualistic in how they saw the world. They increasingly thought of themselves as individual actors. They also became more anxious. Risk—the awareness and preoccupation with possible dangers—is generated by modern developments because the greatly improved ability to make informed decisions in life—on micro- and macrolevels—was accompanied with the responsibility to consider how things could go wrong, worry about such missteps, and deal with them, or at least manage the worrying (and perhaps the worrying about the worrying). This is modernity's hangover. If we live in an old building, we know that tap water might not be safe to drink. We can install a filter, of course, but how good are the filters? Is the cheapest one okay? How frequently should the filters be replaced? We can also boil the water, but that will only get rid of certain germs. It might be safer to buy water at the grocery store, but isn't this nearly a morally reprehensible choice in a world that is both on fire and full of poverty? And what about recent research that shows that "bottled water is packed with nanoplastics?"[3] That can't be good. But how bad is it, really? Maybe it's a moral panic; has anyone studied this? And why are we even wasting cognitive resources on this issue, when—as the never-ending news stream reminds us daily—there are so many much more serious issues out there?

It gets worse. Many of the great challenges are of our making. For instance, we now know all too well that modern capabilities, such as the centralized planning that empowers the state, can lead to grand destruction such as the Holocaust, nuclear meltdowns, financial crises, and climate change—all of which have happened despite (and at times *because*) states act through skilled civil servants, political leaders, military strategists, economists, and external consultants.[4] The growing list of humbling lessons from modern, human-made disasters have moved us away from having an unwavering faith in what rational actors like states can accomplish through science and technology to a present *late* modernity, where modernity is seen as flawed and incomplete at best, delusional or failed at worst.[5] We now understand that many of the sophisticated systems that we were raised to trust—be it water distribution networks, the government, or the Federal Reserve—will sometimes fail spectacularly. We now know that it's delusional to think that we can control the future with expertise.

A recent example of how things can go wrong despite or because of careful planning is the destructive action of my younger sister, Anna. During a backpacking trip in 2012, she joined thousands of young Canadians in a reforestation program that aims to plant two billion trees. Living in a crowded camp in the woods, she sowed thousands of sprouts a day while gobbling up cookies, sandwiches, and eventually DayQuil and NyQuil. According to the novelist Claire Cameron, this undertaking has become a rite of passage for local teenagers, who spend their summer breaks digging, driven by pay slips, opportunities for sociability, and the idea that "planting a tree was always going to be better than not planting one."[6] It turns out that there are exceptions. The kind of tree that most of them plant, the spruce, is so combustible that firefighters refer to it as "gas on a stick." And because they are planted six feet apart, to allow machinery to pass through, flames can spread rapidly across large distances, which they did in 2023, when many of the carefully designed forests blazed up: in the first eight months of that year, 5,881 wildfires consumed 15.3 million hectares. A grand, prosocial state endeavor orchestrated and implemented by experts ended in catastrophe. The enormous wildfires sent toxic smoke all the way down to Chicago, where I had to unpack my leftover COVID masks.

The particular pain of witnessing unintended but extraordinarily harmful consequences of expert planning is quintessentially late modern. To Lucy Easthope, a British crisis responder, it is "a very physical feeling. Everything just drains out, into the feet, into the floor. . . . It's that sense of utter failure."[7] Easthope felt this way in 2017 when the Grenfell Tower apartment block burned in North Kensington, London. The fire ignited late at night in a resident's kitchen on the fourth floor and spread quickly to the top of the building because its cladding panels were highly flammable, even though the local government had recently overseen their installation. Other expert systems meant to bring order to the world also failed: the Metropolitan Police didn't establish a survivor-reception center, local officials were overwhelmed, and work was delayed at the emergency-response center because someone had misplaced the key to the cabinet where the computers were locked up. "No one knew what they were doing," one contingency-planning officer later testified. Most fatally, the London Fire Brigade advised residents to stay put while the flames spread, much like an announcement told passengers on a sinking ferry in Korea in 2014 to remain seated, resulting in hundreds drowning, and emergency-call handlers told World Trade Center workers to stay in their offices after the planes hit.[8]

Even with education and training, protocols for action, and sophisticated equipment and communication tools, highly capable domain specialists will mess up, unexpected things will happen, and overall our ability to manage the present and the future is limited. Not just in the face of unknown unknowns, such as if asteroids head our way or thawed mammoths attack, but also given predictable and seemingly manageable incidents, like sinking ships and buildings on fire. Sometimes organizational expertise even enables disasters, by normalizing risk and thus neutralizing the worries that may propel people to act.[9] The state's confidence in what it could or would be able to accomplish—for instance, in a war on crime—has waned in late modernity. Planners have witnessed their own failures and acknowledged their limitations, and with improved access to information, the state has lost its grip on the narrative—anyone with a television can tell that there's no end in sight to urban crime, which makes it difficult for law enforcement to claim to be fighting a winnable war on it.[10]

The late-modern reckoning is that state control of human activity is elusive, and the best we can do in a hugely complex, uncertain world is to try hard to make things work and avoid catastrophes. It is good to have knowledgeable people in charge, of course, but expertise in a given domain does not equal mastery of it. If the story of modernity is "We've got this," the story of late modernity is a humbler "Let's do the best we can."

The Limits of the Sovereign State

The state has participated in the erosion of its sovereignty by initiating and supporting globalization. For example, by signing free-trade pacts and other international agreements, they relinquished some legal authority over their citizens and corporations.[11] States also funded the development of information technology, which has of course boosted economies and in a plethora of ways improved living standards, but also, as noted throughout this book, further diminished state sovereignty.[12] Information technology has enabled open secrecy, a new force of social change that didn't exist in the world before shadowy groups started tapping into the technological developments of our time.

The three underworlds documented in this book—drug e-commerce, censorship circumvention, and the digital far right—differ in many ways, but they all thrive because of open secrecy: the mixing of tools for anonymity and mass communication. With growing ease, people can speak to one another and to outsiders in semi-public or public channels and organize geographically dispersed collective action, while remaining hidden by anonymity or pseudonymous identities. Even as actors move around in cyberspace like dark, digital nomads, often with powerful organizations on their tails, they can work together to overcome problems, spread solutions, and express and share ideas and feelings about what is happening. Sometimes hundreds of thousands or even millions of people are involved. Such scale makes openly secret groups much more resilient than other cloaked networks. How difficult are they to stop? Consider that the three realms I've analyzed remain active despite being targeted by the world's most powerful agents of social control: Western law enforcement agencies like the FBI and Interpol for the digital drug trade, the Chinese Communist Party (CCP) for censorship evaders, and Big Tech, whose platforms and hosting infrastructure dominate the internet, for the digital far right.

Groups that operate outside mainstream society often have pre-modern or precivilizational characteristics. They are seen as unsophisticated because their worlds appear disorderly and fragile, and people base trust on personal networks rather than rule-based systems—they are the contemporary equivalent to "barbarians" who failed to evolve into formalized societies.[13] Illegal markets, for example, typically have to limit trade to folks who know each other personally or are vetted by mutual connections, because more ambitious organizing is too risky, and peace is always transient; opportunistic crime is rife and police might hammer down at any moment. Through such interventions law enforcement is often able to hinder or restrain market development—for instance, the implementation of structures that support the smooth flow of efficient, dependable, impersonal exchange in mainstream commerce. That is, attempts to streamline illegal trade are hampered by regulatory efforts, and that is a form of policing success, even if the targeted activities are never *eradicated*.

But the state's ability to control social life is undermined by open secrecy. Openly secret networks can easily reorganize and rebuild whenever they are attacked. This way they can maintain their momentum, or even find it reinvigorated, as people are united by difficult but surmountable challenges that sometimes boost morale and stimulate innovation. For example, drug market participants can relocate from a closed market to a new one, or even build a more advanced system for trade. Crackdowns will always create problems and disrupt or even destroy order, but disruption is also positive: it generates energy, movement, compassion and fury, and innovation, all of which can be put to productive use, as openly secret actors have the means to adapt at scale. Friction between different ideas of what is right and wrong sometimes works as grip that produces forward movement in unpredictable directions.[14] The public messaging enabled by open secrecy allows outsiders and insiders to step back and determine how much they want to be involved. For example, after a major drug market crackdown, some people immediately got to work on a reconstruction, while others took a break, only to return in the new marketplace after a period of laying low. Monitoring information about post-crackdown developments did not require insider knowledge, because news was loudly announced, such as when the drug market Silk Road 2 was promoted on social media. As the market's operator at one point wrote in a Tweet: "Whack-a-mole will not work. Time for an open, frank discussion."[15]

Police interventions also failed to stop developers of anticensorship software, who carried on coding, even as key software designers were forced to quit or disappeared altogether. Their work continued on platforms like GitHub or GitLab, where they could discuss implementations, problems, and new projects in encrypted chats. Open secrecy also makes the digital far right resilient—for instance, as they pick up cryptocurrency funding and self-hosting because credit card companies and technology firms refuse to work with them. The latter is a particularly stark reminder of how open secrecy is a value-neutral force of liberation. Its consequences are both prosocial and antisocial, and this book is not a celebration of it but further documentation of how we live in a runaway world in which the state has lost control of the narrative and can no longer claim to know where things are headed.

Open secrecy enables shadowy groups to move beyond the geographical confines and legal control of states. They in some ways resemble nomads that strategically avoided or withdrew from state-ruled societies because they saw them as trouble—for instance, due to excessive taxation and labor regimentation.[16] But open secrecy also gives people the tools and capacities to build statelike order without the state—for example, as operators can "tax" their own participants, in the form of commissions or membership fees, mandate particular systems for payments, communication, and accounting of contributions, and base trust not on kinship but administrative data such as e-commerce reviews and reputation scores, GitHub records, or post histories, all of which are tied to verifiable user identities.

These means of self-administration enable shadowy groups to maintain and expand activities while spending less energy on threats from external, regulatory agents like the police, and they can outlive founders and leaders. When I studied "consumer reports" from drug e-commerce markets, I found that online buyers of banned drugs didn't even mention legal and normative issues—they focused instead on the products and whether these provided bang for the buck. Even considerations of stealthy packaging were assessed in terms of customer service, as just another metric of the overall shopping experience, like shipping speed. By treating their participation in the digital underworld as ordinary consumption, and by contributing to market order by being good commercial citizens who even write reports for other buyers, people made drug trade look and feel normal. Although banned drugs are originally sourced through highly risky processes, on darknet e-commerce markets, legal issues went from being crippling concerns that shape every transaction along the way to an ominous afterthought that fails to stunt organizational development, perhaps not unlike how we live with little consideration and thought about our own mortality. And with law enforcement out of the way, or at least sufficiently sidelined to allow for steady development and long-term planning, actors can attempt to construct worlds to their liking.

What will they build? The many possible answers to this question are fuel for our late-modern neuroticisms. For that reason, much political effort is devoted to reestablishing order or resisting social change. Three approaches are particularly relevant: inertia, doubling down on modern control, and withdrawal.

Inertia

Grand disasters have revealed modernity's delusions and made many political leaders (and citizens) reluctant to talk or even dream about serious political reform.[17] Inertia, attractive for those in power, who have much to lose if things go wrong, becomes an easy sell if the unknowns of the future are frightening rather than exciting and alluring. This late-modern timidness means not only that we might miss out on some prosocial ideas and projects but also that we sometimes stick with dysfunctional practices. A case in point is deterrence, which still underpins the US criminal justice system.

Criminologists agree that people are *mostly* rational and that the state can, to some degree, influence their actions through legal incentives and disincentives. Deterrence works if punishment seems swift and likely: for example, if the cookie jar is transparent, centrally placed in a kitchen full of parental activity, and contains a sole gingerbread man, and the potential thief previously witnessed the speedy punishment of her sibling's failed break-in. A key challenge in the criminal justice system is therefore to increase either the actual or the perceived risk of getting caught. The mere possibility that bad behavior might be punished sometime in the distant future won't do. The logic of deterrence was front and center when Judge Katherine Forrest sentenced Silk Road's creator to life in prison without parole. She said that she was required to send a message to people who were considering getting involved in drug e-commerce that "if you break the law this way there will be very, very severe consequences." In support of this position she noted that "in a study cited by defense counsel . . . the author acknowledges, right towards the back of the article, 'unusually highly publicized punishment events may generate deterrent effects.'"[18]

In fact, the paper's author merely says as a caveat, after documenting the low efficacy of deterrence in crime control, that highly publicized punishment might be an exception: it is possible, he says, because we haven't studied it enough. Judge Forrest's decision, like many others in the criminal justice system, was based not on evidence of deterrence but on conventions. Sociologists call this a ceremonial myth—that is, organizations adopt certain procedures, policies, or structures not because they are the most efficient but because they are assumed to work well and help with legitimization in the eyes of stakeholders. Was Judge Forrest wrong to place her faith in deterrence? Did the life sentence, which was front-page news, convince people to stay away from drug e-commerce? I examined trade before and after the sentence and found that it *increased*—dramatically so. The most likely explanation is that the sentence did send a message but the wrong one: few knew about drug e-commerce before the trial, which even made the front page of the *New York Times*, and the evidence presented in court suggested that Silk Road's creator got caught only because he made a human mistake, not because the technology that enables open secrecy doesn't work. (Ulbricht was pardoned in 2025, after more than ten years in prison.)

In another test of deterrence, I looked at what happened after two globally coordinated police operations took down several e-commerce markets that were created after Silk Road. Following a brief period of reduced activity, they too were replaced and trade carried on. What about individual drug dealers—are they deterred? Did the arrest of a major drug dealer reduce trade by other dealers in the same market? I found that after police apprehended the fifty-five-year-old man behind the pseudonym HollandOnline, who was a top e-commerce seller of MDMA in the Netherlands, the local MDMA trade decreased, but it bounced back after a few months. When I was invited to speak about these cases at the United Nations Office of Drugs and Crime, the host kept a sober expression throughout my presentation, occasionally shook his bald head, and finally stated, with his eyebrows raised: "Ah, well, that was depressing."

All efforts to end drug e-commerce have failed thus far and there is little reason to think that this will change, because the technology that enables open secrecy works well and the pool of buyers and sellers who remain motivated to trade is large, notwithstanding the occasional arrests that result from human error and traditional policework.

Police crackdowns will also continue, even though deterrence doesn't work in the way we wish it did. Why? Not because knowledge of the failings of criminal deterrence is new—it isn't.[19] One part of the explanation is that it is difficult to defamiliarize oneself and rethink firm beliefs that have been reproduced many times over, as we've been told that criminals and everyone else responds to incentives and disincentives. The idea's simplicity and partial truth make it particularly difficult to let go.[20] But a bigger reason we're likely to be stuck with our dysfunctional criminal justice system, and punishment as a crime control to control crime, is that society's contemporary obsessions with crime control is linked to our preoccupation with risk. We differ from our premodern ancestors in that we no longer find the safety and meaning we need in cultural traditions, family life, and religion. Instead, we are burdened with an endless freedom and its evil twin, ontological insecurity: the responsibility to answer all kinds of big and small questions on our own, such as how much to worry about the mercury levels in canned tuna, how to plan for our death, and how to live.

In this context politicians that promise law and order have appeal. Crime is in this environment a political resource—leaders can win popular support by aiming to punish bad guys and/or minorities that are framed as bad guys. What's more, because we don't want to worry about the unintended consequences of social change, and perhaps also because good leadership is associated with decisiveness and surety, we're unlikely to see heads of state say, *I'm terribly sorry but it looks like we've done it the wrong way. We don't really know what the best alternatives are, but we will try something else, let's hope for the best.* Even with a professional spin, uncertain wholesale reform in the criminal justice system is a difficult pitch, even if it is honest and evidence-based. So instead, we just carry on.[21]

Doubling Down on Modern Social Control

Another way of resisting change is to crack down harder and "smarter." A case in point is the efforts of the Chinese Communist Party (CCP), which worries more about risk than most organizations. It fears that with just a few wrong steps, its reign will collapse, like that of the Communist Party of the Soviet Union, whose fall it has devoted great resources to learning from.[22] In yet another example of how tricky it can be to navigate social change, despite or perhaps because of an abundance of scholarship and available expertise, some CCP members argue that political reform is essential, while others say it should be avoided at all costs.[23] Over the past decade, however, it has become clear that the conservative faction won: Xi Jinping favors tightening control, drawing on modern design and implementation of surveillance systems.[24] Here's an example of hardcore modern social control:

> To all City Officials and Designated Responders,
> Considering the ongoing pandemic crisis, we issue directives to ensure the safety of our city and its residents.
> 1. Execute a citywide lockdown, penalize violations. Detain stray animals.
> 2. Designate officials to supervise city sectors, ensure within-zone compliance.
> 3. Order residents indoors, lock residences.
> 4. Implement contactless delivery systems for essentials.

5. Position law enforcement to ensure adherence and monitor city access points.
6. Perform daily health assessments and have street monitors confirm residents' well-being.

Using surveillance, administration, and coercion when needed, the state establishes total, utopian order. The guidelines are not from a Chinese regional office during the COVID-19 pandemic and ensuing "lockdown" but from a seventeenth-century French town. I have rewritten the text for tone and clarity, but the key points were published hundreds of years ago, in early modernity.[25] Why is the logic so familiar to us? It is not just because we've lived through a pandemic, it is also because faith in coercive social control remains central in contemporary autocratic states. Michel Foucault, who dug out the original text, argued that the directive is an example of a style of social management that is dated, not for normative reasons, but because excessive ambition and scale hampers its effectiveness, just as it is infeasible to employ one police officer for every noncop citizen.[26]

China's Zero-COVID strategy, implemented in 2020 through 2022, is close to the French plan. It consisted of compulsory testing, curfews, and separation of the ill and healthy, even within the same families. While the methods weren't unique, they were carried out far more rigorously and intensely than in the West, and they worked well for a while. The strategy limited infections much more effectively than in the United States and Europe, even at times allowing life to return to normal, a great source of pride for many Chinese people I spoke to.[27] But, like Foucault would have predicted, this strategy turned out to be unsustainable, as persistent outbreaks and more infectious variants necessitated lengthy lockdowns of whole cities, which devastated the economy and disrupted life for months, until some people literally started banging pots and pans and screaming out of their windows.

The CCP is devoted to making "better social systems," unlike Western leaders who prefer inertia. And it is possible that tools that didn't exist in Foucault's time can work: machines can supplement conventional human tactics, such as infiltration of civil society groups, to make large-scale repression effective and affordable.[28] An investigation of more than one hundred thousand leaked government documents found that the Chinese state has built a contemporary, techy version of the surveillance system imagined by the French village administrators, which uses facial recognition technology, phone tracking towers, administrative records, travel histories, iris scans, DNA tests, voiceprints, and in some cases, blood samples. The goal is to match the data with surveillance camera feeds and, with the help of artificial intelligence, automatically track individuals, even in large crowds, and predict who is likely to "cause trouble."[29] The hugely complex system requires lots of person power—it is not a dystopia on autopilot—but the CCP has the resources and legitimacy to keep it running.[30]

As noted in chapter 2, social control methods have also been given technological updates in the West. An example is American mass surveillance, which has a surprising origin story.[31] In August 2005 a roadside bomb in the Iraqi town of Haditha hit an American amphibious carrier. The blast overturned the thirty-one-ton vehicle and killed the fifteen people on board. An increasingly sophisticated insurgency killed hundreds more by the end of the year—it was a clash of forces that stimulated action, movement, and innovation.[32]

The new director of the National Security Agency (NSA), General Keith B. Alexander, a tech-savvy, self-described "numbers guy" with four master's degrees, decided to amp up surveillance by collecting, tagging, and storing as much data as possible on digital human activity—phone calls, texts, social media usage—a method he later introduced at home, on the grounds that this surveillance averts cases of terrorism.[33] The goal of the surveillance in Iraq and the United States was to tap the free-flowing information that people create by living their lives.[34] The NSA expressed its aspirations well in an internal PowerPoint file that was leaked by Edward Snowden: "Sniff It All," "Know It All," "Collect It All." As with Zero-COVID, the goal is to accomplish what Foucault deemed unrealistic: near complete, all-seeing rule.

Can the doubling down on modern social control strategies work? Qian Xuesen, a revered Chinese rocket engineer, has argued that societies can be designed as self-correcting systems.[35] One person who agrees is the artificial intelligence developer Ilya Sutskever, who warned that "AI has the potential to create infinitely stable dictatorships." Automated AI agents are fast becoming a useful productivity tool in administrative work and may one day help states create the digital equivalent to one cop per citizen. The efficacy of systems that double down on modern social control is difficult to test, which ironically means that although they are based on science and technology and the view that social engineering is possible, they are also grounded in *hope*—hope that developments in hardware and software can help the state establish near complete order, by bringing digital legibility to messy human life.

The promises of automation and convenience have emerged as a key influence on our behavior. Modernity's intensifying obsessions about efficiency introduced factory-based principles and methods into the realm of domestic life.[36] These eventually targeted our minds and bodies, to the extent that wasted time or unexpected inconvenience, such as a closed grocery store or delayed delivery, became a physical, emotional experience. For my students at the University of Illinois, who are used to organizing their lives with slick software, convenience is now expected. I sometimes get questions about why paper and exam grades are returned separately rather than presented in an online gradebook complete with a full overview of all graded deliverables and updated estimates of the final semester score. This is indeed doable. But it requires that someone sits down and goes through new grades, calculates estimates based on assignment weights, enters the figures into a spreadsheet, exports it as a CSV file, exports the existing gradebook as another CSV file, and then uses the university's Grade Import Tool, developed by Wade Fagen-Ulmschneider and Karle Flanagan, which matches the two files based on student ID numbers and creates yet another CSV file, which is now formatted to meet system requirements, such as having six specific columns per row for grade imports and can be uploaded to the online learning system. After the next assignment the process would need to be repeated. The convenience of having all grades in one place masks the work behind it: on the receiving end, it arrives with a click, and the ease suggests that the effort on the other side isn't too different.

Perhaps I'm no better, as I prefer the "convenience" of not doing all that extra work. Some drug dealers feel the same way, opting out of the sophisticated e-commerce trade discussed in earlier chapters, which requires manual encryption of messages—nearly as annoying as my grade-entering system—and instead sell on mainstream social media platforms, which they reckon are "safe enough" for small-scale and sporadic exchanges. Technology companies are well aware of our preference for convenience and do what they can to keep us within their ecosystems of services, such as by making it a pain to mix Apple and non-Apple products. Convenience can thus be used to manage (i.e., control) our behavior. But it can also make it easier to resist and open up new opportunities, even new ways of living.

Jeremy Rifkin has argued that "privacy has lost much of its appeal," as younger generations are accustomed to digitally sharing "every moment of their lives."[37] Another reason people might accept omnipresent, complex surveillance is because it is too overwhelming and too tricky to fight. In China, internet censorship has worked well for long in part because people are aware of it and because it hasn't been too onerous, and in the West rallies against snooping seem unlikely now, years after the initial fury, when Snowden's revelations gained widespread attention the world over.[38] But when people are given a convenient way to evade surveillance, they often take it. When I asked my Illinois students what they thought about Rifkin's statement, as noted in chapter 2, they said that they experience presumed surveillance as intrusive and overwhelming. It is no coincidence that in this context, apps for encrypted communication, which make it remarkably easy to hide, have become popular. Perhaps for the same reason as politicians who campaign on law and order do well in risky times, people who live in surveillance capitalism find privacy tools appealing. Apps for encrypted messaging are now used not only by participants in the three shadowy realms I've discussed in this book but by a growing swath of the general population: Signal, the most popular app along with Telegram, has been downloaded more than one hundred million times.[39] Many have even found their elderly parents on them.[40]

Rifkin might be right that people care less about privacy than they used to, but he might also be out of touch with the zeitgeist. In any case, there are clearly millions of exceptions, and they make up a powerful force. It was the feeling of eyes on one's back that gave rise to open secrecy, which now undermines state control and has transmuted into a driver of social change. Open secrecy came about thanks to the persistent efforts of people who deliberately fought surveillance, often at great risk, but also because of the increased convenience of doing so, which has helped spread cloaking tools. Examples include when police interventions in China's anticensorship community were followed by widespread copying of circumvention software in solidarity with the original developers, and when people who are fed up with excessive social control seek out the tools to connect to the open internet. People are more likely to resist unwanted state intervention in their lives if it isn't too risky to do so.[41] It also helps if it's easy.

Withdrawal

A third way to avoid change and alleviate late modernity's discomforting developments is to withdraw from them. For example, the Chinese Communist Party knows that living well in late modernity isn't just about material considerations and tries to harness and guide the energies, passions, and aspirations of the Chinese people.[42] By presenting curated pieces of cultural heritage, select nationalist narratives, and political ideology that justifies one-party rule, the CCP offers a politically safe meaning structure. These spin-doctoring efforts are combined with repression of alternative and diverse—and potentially disruptive—interests that contemporary people draw on to make meaning in their lives, be it vipassana meditation, K-pop fandom, software development, gaming, Sicilian food, or Catholicism. Such a dramatically expanding array of meaning might make people harder to control, and in response to this growing heterogeneity, the Party cracks down on cultural offerings and pitches a vision that is based on nostalgic yearning of a glorious past and dreams about a future of empowerment, the "rejuvenation of the Chinese nation," which Xi himself has framed as "the greatest Chinese dream."[43]

In the West the political right is likewise promising to engineer a future based on a mythical past. For some people the shifts of late modernity—changes in values, for instance, growing outrage over police brutality; attitudes, such as diversity as a goal and an expressed belief in meritocracy; the economy, which appears more inclusive in hiring and marketing strategies; and even pop-cultural taste, which has become less exclusionary (the rapper Kendrick Lamar appeals to all class levels, for instance, because today's elites aren't highbrow snobs but rather "cultural omnivores")—arouse the feeling of a loss of status and privilege based on race and gender, which partly explains the rise of the political right.[44] Because it hurts to lose something valuable (behavioral economists call this loss aversion), people who long for the privileges of yesteryear are often drawn to figures that promise to turn back the clock—for example, by cracking down on nonwhite immigration and reversing liberal policies about diversity and inclusion.[45] A case in point is when the operator of Gab promotes "The Biblical Order of the Family," which puts Jesus Christ at the top, followed by a husband who "Lead[s] the Family," and a wife who provides "comfort" and "teach[es]" and "nurture[es]" the children. Changes brought about by modernity can't be stopped, but they can be withdrawn from.

On the far right the most extreme idea is to construct a "white ethnostate." What that would look like differs from group to group, but one inspiration are the Nuremberg Laws that were enacted in Germany in 1935, which, among other things, forbade marriages between Jews and gentiles. Central to the idea is the belief that in order to preserve "white culture" and genetic purity, white people need to drastically alter Western societies or even build ones from scratch. A Stormfront text titled "White Nationalist Construction Manual for a White Homeland" proposes several criteria for "white" citizenship, including having solely European ancestry, exhibiting physical characteristics deemed typical of white Europeans, and belonging to specific Y-DNA haplogroups (branches on the paternal tree of humanity) believed to have originated among ancient European populations. Individuals would also be required to identify as heterosexual, and while various pagan/folk beliefs would be allowed in addition to Christianity, religions like Islam and Judaism would be banned, as would interracial marriage and reproduction. The homeland would be governed by elected white representatives and have policies ensuring racial homogeneity. What would be done to current residents who fail to meet these criteria is left unsaid.

To many male far-righters, inertia in changing times is not an option. They say that nonwhites are taking their jobs, women, and land while their cultural space is being encroached on and adulterated in ways that undermine white unity. A recent study indicates that to some believers in this camp, racism is a zero-sum game.[46] It found that white Americans who believe that anti-Black biases have dropped over the past six decades also believe that anti-white biases have increased, and strong beliefs (measured by ratings on a ten-point scale) on both ends were statistically associated. Soberingly, the study also found that white people now see anti-white bias as a bigger social problem than anti-Black bias. This logic is widespread throughout the digital far right. For example, recall that on Stormfront, after media coverage of police killings of Black people, members say that the "real" issue is anti-white crime, which they claim is much more prevalent.

Far-righters worry about change, but they advocate for neither inertia nor a doubling down on modern social control. Instead, they call for a future inspired by the past and the restoration of old hierarchies based on race, ethnicity, and gender, and privileges that they believe are being or have already been stripped away by progressive politics, which are, they say, ushered in as a camouflaged attack on the "white race."

· · ·

In late modernity our collective psyche is preoccupied with risk. Efforts to improve humanity through careful, data-driven planning have on numerous occasions failed spectacularly; rather than bringing order to the chaos of the world, they have introduced unprecedented horrors, such as the Holocaust, plagues, climate change, and the prospect of nuclear war.[47] The nation-states that have driven most of modernity's development have in this period lost the ability to govern the direction of change, in large part because of their own engineering of global flows of people, information, and capital.[48] State control is further eroded by the emergence of open secrecy. The newfound means to communicate and collaborate publicly and covertly at the same time have empowered shadowy groups to the extent that they can no longer be reined in by conventional mechanisms of social control, and thus they too contribute to the fast-paced dynamism of late modernity, which is heading in unforeseen directions, with no one at the wheel.

11 *Embracing Ambiguity*

People in the three underworlds investigated in this book—the darknet drug trade, black markets for censorship circumvention, and the digital far right—are devoted to collective goals that override legal and social norms and are pushing for change. Some of these actors participate in drug e-commerce to add recreational pleasure or entrepreneurial excitement and enrichment to their days. In autocratic parts of the world software developers find information restrictions so onerous that they risk their personal safety to build tools that ease access to the open internet. Through iterative action, as I call it, they contribute to a global struggle for individual and collective liberties in places where the state rules through censorship, propaganda, and coercion. Far-righters, the darkest and most dangerous of the three realms, worry about the perceived declining status of white people (in particular white men) like themselves and find strength by joining a vengeful, misguided fight against multiculturalism and the racial and ethnic Other.

How do we create a world in which people are free to apply their energies to what they want while effective systems of social stewardship minimize the potential harms? How can we find the right balance between liberty and control? There is no equilibrium, no sweet spot or perfect balance: human societies are too variegated, complex, and dynamic for that. Moreover, ideals of governance differ widely. The great challenge for any government is to support social progress while also maintaining order, and part of the task is to help people channel their passions in prosocial directions.[1] Our digital time is well suited for the spreading of outrage, about social injustices, and hope, for a new and better future, such as when people across the Arab world rose up in 2010 in response to the resonating despair of Tunisian fruit and vegetable vendor Mohamed Bouazizi. He was so frustrated by police corruption, humiliation, and the confiscation of his wares that he set himself on fire, expressing a despair about the status quo that resonated widely and literally started a revolution.[2] But it's often unclear where our passions should go, what we should fight for, and what exactly brings them out of us. Anger and other strong emotions are sound responses to what we experience, and have much to say about our world, but these emotions don't explain themselves very well, they just show up, demanding attention and action.[3]

As rational planning and secularism expanded in the modern age, traditional roots of meaning wilted and our lost contemporary souls now try to find substitutes, in self-help literature, therapy, sports, work, lifestyles, and our poor romantic partners who have to stand in for everything that family, religion, and community used to offer—friendship, reason for being, professional advice, comfort, familiarity—while also offering excitement, novelty, erotic mystique, and tech support.[4] In that chaotic search for meaning, open secrecy has made it easier for people to establish and sustain underworlds like the three discussed throughout this book, which for some folks are a transient interest, others a yearslong commitment. Open secrecy runs many other electronic underworlds, such as online communities focused on sexual kinks, file piracy, child pornography, Islamist terror, democracy promotion, the distribution of copyrighted research papers and books, LGBTQIA+ rights, incelism, and banned literature.

Empowered by open secrecy, these groups are all able to thrive beyond the reach of law enforcement and other agents of social control. Members of underground groups have always had ways to identify one another and connect, of course—with secret handshakes, for instance—but open secrecy makes such networks scalable, more able to communicate, collaborate, and broadcast ideas and emotions, in public, with masked identities. For the same reasons open secrecy makes shadowy groups more influential, as participants can now build lasting ties, speak freely to outsiders without fear of legal or other repercussions, and plan for the long term. For these communities coercive regulation such as police crackdowns is ineffective. Alternatives are needed.

Would You Like a Purple Haze Latte?

Digital drug trade is a fascinating world. Vendors sell illegal substances in public, and buyers openly share product pros and cons, trip reports, and discuss customer service issues, as if they were buying sneakers on eBay, all because criminal entrepreneurs had cracked some sort of code: by joining encryption and mass communication, they enabled powerful new combinations of secrecy, security, and openness. As I read through discussions among darknet drug market actors, I discovered that many early adopters saw these markets not just as platforms for exchange but also political projects about personal liberty. The cathartic joy of newfound agency and a calling to something big and important explains why participants were willing to talk to me, first as a journalist and then as an academic. They weren't hiding any longer.

People tend to resist social control they find repressive in ways that minimize their risk—for example, if an authoritarian government outlaws protests, people might agree to leave their banners at home and simply all go out for a walk at the same time.[5] Open secrecy lowers the risk for partaking in banned and controversial activities, and thus enables a more forceful challenge to the status quo. For example, a man in his mid-twenties who regularly purchased drugs online told me that every order he placed—more than sixty in total—was delivered, and he claimed that drug laws no longer impaired his recreational choices. Another person told me that his order was intercepted, but because the police were unable to prove who had placed it, as anticipated, they dropped all charges. What could have been a lesson on the risks of illegal trade instead convinced him that drug e-commerce works. So he carried on. Initially I was sympathetic to the market communities. The war on drugs has done far more damage than good, and extending it to the digital realm will also perpetuate the waste of lives and resources.[6] I surmised that drug e-commerce might represent a kind of de facto legalization of drugs and a source of much needed disruption, in the way that unstoppable file piracy contributed to the rise of streaming services, or how websites for pirated academic works, hopefully including this one, might shift academia toward open access publishing.[7]

Could it be that illegal e-commerce platforms, with customer reviews and sometimes detailed product testing of dangerous illegal substances, are in the public interest? One piece of evidence presented by the defense in the trial against the Silk Road founder was testimony from Dr. Fernando Caudevilla, a Madrid-based family doctor and long-anonymous Silk Road member. "DoctorX" spent up to three hours a day on the Silk Road discussion forum, providing information about the harms associated with certain drugs and guidance on dosage and administration.[8] Caudevilla started out as a volunteer but was eventually hired by Ross Ulbricht—earning $500 a week. He claimed in a sworn statement that he had autonomy in his job and acted in good faith. Indirectly, he helped regulate the market: "I espoused views that Silk Road users should not use or buy certain drugs . . . particularly new synthetic drugs that have not been tested in humans and that have a higher potential for harm compared with other drugs)." Most important, Caudevilla helped drug-takers make informed decisions. Below are shortened examples of the kind of questions DoctorX received, and the answers he offered.[9]

Q: I go to a Techno festival once a year . . . I keep [meth] in the fridge or in the freezer, well packed. Is it safe to take it after a year?

DOCTORX: Amphetamine and amphetamine derivatives are simple stable molecules. Their rate of degradation over time is very low and they can keep their properties during years if they are kept in a dry dark place out of direct sunlight. There is no need to keep them in the fridge (in fact moisture can facilitate degradation).

Q: I'm having hand surgery next Friday and am an occasional heroin user (snort, don't shoot). Should I stop using at some point before surgery so I don't mess something up with the meds they will give me for surgery?

DOCTORX: If, after surgery, you are prescribed opiates and you have developed tolerance as a consequence of regular use of heroin . . . you would need higher doses.

Q: I have type 1 diabetes and I am wondering if there is any information connected to MDMA and its effect on blood sugar? I have never done MDMA but am interested in exploring it.

DOCTORX: MDMA does not have a significant effect on glucose blood levels. There are no specific studies on diabetic persons but, according to MDMA pharmacology, dramatic changes in glucose are not expected . . . Most people feel like, on MDMA, it is easy to keep control on what you feel, what you think and what you do (or at least easier than other drugs). But the positive mood could make you feel forgetful and carefree. As MDMA effects last for 4–6 hours, one possible strategy is to set an alarm clock in hour 2–4 to remind you to test your sugar. I think with that, it should be enough. If you are with some friends that know what you are doing it should be great. You should use moderate doses first times (60–80 mg) and be cautious with dosage in general (not over 120 mg).

DoctorX offered professional advice—as a physician and academic familiar with research on banned drug use—in a space with contested perspectives. Warnings of the harms of drug-taking from the expert systems people are raised to trust are often dumbed-down messages about all the things that can go wrong, while subcultural tales of good and bad drug-taking practices are based on anecdotes and often lack crucial nuance—for instance, how drug-taking can affect an ongoing depression and scheduled surgery.

DoctorX did not impress Judge Katherine Forrest, however. DoctorX was "particularly despicable," she said, as he did "positive marketing" on the Silk Road market for harmful substances that "we have deemed in our democratic process to be unacceptable," at great cost to "those trying so very hard to get away from [them]." Forrest based her statements on the same DoctorX posts I quote from above and cited one of them as an "example of the problem."[10] She said in her judgment:

> [In one message, DoctorX] is told that an individual . . . is interested in exploring [MDMA]. The individual discloses that he has Type 1 Diabetes. DoctorX states that MDMA would be okay nonetheless, that "dramatic changes in glucose are not expected." He states that a danger is that MDMA could make the user forgetful, that he might forget to test his sugar, so he recommends the individual set an alarm clock. He states: "I think with that, it should be enough." This doctor has got a guy with Type 1 Diabetes, knows nothing else about him, about to try MDMA. This is breathtakingly irresponsible.

People who are on the fence about trying drugs like MDMA will often wait until the "right moment," however they define it, to do so, and Judge Forrest was right to say that DoctorX helped this person find his.

But isn't a brief online consultation with a doctor better than a blind leap of faith? We're often told to consult medical professionals—for instance, when we deviate from conventional diets—but their time is scarce and being able to correspond directly with a doctor is a privilege. DoctorX ignored the issue of addiction, as Judge Forrest noted, but that's likely because MDMA isn't addictive in the way alcohol or stimulants are. Drugs are not all the same. Another DoctorX comment that people might find more problematic is one in which he described MDMA as an incomparable drug that "combines mild stimulant properties, subtle psychedelic effects [that are] easy to manage, and a deep emotional aspect." DoctorX's words here read like an endorsement, even a recommendation, which carries significant weight because of the trust people have in health professionals. But the advice is in good faith, DoctorX appears to be aware of his status, and treats people as autonomous beings who can think for themselves and make their own decisions.

But, but, but. It's tricky to defend convenient drug distribution in the midst of an overdose epidemic. In 2023 alone, 108,000 drug overdose deaths occurred in the United States, mostly from opioids.[11] Particularly potent killers are synthetic opioids, like fentanyl, which killed 75,000 people that same year. Fentanyl is so strong that two doses similar in size to the naked eye can be the difference between life and death. As one person in a drug market forum wrote to another, who tried to measure his dose: "OMG dude you just eyeballed a tiny little line of pure fent? Lol do you know how dangerous that is? . . . You can easily kill yourself with this stuff. Or you can be smart and have a good time!"[12] Opioids and opioid-based drugs are so addictive that they undermine self-control in the way milder drugs do not.

Fentanyl remains far less popular on darknet markets than cannabis and other milder drugs, but research I've done suggests that people who get hooked on opioid pills switch to fentanyl when the former become too expensive. This makes it difficult to support the idea that electronic markets for banned drugs is a good thing because it reduces harm and fast-tracks the end of the war on drugs. But regardless of moral deliberations and what Judge Forrest or I may think, it's clear that cracking down on darknet markets won't work, because with open secrecy, drug vendors and customers can simply relocate to other websites, as they have done so many times before. Law enforcement must instead adapt its approach to the particular cultural characteristics of digital drug markets.

One experiment offers some ideas. In June 2017 the Dutch National Police took control of the drug e-commerce market Hansa and kept it online for nearly a month, to collect data on its users. For that period the police allowed most trade to continue as usual as it "would have taken place anyway . . . on a different market," except that they banned fentanyl.[13] By doing so, the police (1) acknowledged the futility of trying to stop digital drug trade as a whole, and (2) suggested that its harm can be reduced by restricting the drugs on offer. Several markets have demonstrated a willingness to regulate what their participants buy and sell. Silk Road prohibited child pornography, weapons, and stolen bank card data; Pandora disallowed products and services that could "harm people"; and Darknet Heroes League banned fentanyl, following the same logic of the Dutch police: "Due to recent deaths and the threat to customer well-being . . . we will no longer allow the sale of fentanyl and its related analogues on our market."[14]

The ban on fentanyl as well as the involvement and eventual hiring of DoctorX on Silk Road are not anomalies. The five markets I've studied—Silk Road and four other early darknet markets—all had threads for talk about harm reduction. The largest market in 2024,

Abacus, had on its front page links to a PDF version of the extended six-hundred-plus page version of the book *The Drug Users Bible*, whose subtitle is *Harm Reduction, Risk Mitigation, Personal Safety*. Whether market operators seek to reduce harm out of the goodness of their hearts or not is irrelevant. What matters is that if law enforcement promises to crack down on markets that facilitate trade in opioids, perhaps risk-conscious operators might ban such trade. Rather than treat all drugs as the same, as Judge Forrest did, states and their police forces should acknowledge the differences among various drugs—on which there is a mountain of peer-reviewed research—and nudge buyers away from markets that kill. The only thing MDMA and fentanyl have in common is that they have been classified as Schedule I controlled substances—if they were animals, they would be different species. MDMA has psychoactive and empathogenic effects, while fentanyl is a synthetic opioid with strong analgesic and sedative properties.

Some people want the state to legalize certain currently illicit drugs. Too much of anything is problematic, of course. A mild drug like cannabis, which can ameliorate pain, anxiety, and inflammation, can also be addictive, interfere with biological brain development if consumed at too early an age, trigger psychosis for people who are genetically predisposed for schizophrenia, as well as reduce working memory, learning, and sleep quality.[15] But even with these caveats in mind, cannabis use is much less harmful than a prison sentence, which can ruin individuals' lives, break up families, and fracture communities. Many drug effects are understudied—for instance, if they make life more enjoyable, not merely by reducing bad things like pain but also by adding good things like fun. Yet is full legalization of cannabis or other currently overcontrolled drugs a good idea?

A coffee shop that I like to work at in Chicago—it is semiquiet, has lots of daylight, and a large wooden table that does not wobble—

offers the option to add THC or CBD to any beverage on the menu. According to the barista, about 15 percent to 20 percent of customers request it. What will be the consequences of the normalization of cannabis consumption and, in particular, the commercialization and active marketing of marijuana-infused products like the Purple Haze Latte in that shop? The modern neurotic in me thinks, as people around me have voiced, *I'm not sure if this is a good idea.* Chaos ensued after Oregon decriminalized possession of small amounts of harder drugs like opioids, meth, and cocaine in 2020.[16]

What went wrong? Part of the explanation is that the pendulum swung back too far. Sociologists have long argued that a sudden evaporation of legal or normative boundaries can generate a state of anomie, where people don't know what's right and wrong, what's acceptable and unacceptable, and therefore they do things they normally wouldn't—for example, when "ordinary" men find themselves doing horrendous things at times of war.[17] The idea is not that pared-back law brings about senseless anarchy—a greatly exaggerated thesis that is loved by Hollywood filmmakers and politicians as it sells tickets and wins votes—but rather that people who are hooked on drugs like fentanyl will struggle to make the right choices when given complete social and personal freedom. But even then, the drug law reform in Oregon *was* a move in the right direction, because although any society struggles to find the right balance between personal liberty and social control, we can be sure that drug use should not be treated as a crime and improved access to milder drugs is not going to upheave order. At the coffee shop in Chicago, most of the customers who visit are not newly enslaved by THC and now jettisoning their life plans, but rather they come here occasionally because of its unique offerings, just like some people travel for cronuts. The list of moral panics is as long as it is amusing—including the predicted terrors of radio and gin, both of which were deemed unusually addictive in previous cases of hysteria.[18]

Demolish the Great Firewall

Protests are common in China, but they are typically regional and about material issues such as unpaid wages or improper land sales by local officials; nationwide demonstrations are exceedingly rare.[19] One exception, the short-lived "blank paper" movement in response to Zero-COVID regulations in 2022, which included public calls for regime change, burned out quickly. But protests come in many shapes and forms, and underground a growing number of people defy the state in search of meaning in art, history, and traditional religious practices that predate the founding of the Chinese Communist Party (CCP) in 1921.[20] And as I've documented throughout this book, people are building and using ladders and airports to get over the firewall and access the open internet, our time's cultural snorkel.

China scholars I've spoken to, the work I've read, and my own findings suggest that large-scale calls for political change in China, expressed in banners, slogans, and marches in the street, are exceedingly unlikely to materialize any time soon. But people who connect to the open internet are, regardless of their goals or interests, part of a "nonmovement."[21] As noted in chapter 9, the term describes the collective action of unorganized and dispersed people who contribute to social change through subtle, mundane, and seemingly inconspicuous day-to-day behaviors that add up—for instance, when women in Iran protest enforced veiling by wearing their headscarves loosely, partially revealing hair that is supposed to be obscured, or when people protest private property rights of land by "stealing" wood.[22] Such nonmovements can have a significant impact on social control, even if they are uncoordinated, because subtle, collective protests undermine state legitimacy. And because the risk of punishment is low, many may opt to join.

The mainstreaming of censorship circumvention in China has political power even though many participants are explicitly apolitical or even generally supportive of the CCP. This apolitical non-movement is an odd coalition. The software developers who make and maintain censorship circumvention tools are a community—they are united through a shared commitment to open-source ideas and idolized figures; they use subcultural language to describe and think about the world, and so on. But the people who merely want to purchase access to the open internet—airport users—are united only by their dislike for internet censorship. This is a fickle source of solidarity—not unlike the terror that ephemerally united New Yorkers on 9/11, as seen in Patrick Witty's famous photograph of a diverse mix of shocked onlookers who were momentarily bound by a collective experience—but if frustrations about online access fester, transient unity might transmute into an actual movement.

The reliability and popularity of ladder technology—which has been available since at least 2012—suggests that it is in the CCP's interest to make concessions. This might seem unlikely, but the Party often responds to the people's demands on a regional level, and more generally, it claims to be open to change.[23] "History never ended, nor can it ever end," Xi said in a 2016 speech marking the anniversary of the Party's founding, in reference to the claim that the universalization of Western liberal democracy signaled a kind of evolutionary endpoint in governance. Xi added: "The Chinese Communist Party and the Chinese people are full of confidence that they can provide a China Solution to humanity's search for better social systems."[24] A "better system" from the perspective of any state is one that preserves and empowers itself, and in the case of China and the CCP, that might require the leadership to dial down coercive social control, in particular if it no longer can claim to improve living standards for the people. A change of tack can be unsettling—perhaps especially for strongmen whose legitimacy is based on decisive leadership—but all the political talk about searching for good social systems might make it easier. And the Party likely has the administrative capacity and popular support to allow free-er speech while reining in political dissent, as it did under Jiang Zemin and Hu Jintao.[25]

Coercive rule, like a strictly enforced ban of particular software or severe punishment of a dissident hacker, can be less oppressive than more subtle forms, such as surveillance, because the latter ingrain discipline and compliance in the people, who internalize ideas of "ideal" behavior and start regulating themselves at the expense of their autonomy, as if they are simply doing what they want as free human beings, not what they are being told. People know what they do and why they do it, but they are often unaware of the social consequences of their actions.[26] For the CCP, then, granting more freedoms and rights might mean not less state power but more of it, as the Party becomes less visible and frustrating while remaining effective. Allowing people to consume the content they want—which is mostly apolitical anyways (see chapter 6)—and to converse more freely while restricting the distribution of political work might thus support the Party's survival.

Fight the Far Right

Human history isn't locked in on prosocial progress, but it might be true that things are more likely to gradually get better as we move through a rocky trajectory of trial and error. Open secrecy empowers shadowy groups, some of which are dangerous and hard to defend, but the information technology they use is, as seen in chapters 1 and 2, a general source of liberation that has led to formidable collaborative projects that are clearly prosocial, such as Wikipedia. That capacity for collective action can be harnessed to contest the growing influence of the far right. The reelection of Donald Trump has emboldened them, but their views remains peripheral and per definition extreme. There are many out there who would like to join the fight against their dark forces, and by smoothing pathways to participation, such a countermovement might prevail. Research on radicalization suggests that many young people who join the far right do so because it is a way to be part of something "bigger and better than themselves."[27] The fight against the systems that promote hate and drive people to kill is no less grand than the fight against "white genocide" and has the bonus of being grounded in reality.

Far-right sites like the Daily Stormer are dangerous not only because they spread dangerous ideas but also because they organize real-world action, such as antisemitic trolling campaigns. Cases of countertrolling are instructive as ways to push back. For example, recall that when white supremacists got #whitelivesmatter trending at the start of the Black Lives Matter, a larger and more tech-savvy group of K-pop stans spoiled the effort by using the same hashtag in messages with fancams of K-pop stars singing and dancing. When the tag changed to #whitelifematters and then #whiteoutwednesday, the stans regrouped and reengaged.[28] When white supremacists marked Jews as targets on social media with "(((echoes)))," thus subjecting them to concerted online abuse as far-right "troll armies" attacked by sending death threats and hate mail with references to the Holocaust, many started self-bracketing themselves to express solidarity and confuse the far-righters.[29]

These anecdotes point to the untapped energy of well-connected ordinary folks. While digital natives like K-pop stans understand their power and move more swiftly and smartly than most, the (((bracketeers))) represent an effective kind of slacktivism that anyone can do. Rather than leave the far-right threat entirely to law enforcement, technology companies, and perhaps nongovernmental organizations, ordinary people can engage in such prosocial vigilantism, perhaps learning from the far right itself, which has been soberingly successful at converting growing support into in-person gatherings and the mentioned trolling campaigns. Guidance from a trusted source is particularly important for channeling the help of those who want to participate in low-effort initiatives, because they might not know where they are needed or how to assist in disrupting a far-right campaign or deflating a meme. Putting this idle goodwill to use could have saved Pepe the Frog from becoming a far-right symbol, but more important, such collective public actions send the message that far-right views are, despite mainstreaming trends, still on the fringe.

Those with an above-average interest in countering the far right can do more. Hackers with good intentions—such as those who work with Distributed Denial of Secrets—have made data from far-right sites available to the public. Open Measures, a platform designed to assist journalists, researchers, and organizations focused on social good, has compiled tens of millions of far-right social media posts in searchable collections, which opens doors for scholars at every level. People who have the necessary research skills can help in the fight against the far right by bringing attention to the threat and broadening our understanding of how the realm works—like I have tried to do in this book. With some guidance those with the willingness to learn can be steered in productive directions. For example, much like information hubs for darknet markets offer facts and advice on available vendors and encryption practices, an information hub for far right–countering vigilantes can include research questions that might be answerable with the data we now have access to. The technical, analytical, and organizational skills developed through such activism can also be transferred to a professional career—many universities and companies would be happy to enroll and hire a hard-working, tech-savvy person who has devoted her time to fighting extremism.

Another way to help is to reach out to the extremist Other. We know from research that on average intergroup contact reduces prejudice.[30] Such connections are difficult to organize, because we are drawn to people like ourselves, but they happen often in settings like educational environments and urban communities (which is why diverse workplaces and living spaces are prosocial). With effort and intent, intergroup contact can be targeted at the people who need it the most. A case in point is Derek Black, whose father founded Stormfront. Derek too was involved in white supremacism and at one point spoke of infiltrating politics as the way to "take the country back." He enrolled at the liberal New College in Sarasota, Florida, hiding his family background, and blended in well until being outed by a senior student. Most of Black's peers severed ties with him immediately, but one friend, Matthew, an Orthodox Jew, chose to engage. He began hosting weekly Shabbat dinners with Derek and other students. One of Matthew's roommates, Allison, who initially kept her distance, started challenging Derek's claims about white supremacy with data on racial disparities and discrimination.[31] The blend of social interaction, intellectual engagement, and good-faith debates over dinner transformed Derek. By graduation, he had repudiated white supremacism, to which, in a bridge-burning act, he published a farewell letter on the website of the Southern Poverty Law Center, which has long been a nemesis of Stormfront and Derek's father.[32] The kind, honest, and open-minded deliberation between Derek, Matthew, and Allison is rare in today's polarized society, and is contingent on trust in objective sources of information, which most members of the far right reject. But it shows that engagement can be organized.[33]

I know this firsthand, thanks to a chain of absurd events. In 2013 UCLA graduate student Michael LaCour was at a political science conference in Chicago. Like other attendees, he had flown in to talk about academic stuff, drink local brew along the river, and perhaps take a stand on the city's deep-dish pizza. LaCour was known for occasionally cornering colleagues with his iPad and showing off enchanting visualizations of his ongoing research, and many were impressed.[34] In one study, LaCour found that people who received brief home visits from gay canvassers, who initiated a conversation about exclusion and discrimination, became more accepting of the idea that marriage is not just for heterosexuals. And the effect lasted.

This was a breakthrough in the world of social science: LaCour had found a practical intervention that could reduce prejudice. The study was published in *Science* and covered in the *New York Times* and on *This American Life*, and LaCour received a tenure-track job offer from Princeton. The only wrinkle was that all the data was fake.

The job offer was rescinded, and LaCour no longer goes by that name. But there are more twists to the story. Two of the scholars who discovered the fraud had already designed a replication of the study—back when they thought it was real—and having done all the preliminary work, they decided to go through with it. They found that door-to-door political canvassing *does* reduce prejudice (in this case, the topic was transgender rights). Fake research led to real findings. A few years later, I was recruited to a small team at Monash University in Australia to study the far right. We were looking for ideas, and with the LaCour scandal on my mind, I suggested that we replicate the replication of the fraud. We did and found a similar effect for Islamophobia: people who participated in an open, good-faith, nonjudgmental conversation about Muslims and Muslim immigration and shared their own experiences of being excluded and judged for who they are—which most people have endured at some point in their lives—scored significantly lower on measures of prejudice in follow-up surveys than in a baseline survey conducted before the visits. And the effect lasted for months.[35] Engagement worked for Matthew and Allison, it worked for the authors of the replication study, and it worked for us in Melbourne. Outreach can also work in open secrecy. The people on the digital far right can be reached with just a few clicks.

Into the Wild

Our ability to control the world is improving in many domains. One example is Bennu, whose full name begins with the number 101955, a five-hundred-meter-wide asteroid, a mix of boulders and gravel barely held together by its own microgravity.[36] In 2020, NASA managed to briefly land a spacecraft on it, collected fistfuls of soil from its ground, and sent the sample back to Earth for research. The vehicle then headed toward another asteroid, 99942 Apophis, which was once given a 2.7 percent probability of hitting our planet. Can we apply similar principles and methods—data collection and analysis, theory building, and expert interpretation—to make sense of social life? If we can predict and forecast an asteroid's flight path up there, and a hurricane's strength at home, can we apply science to make sense of and improve human societies and thus build a more harmonious future? Is anything, in either the physical or the political world, really random?

Chance *is* a little overrated. It doesn't determine the outcome of a dice throw, for example—the laws of physics do. Gravity pulls each cube toward the ground, and their initial velocity and spin, which are imparted by the force of the throw, determine their trajectory and rotation while angular momentum influences how they spin in the air. Upon contact with the tabletop (or other surface), friction affects how the dice bounce, roll, and ultimately halt. Perhaps there are analogous laws of human behavior? William Shockley and Qian Xuesen seemed to think so. These two esteemed scientists in the fields of semiconducting and rocket propulsion believed that their know-how of physics and machines made them uniquely capable of problem-solving in the complex system that is human society. They believed, like so many Enlightenment thinkers of the past, messy social life can be made legible and thus be controlled, evaluated, and optimized in the same way that we can improve science by learning from our mistakes and move toward perfection, or at least make gradually better versions.[37]

The delusions linger. We tend to respect numbers, particularly when they are expressed in mathematical formulas, which signals expertise and certainty, but too often calculated probabilities are meaningless, such as when people "estimate" the risk of human extinction owing to uncontrollable developments in AI, the timing of the next financial crisis, the risk of war, the long-term consequences of Brexit, and so on. Serious conversation about such topics is important, of course, but there are far too many unknowns involved for meaningful quantification. What's worse, by putting figures on what are truthfully ignorant guesses, we add a semblance of insight and accuracy that we don't have.[38]

Consider this possible future: The social and economic trajectory of the United States took a remarkable turn in the 2040s. A study had found that the drug semaglutide can help people reduce their weight by 10.9 percent after six months.[39] Because 41.9 percent of the population was obese at the time, public health advocates and insurance lobbyists argued that the government should pay for the drug.[40] Disregarding cautions about unknown long-term effects, it did, noting the popular support for the idea and the predicted fiscal boost of a healthier population, and millions of people started taking it. As semaglutide reduces appetite, consumers ate less, and the content of their meals became more important. Combined with the plummeting popularity of meat among the climate-conscious Gens Alpha and Beta, the drug trend therefore caused a spike of interest in legume-heavy vegetarianism.

One benefactor of the trend, which was gradually picked up by celebrities, restaurant chains, and TV chefs, was the thirty-one-year-old YouTube influencer Suhani Jain, who had thus far been known only in niche circles for her experimental dal dishes but became tremendously popular after Taylor Swift guest-hosted one of Jain's episodes, which featured "Taylor's version" of *paruppu kadaiyal*. Riding the wave, several "dal-fluencers" emerged, and the Indian government, sensing an opportunity to boost its soft power, invested heavily in Indian and Indian-American pop culture, whose "nu-bhangra" scene became a global phenomenon, partly due to widespread K-pop fatigue. Years later, political scientists attributed a sudden and salient change in people's attitudes about diversity to what they dubbed the "Suhani shift"—the tipping point when an aspiring immigration society overcomes polarization issues and turns into a true melting pot. Reinvigorated by a healthier, larger, and more diverse population, the US economy grew rapidly in the following decades, far exceeding those of other developed nations.

This fairytale is partly based on real data and can, with guesstimations and cheeky imputations, be expressed in probabilistic terms. Such a calculation would tell us that although each event might seem plausible on its own, the compounding probabilities render the entire sequence vanishingly unlikely. But the point is that this chain of imagined events is how social change comes about: thanks to an eclectic, chaotic blend of cultural trends, economic factors, innovative and motivated individuals, technological capabilities, happenstance, people making decisions about what is right for them, shower thoughts, and unintended consequences of all the possible combinations. No one can plan for a future that is as chaotic as this.

The reason the Suhani shift story sounds absurd is not that it is unlikely: historical events are often far more unbelievable and seem logical and sensible only because we see the past in terms of coherent narratives, just as I say that I discovered sociology by reading during night shifts at a hotel in Norway.[41] We can't use science to figure out what is going to happen in our human societies. We should be wary of people who think otherwise, even if they are experts in particular domains—and particularly if they have the resources to make things happen. Government-sponsored semaglutide and population growth in a time of AI outsourcing might instead lead to mass unemployment, depression, alcoholism, suicide, opioid abuse, calls for a return to a mythical past, increased support of the far right, and withdrawal from climate agreements.[42]

The upside of uncertainty is that it is a good place to be for new thinking. In ambiguous situations people have to seek and explore without having a goal in mind or clear sight, and that struggle often stimulates innovation. Our most celebrated writers, for example, develop their characters and plots as they type into the unknown. They have ideas, sometimes a rough outline, but the valuable work, the art, happens in the wild.[43] The same is surely true for our personal lives, which would lose their magic if they were planned out in advance, and it is often true for organizations like states and firms.[44] An inquiry into the failures of the war on drugs, for instance, might ask, Does punishment work? If not, what are the alternatives? Can the issue of harmful drug use be handled by institutions other than law enforcement? If so, what do we do about all the police officers and other professionals who have devoted their careers to drug policing? And what do we tell the people, in particular those who feel anxious about change and are drawn to politicians who promise law and order? Do we say that we have been wrong about how crime control works but are now doing the best we can to find better solutions? A general awareness of risk and related reflections are healthy, as the world is indeed full of dangers, and any kind of social experimentation must be accompanied by serious consideration of the things that can go wrong.[45]

But another source of risk is to repeat the modern lie that the future is in our hands. It isn't. Oftentimes the wise interpretation, even for experts, is that we don't know what will happen when we depart from our old ways and try to make things better. But the admission of ignorance is the honest way to live.

·　·　·

The technological wonders of modernity created new ways of living. Interaction was no longer dependent on people being in the same physical and temporal location, as orders, offers, and words of love were increasingly transmitted not face-to-face but through telegraphs, phone calls, and binary digits. The resulting data trails are now assembled to measure our past behavior and predict tomorrow's. This is surveillance capitalism: an economic and political system in which companies and states benefit from the collection, analysis, and sale of personal data.[46] People who yearned for cover from the omnipresent surveillance of late-modern life built encryption systems, fought for the right to hide, mixed tools for secrecy with the ability to communicate and collaborate openly and widely, and helped spread the new technology combinations to markedly different domains, including banned trade, anticensorship activism, and hate-based communities. This medium—open secrecy—has a message: shadowy online groups can no longer be controlled by coercion, whether by conventional brute force, algorithmic prowess, unrivaled computing power, or novel surveillance techniques.

Does open secrecy spell a return to the internet's anarchistic origins? The internet was constructed with military funds and the technical work of elite researchers in academia and industry, but most of the early users, who were freed from intergenerational Cold War paranoia and energized by the potential for global connectivity, made cyberspace an aspirational world of worlds, with unique cultural characteristics and a plurality and vibrancy that seemed unnavigable and ungovernable to outsiders but made sense to local netizens who knew where to go. The present-day internet is a far cry from this anarchy. Instead, it is dominated by a handful of enormous technology firms who, like intelligence agencies, extract data from social life in order to shape it, control it.

Open secrecy does not disrupt this structure. But it brings back some of the internet's early lawlessness, because it undermines the state's ability to watch, administer, and control its citizens and thus diminishes its sovereign power, a trajectory already well under way in a globalized, late-modern world. What's new is the scale of cloaked activity that is enabled by information technology. Shadowy groups that move in open secrecy are far more capable than people who lurk in the literal dark, always on the verge of being discovered, because openly secret communities have the means to speak out, connect and collaborate, bounce back, rebuild, mass-communicate outrage and hope, distribute political ideas and solutions to practical problems, and transmit capital. They can carry on, over years and decades, even in the face of continuous pressure from the world's most powerful organizations, such as the FBI, the CCP, and Big Tech.

Open secrecy is a force of change, a bouquet of unknown consequences. Some of the discussed underworlds might wilt—for example, if the far right loses its appeal, as often happens to radical parties that win elections and become part of the mainstream. Others will bloom. How do we cope with the unknowns? How do we operate in a world that is increasingly uncontrollable? What can we do? Worries about such questions may lessen once we remember that we live on even though we know very well that our personal lives are full of painful and joyous surprises, and will continue to take unexpected turns. Late modernity tells us that no one was ever in control of social change—we just thought (or hoped) someone was. We've now been freed from this delusion and can see that no one is at the steering wheel, we are all just doing the best we can. Handling the juggernaut of social change involves admitting that we are moving through the unknown, which is difficult but honest, invites new thinking, and perhaps fosters unity through our shared human vulnerability.

Open secrecy reveals some things we would rather keep in the dark, but it also brings out the truth of what is going on in the social world and can help us see ourselves. This is who we are. This is what we have to deal with.

Epilogue

The Digital Public Square Is Dead

Humans stand out on this planet in part by how they use tools to transform their social worlds. A case in point is the invention of writing—perhaps the first information technology—which we use to encode important and meaningful bits of life. We started writing after roughly 50,000 years of orality, and the practice gradually transformed how we think and engage with each other and our surroundings.[1] With writing we could develop, revise, and distribute complex arguments across time and space, and without all the context provided in oral communication—consider how we convey irony with verbal tone, gesturing, and facial expressions—we were forced to develop a precise and more expansive vocabulary.[2] This enriched our lives; if nothing else, we learned to complain with granularity.

We don't know when writing was first used to make art, or when the earliest love letter was delivered—perhaps because its affections were unrequited—but we do know that premodern writing was used to record and transport valuable information, for instance in the form of lists. That tells us that writing was also a tool that benefited actors who had stuff to count, such as iron tools, military assets, economic transactions, and perhaps most importantly, people, be it followers, slaves, or personnel. Writing thus enabled effective administration of material and human resources, and aided the development of settled societies and eventually formal states.[3] Governments could, by mandating and collecting names and addresses, keep track of where "their" people lived, their age and gender, their possessions, and data that enabled taxation, conscription, and labor mobilization and distribution. Realizing that people are a source of power, early states devoted much energy and many resources to boosting their ranks and avoiding their depletion, in particular when nonstate living was a real alternative with many attractions.[4]

An example of how the state became the protagonist of modernity, from the 1700s onward, is how it absorbed a growing mass of economic life into its domain and gradually made itself an indispensable custodian of commerce.[5] By introducing material and intellectual property rights, mandating labor and business contracts and standards, issuing regulatory guidelines, and supporting and enforcing global trade, most exchanges were made state affairs. The more "developed" a state was, the more of the economy was regulated (including so-called free markets, which require more regulatory work than the name implies). The state's deep involvement in economic matters is perhaps most evident in the struggles of those who resist it.

Informal exchanges are almost entirely out of sight in rich countries, where even ice cream trucks need permits, and in areas of less affluence, public participants are vulnerable. One example is found in Egypt, where wheeled hawkers of food, drinks, and garments set up shop in locations with heavy foot traffic, such as train stations. These unlicensed businesspeople are often forced on the run. Elites say that their presence makes cities seem dirty and backward; owners of formalized stores complain that they can't compete with street prices; and the state worries about public disorder, the inability to control what people buy and sell, and, of course, tax evasion. Local law enforcement therefore attempts to "clean up" central city districts by physically removing street vendors, and courts punish them with fines and prison time. But people roll their carts back to the square, or are replaced by colleagues, and trade picks up, until the state cracks down again, and on it goes.[6]

Liberty at Scale

This book is about how recent advances in information technology enable new ways to organize social life, outside the state, much in the same way writing and administration helped state formation in early modernity. That is, while information technology first empowered the state, as it still does in many ways—for instance, by making mass surveillance possible—information technology is now also helping people carve out digital spaces in which they can operate freely, outside of the state's regulatory reach. In these novel geographies of power, openly secret groups use information technology to effectively govern themselves. They can recruit members; collect taxes in the forms of commissions, donations, or sign up fees; and when needed, discipline rule-violating actors by kicking them off their platforms, or the opposite, when they reward modal behavior, such as in public customer reviews or statements to people inside or outside of the community, for instance when drug e-commerce operators post on social media. Such openly secret domains are powerful enough to influence social change because they enable large-scale activities.

Widespread participation has helped the three openly secret underworlds I've studied survive. The digital drug trade discussed in chapters 3 and 4 has expanded far beyond state control since it began with Silk Road in 2011, and I have in my ten years of researching this domain seen no signs of the cat being bagged. The relatively frequent turnover of markets, due to crackdowns, hacks, and exit scams, has done little to deter participation in the darknet economy but much to stimulate innovation and has contributed to order by preventing power concentration, where one or two markets dominate and then create chaos and confusion when they collapse. One recent example of the darknet economy's resilience is the information hub or Reddit-like portal Dread, which has now been available for more than six years and continues to connect pseudonymous buyers and sellers of drugs and markets, giving them a place to mingle, and after another market crackdown, figure out where to go next.

Platforms that enable openly secret hacktivism, discussed in chapters 5 and 6, are also populous enough to overcome major setbacks. One of their peculiar threats demonstrates that connected groups are not necessarily in support of greater liberty, for the people come in many colors: a large Chinese network of techy *pro-state* vigilantes works to dox anticensorship developers and airport providers, even airport consumers, and in other ways hamper their efforts to connect to the open internet. These counteractivists are outnumbered and likely incapable of achieving their goals, but they are yet another illustration of how openly secret collective action is value neutral.

The most sobering case of antisocial open secrecy in this book was discussed in chapters 7–9 on the digital far right, which has leveraged its sizable base of supporters to promote dangerous ideas and organize concrete action—such as by casting votes. The night before the November 2024 election, Gab's Andrew Torba wrote: "The stakes could not be higher. We have a duty . . . to our families and to our country to show up and vote . . . if men turn out to vote, Donald Trump is poised to win this election. If you are a man, go and pull the lever." The comment was reposted 600 times and viewed 131,000 times.

Many of the people Torba reached with that message and others like it might have been decided voters. But considering that far-righters distrust political institutions—including when they are under Republican control—Torba's extra nudge might have turned some skeptics. A more sobering influence of the digital far right is how prominent actors like Torba display dangerous ideas, such as concerns about demographic change and immigration, or carefully crafted, "smooth" white supremacist messaging (an example from a Gab post shared by Torba: "I don't think one race is inherently superior to another, but I do believe that each race has unique qualities and contributions to make. I think it's natural and healthy for people to identify with and prioritize their own kind.").

Does He Mean What He Says?

Far-right narratives have been tuned up and increasingly normalized by mainstream figures who harness their popular appeal to win attention in an oversaturated media landscape. In the United States, one of the first who figured this out was Tucker Carlson, whose prime-time programming on Fox News vilified nonwhites and promoted conspiracy theories with such rhetorical effectiveness that his show became television's most popular, and Stormfront's Don Black started studying his episodes to better his own messaging.[7]

Another is Donald Trump, who arrived on the political scene around the same time as strongmen around the world were gaining popularity and a few months after the United Kingdom had voted to leave the European Union. The rise of destructive disruptors like Brexit campaigner Nigel Farage in the UK and Trump in the US stems from decades of neoliberal austerity and growing economic inequality; these social conditions, which seemed particularly tough after a golden postwar period of good jobs and low unemployment, fueled a cultural backlash against liberal policies. Trump exploited the strong (albeit often subconscious) yearning for the past by attacking immigrants and "woke" progressives who were moving the country in the "wrong" direction, and by refusing to denounce far-righters (for instance, after the "Unite the Right" rally in Charlottesville in 2017 and the Capitol attack in 2021), who in various toxic ways called for a similar restoration of a social order that benefited people that looked like them.[8]

A third example is the world's richest man, Elon Musk. Musk supported Trump's 2024 campaign with about two hundred million dollars from his personal funds, and what's perhaps even more valuable, his public presence and vocal promotion of a new Trump presidency by attending Republican campaign events and speaking through the social media platform that he owns, X.[9] In the same period, Musk's social media messaging increasingly overlapped with the far right. Despite his claims to be a moderate, Musk's posts are well aligned with far-right tropes, such as when he wrote that the Jewish businessman George Soros "hates humanity," called low birth rates "a much bigger risk to civilization than global warming," accused the Biden administration of actively facilitating illegal immigration to win future votes, reposted a social media comment that claimed that Jewish communities push "hatred against Whites" (Musk called it "the actual truth"), and when he displayed a Nazi salute twice during a Trump 2025 inauguration event.

Musk might mean what he says. But he might also be maximizing his influence by speaking to multiple crowds. This is possible because we live in a confusing post-truth society where emotional appeals and personal beliefs often outweigh objective facts. And in this context, moderates who admire Musk's entrepreneurial accomplishments may dismiss his extreme statements as banter, trolling, or honest mistakes (he apologized for that post about Jewish people hating white people). Far-righters, by contrast, may take the same exact words as validation and support, such as when Stormfront members debate whether Musk's concern about low birth rates is code for concern about *white* birth rates, or when Gab's Torba praises Musk for allowing and even reposting extremist language on his own social media platform: "I have to thank Elon Musk for mainstreaming the free speech movement and normalizing sites like Gab." (Musk has to my knowledge never said anything publicly about Gab.) This ambiguity—does he mean what he says?—allows Musk to avoid accountability while reaching people on both the far right and moderate right.

Big Tech and Washington

The ability to connect with a wide range of people can be effectively turned into real-world political power with the help of digital platforms. This was recognized early by the campaign of a young, tall, and Black senator in Illinois. Barack Obama became a serious contender for the Democratic nomination with the support of technologists, such as one of Facebook's non-Zuckerberg founders, Chris Hughes, who took a leave of absence to join the Democrats' campaign in 2007. Hughes helped create My.BarackObama.com, a social network for Obama supporters that mobilized and organized support. By the time the 2008 campaign was over, people had used the network to plan 200,000 offline events, and users had created more than two million volunteer profiles, and formed 35,000 groups.[10]

Obama embraced the tech industry as president, too, creating three Silicon Valley–inspired positions in his administration: a chief technology officer, a chief data scientist, and a chief performance officer. The *New York Times* called him America's first truly digital head of state: he was active on social media, shared music on Spotify, held Reddit AMAs, and built strong relationships with Mark Zuckerberg, Bill Gates, and Steve Jobs.[11]

Since then, the tech industry has also built strong ties with the right. Alphabet, for example, has worked hard to shed its image as a company for Democrats, in particular when Clinton lost to Trump in 2016. The company sponsored conservative think tanks, contributed millions of dollars to Republican campaigns, met with Republican leaders, made several visits to the Trump Tower in New York City after Trump's first election win, and arranged events, at one point spending more than fifty thousand dollars on a party primarily for Republicans.[12] Meta's Zuckerberg, meanwhile, had several personal meetings with conservatives, including with Senator Lindsey Graham of South Carolina, Tucker Carlson, and Jared Kushner, who arranged a meeting with his father-in-law. Zuckerberg told Trump that he generated more engagement on Facebook than any other world leader, and the flattery worked; the following month, Trump invited Zuckerberg to the White House.

In 2024, sensing that Trump might win the election, Amazon owner Jeff Bezos killed the *Washington Post*'s tradition of endorsing a presidential candidate, a decision the newspaper's former editor called cowardly.[13] Around the same time, Zuckerberg said that Meta would reduce political content on its services, claiming that's what the people want, echoing the company's earlier efforts to make Facebook a sanitized space by filtering out fine-art nipples. Both executives, and several other tech leaders, donated money to Trump's inauguration fund and visited Trump's Mar-a-Lago headquarters, where Musk spent so much time that *The Onion* joked that Trump had to lock the bathroom door to get away from him.[14]

Because Big Tech's lobbying involves shaping the products and services they offer and we use, the courting of Trump and other politicians influences people's daily lives directly. That may explain why many people want out. When users began leaving Musk's increasingly toxic social media platform after Trump's 2024 win, many passed on Meta's apolitical alternative, Threads, and instead moved to Bluesky—which was seen as more independent. Similarly, growing concerns about surveillance capitalism have, as noted earlier, made hundreds of millions sign up for encrypted communications spaces like Telegram and Signal.

Coffeehouses and Saloons

People have always preferred digital environments that support user autonomy, transparency, and trust, but convenience matters too. When surveillance-enhanced services are slick and surveillance-evading ones are cumbersome, many people pick the former most of

the time. But the same technological advances that enabled open secrecy have made it easier to build digital enclaves that are more attuned with what people want while having Big Tech–like functionality and aesthetics. That is, comparing Bluesky and Threads, both of
which have tens of millions of active users, it's not obvious that the
former only has a few dozen employees while the latter is one of the
richest companies in the world.

Democratized platform technology enables administration of
large groups without the state, and without Big Tech. This has, unfortunately, given rise to places like Gab and has generally empowered
people who hold far-right views. But it might now be empowering a
far larger group of people who don't, but who similarly seek to build
digital worlds that are less dependent on corporate interests and safe
from political influence (and kowtowing).

A central reason why political discussions on mainstream social
media platforms so often go down in flames is that moderates are put
off by the intensity of disagreements from people with more hardened and extreme views, which dominate, and thus they opt out.
People who deliberately engage with the other side are often met
with hostility and thus end up with their existing views reinforced.[15]

One proposed solution is for moderates to take a deep breath and
go back in and together crowd out the loud extremists—which are in
a minority—and thus collectively make the digital public square a
place for cordial good-faith debate. Such utopian ideas are valuable
because they help us imagine how things could be different, and
what people can accomplish with information technology.[16] It reminds me of the argument that if people cut back on TV watching
and spend more time on collective prosocial projects, they can build
numerous Wikipedia-sized projects a year.[17] People *do* build incred-
ible things together—for instance, the three cases in this book, which
are all impressive from a purely practical perspective, and so is Wikipedia. But the flow of people who left X for Bluesky suggests that

many people on social media don't want to spend their time and energy elevating moderate perspectives on contested social media platforms; they are just sick of those places and ready to withdraw from them and build their own digital worlds. Those enclaves, I contend, can become sources of prosocial change.

A digital world with multiple social platforms—each one with its idiosyncrasies and internal differences, logics, and challenges—may look less like a public cybersquare and more like a digital version of how people in early modern Europe who disliked the activities that dominated public arenas and gatherings instead came together in coffeehouses and saloons, some of which were exclusive to particular professions, trades, classes, and political parties. These places became alternative centers of social interaction between writers, merchants, and members of the middle class, with discussions focused on literature, art, and eventually, economics and politics.[18]

Digital coffeehouses or saloons can drive prosocial change by fostering open discussion in spaces that are less weighted down by toxic talk. Participants will be aware that they are in an echo chamber, which will temper overconfidence in the appeal of their ideas, also helped by algorithmic autonomy and transparency. The digital far right is an example of how this isn't inherently good. But it might be time to give up on the idea of a digital public square where people can meet and interact across their differences, and instead accept that a digital world of multiple platforms for interaction also represents a form of plurality, one that might work better than the failed experiments that started with Facebook. A world of digital saloons will be one in which some dark places are visible. But they will be outnumbered.

Acknowledgments

One of my sisters asked me if it was difficult to write this book all on my own. The truth is, I didn't. I have been fortunate to have the support and guidance of many colleagues, mentors, and peers—junior and senior alike.

I began writing what would become this book sometime in the 2010s at Boston College, where my dissertation advisor, Stephen Pfohl, encouraged me to pursue the project. His invaluable advice on rough drafts (which I hope no one will ever see) got me going. I also benefited from the perspectives of other BC faculty during this period: Wen Fan, Natalia Sarkisian, Brian Gareau, and Sara Moorman all offered feedback on various parts of this project, and Sarah Babb is partly to blame for my transmutation into an economic sociologist. Above all, I owe my deepest gratitude to Juliet Schor, who taught me everything I know about being a scholar. She remains my greatest influence—both in how I think about the world and strive to make sense of it through my writing and teaching.

My graduate research was funded by the National Science Foundation, and the University of Illinois at Urbana-Champaign provided crucial support during my four years as an assistant professor, including a grant that allowed me to dedicate an entire year to this manuscript. My students were instrumental in engaging with and discussing material that later became part of this book. I am also grateful for thoughtful feedback from my UIUC colleagues Tim Liao, Anna-Maria Marshall, Zsuzsa Gille, Jeffrey Martin, Melissa Ocepek, Dede Fairchild Ruggles, Jose Atiles, Matthew Soener, and Richard Benton. And I have found great inspiration in the work of my UIUC colleague Asef Bayat.

I have been fortunate to share this work with scholars placed elsewhere, including Diane Vaughan, Frank Dobbin, Michele Lamont, Kathleen Blee, Dan

Lynch, Minxin Pei, Alexandrea Ravenelle, Sida Liu, Borge Bakken, Kristen Davis, Temily Tianmay Tavangar, Rod Broadhurst, Marie Ouellet, and attendees at invited talks at Monash University, Rutgers University, Oklahoma State University, Purdue University, SUNY Albany, Australian National University, UC Irvine, and my alma mater, the University of Hong Kong, which recently brought me back.

Link_IL played a pivotal role in shaping the project by suggesting that ladder technology was a valuable empirical case to include. Philip Zimmermann helped clarify my understanding of encryption in the age of mass surveillance, the GFW Report welcomed questions about their research on Chinese ladder technology, and my dear friend Suhani Jain provided invaluable knowledge from the tech world. Suhani's unexpected passing in 2023 was a great loss for the universe.

I would also like to thank my participants, who generously shared their experiences and helped me tell this story. Talking with them reminded me yet again that no matter how big my datasets are, qualitative research methods remain invaluable.

My research assistants in Boston, Urbana-Champaign, and Hong Kong, most of whom started as my own students, were indispensable to the progress of this work. I am deeply grateful for their energy and diligence. Their names: Cindy Zhang, Nick Loeper, Sze Ching Tang, Loong Kuan, Grace Tyson, Ilan Valencius, Josie Morales-Thomason, Isabelle Luke, Yitong Liu, Laura Tao, and Ruifan Yang.

I am indebted to the team at UC Press, including Aline Dolinh, Julie Van Pelt, Teresa Iafolla, Katryce Campbell, Chloe Wong, Neal Swain, and especially Naomi Schneider, who believed in this project early on, even when I was a first-time author with only the barest outlines of a book.

I also owe much to my developmental editors, Dawn Elizabeth Culton and Juliana Froggatt. In particular, Juliana's careful, highly professional reading, insightful comments, and multicolored annotations made the manuscript revisions much more manageable. The excellent copyeditor Amy Smith Bell saved me from myself. I have also benefited from feedback from nonacademic readers, including my sister Anna Ladegaard and, of course, mom (Kirsti Ladegaard).

The people above all had a direct impact on the research or writing process. But outside of this academic sphere, I also leaned on my globally dispersed friends, my parents, grandparents, siblings, and extended family, and my partner Junghyun, all of whom reminded me that there are many worlds of meaning out there. I love you all.

Case Selection and Data

I selected three different empirical cases for this book because I wanted to emphasize that open secrecy is a broader phenomenon, a force of social change that has many different consequences, across many different domains. In particular, I wanted to stress that my argument isn't normative. I found that many books make the case that information technology is a prosocial or antisocial force of social change, but I believe it is both. At the same time, I didn't want to cop out of the debate, as Marshall McLuhan did in his analyses about technological change. I therefore decided to present a case that I have mixed thoughts about (chapters 3 and 4 on drug markets); a case that many people, myself included, will likely see as a prosocial struggle for freer speech (chapters 5 and 6 on censorship circumvention); and finally, a case that is sobering and deeply disturbing (chapters 7, 8, and 9 on the digital far right). I could have included other cases in this book, such as child pornography networks, as they continue to operate despite considerable law enforcement pressure and moral condemnation from all corners and segments of society. But it would have been difficult to analyze child pornography networks and avoid exposure to such content. File piracy was another alternative, but it has been studied extensively, although not conceptualized as a case of open secrecy, and as a force of social change it was more relevant a couple of decades ago.

Case 1: Drug Trade on the Darknet

Open secrecy enabled the development of digital drug trade, exemplified by Silk Road and subsequent platforms. These markets were created in the image of free markets, where participants were expected to behave as atomized, rational actors focused on maximizing gains and minimizing costs. Over time, the countercultural logics and deeply personalized networks that characterized traditional drug markets—such as kinship, friendship, sharing over profit-making, anticapitalist sentiments, and community solidarity—were gradually replaced by quantitative reputation systems, professionalized ties, and decreased interest in sociability. This cultural transformation was enabled and at least partially driven by open secrecy, allowing for the creative entrepreneurship of individuals with libertarian values and reshaping the drug trade landscape.

The data for this case primarily included interviews with drug dealers and customers, and information scraped from darknet drug markets and related online communities. I contacted the potential interviewees directly, on the Silk Road market website or its online community. People were surprisingly responsive, likely because anonymization technology made them feel safe and perhaps because talking to me was much less risky than the other things they were doing there, with the same usernames. To estimate trade and activities in the market forums, I downloaded and extracted data from key original sources. To measure trade and seller movement after Silk Road was shut down, I collected daily data from Silk Road 2, Evolution, and Agora, from October 2014 through September 2015. Agora lasted throughout the period, but Silk Road 2 was shut down in early November 2014, and Evolution closed in the middle of March 2015. For the analysis of identity verification and post-crackdown mobilization, I collected data from the discussion forums associated with Silk Road and Silk Road 2, Agora, Evolution, and BlackMarket, another early darknet market. For the analysis of information hub activity, I collected visitor data from three market-independent forums (two were on Reddit) and two websites for practical information related to the darknet economy (e.g., market uptime measures). In sum, I collected and analyzed nearly one million market transactions and three million forum messages.

Case 2: Fighting Censorship

I decided to include activist technology in autocratic states as the book's second case because the bigger story about open secrecy is highly relevant to the literature on social movements. While much has been written about how information technology can aid collective action, none of the books or articles I have reviewed have discussed the new combinations that enable open secrecy—that is, the particular technologies that make digitally organized group action nearly impossible to stop—nor have they linked their empirical cases to broader themes of modernity and undermined state power, which is not inherently prosocial. I decided that open secrecy in autocracies like China and Iran is worth thinking and writing about because they pose unique challenges to shadowy groups. Darknet markets and related communities, which primarily operate out of Western countries, have formidable opponents—law enforcement agencies like the Federal Bureau of Investigation (FBI) in the United States and the National Crime Agency (NCA) in the UK—while autocratic states are less restrained because they rule by law rather than operating under rule of law. Moreover, because autocratic states see legitimacy threats as existential threats, their resource allocation differs from Western policing.

Data for this case was scraped from publicly available code-sharing platforms, open chat groups or "channels" dedicated to testing of airports, discussion forums for tech issues that covered ladder technology, and interviews with developers, airport operators, and other tech-savvy actors who were part of the ladder community or related to it. I took great caution to avoid putting them at unnecessary risk. I did not ask any identifying questions and omitted such data from my notes when it emerged. I did not store any information on my participants—not even their digital pseudonyms—and deleted all chat logs. I will not discuss how I found them.

Case 3: The Digital Far Right

I included the digital far right in this book because it brings attention to how open secrecy is not a prosocial force of change but rather evidence of how technology-driven liberation is value-neutral and can be dangerous. The digital far right thus serves as a reminder of how social control is, despite the connotations of repression, not something to get rid of or avoid at all cost but rather a necessary ingredient in a healthy society. (Most sociologists would also say that all social life includes some informal or formal system of regulation.)

Although I devoted three chapters to the digital far right—one more than the other two cases—this case is in some ways the most limited. I perhaps should have included a chapter dedicated to gender, another one that links the digital far right and far-right ideas in mainstream politics (e.g., the influence of Stephen Miller on Republican immigration policies), and one on how open secrecy supports global linkages in the larger far-right realm. The focus on the United States is partly explained by the fact that I have spent most of the past decade on the American East Coast and in the Midwest but also because the digital far right has legal protections in the United States that it doesn't in Europe. This means that the regulatory pressure differs in interesting ways that in my view warrant the case's inclusion in this larger story about open secrecy. I decided to focus on Stormfront, the Daily Stormer, and Gab because they have for several years been the largest far-right sites in the world, they are independently run (unlike sections of larger platforms, such as subreddits), and they have aesthetic and rhetoric differences that seemed worthwhile to dissect. They also offer a more accurate representation of the heterogenous far-right landscape.

The data for the far-right chapters were collected using web-scraping techniques in the period 2019–24. The Stormfront scraping was done in several steps. First by me, then with the help of Ruifan Yang, a student at Boston College, and then by Loong Kuan Lee, a PhD candidate at Monash University, who did most of the heavy lifting, until we had a complete archive of all English-language posts: about 10.4 million. Gab posts from 2017 to 2021 were purchased from Open Measures. The Daily Stormer data—about fifty-five thousand articles—I scraped myself in 2024.

Notes

Chapter 1. Invisible Forces of Liberation and Control

1. I use the internet as an umbrella term for all variants of the global system of interconnected computer networks that includes the World Wide Web, email, SWIFT, etc.

2. Kurzweil (2010, p. 312).

3. Quoted in DDSN Interactive (2021).

4. Elias and Foucault in Van Krieken (1990).

5. Hansen & Reich (2015).

6. Van Dijk (2020).

7. My most recent temptation: motorized curtains that activate at sunrise.

8. Hobsbawm (2010).

9. McLuhan (2017).

10. Sassen (2000).

11. Castells (2015); Tufekci (2017).

12. Scott (2020); Bauman et al. (2014); Zuboff (2019).

13. Beckert & Wehinger (2013).

14. Arlacchi (2002); Beckert & Wehinger (2013).

15. Both Gab and Stormfront—US-focused far-right communities—have hundreds of thousands of users.

16. Novos & Waldman (2013); Steel (2009); Greco (2023).

17. Giddens (1986); Beck (1992); Bauman (1993); Scott (2020); Zuboff (2019).

18. My thinking here is influenced by Nelson (2020); Small (2011); and Grigoropoulou & Small (2022). People who want more information about the topic models I use in the far-right chapters (chapters 7, 8, and 9) can look at the

discussion of inductive-deductive topic modeling (IDTM) in Ladegaard & Rieger (2024).

19. Ladegaard & Rieger (2024).
20. Following Emerson et al. (2011).

Chapter 2. The Three Acts of the Information Age

1. Mann et al. (2008); Ottoni & Izar (2008).
2. Isaacson (2014).
3. Scott (2017); Geertz (1973).
4. Castells (2015).
5. Hauben & Hauben (1998).
6. Fischer (2023).
7. Kay & King (2020).
8. Krugman as quoted in Halpern (2013).
9. McPherson et al. (2001).
10. Ladegaard (2018a).
11. Sunstein (2009).
12. Sanchez (2019, August 21); Caramanica (2011, October 24).
13. Quoted in Martin (2022, September 14).
14. Rheingold (2000).
15. Turkle (2012).
16. Chayko (2008).
17. Cole & Griffiths (2007); Preece & Ghozati (2001); Ladegaard (2019b).
18. Benkler (2010); Shirky (2010).
19. Marwick (2013).
20. As reported in Coscarelli (2020, June 22).
21. Quoted in Petrusich (2020, June 5).
22. Abdulla (2011).
23. Castells (1996); Tufekci (2017).
24. Bennett & Segerberg (2012).
25. Benkler (2006); Shirky (2010); Wright (2020).
26. Nelson et al. (2022).
27. Berlin (2013).
28. Quoted in Zuboff (2019).
29. Lianos (2003).
30. Tufekci (2014).
31. xAI (2024); Wolfram (2023).

32. Mayer as quoted in Levy (2011).

33. Isaacson (2011).

34. Chayka (2024).

35. Schüll (2012).

36. Quoted in Scheiber (2017, April 2).

37. Quoted in Carr (2013, February 24).

38. Kramer et al. (2014).

39. Bond et al. (2012).

40. Scott (2020).

41. Schneier (2015).

42. Snowden as quoted in Leon (2019, October 28).

43. Alexander (2013, September 26).

44. Pei (2024).

45. Pei (2024, p. 242).

46. Defense Innovation Unit (n.d.).

47. US Department of Homeland Security (2020, December 22).

48. In-Q-Tel does not disclose how much it invests in individual companies, but according to the *Wall Street Journal*'s anonymous sources, the amount was "at least" $120 million a year as of 2018, with money from the CIA, the FBI, the NSA, and the Defense Department. Early recipients included the software company Palantir, which specializes in big data analysis and has won several national security contracts. See Copeland & Brown (2018, November 12).

49. Reagan National Defense Forum (2019, December 20).

50. Bezos as quoted in Waters (2019, December 8).

51. Schmidt (2020, February 27).

52. Varoufakis (2024); Bremmer (2021, October 19).

53. Wolf (2017, November 14).

54. Grind et al. (2021, February 6); Big 5 market cap growth from December 2022 to November 2024, Statista (2024, November 27).

55. Norges Bank Investment Management (2024).

56. Scott (2020).

57. Rosenberg (2018, April 22).

58. New Scientist & Press Association (2018, April 5); Laterza (2021).

59. Isaac (2024, April 24).

60. Romero (2018, December 31).

61. Karpathy as quoted in Fridman (2022, March 2).

62. Wu (2018, February 16).

63. Vogels (2021, July 20).

64. Geiger (2018, June 4).

65. Pew Research Center (2016, November 4).

66. Bauman et al. (2014).

67. Nicas et al. (2021, January 13); Zuboff (2019).

68. Giddens (1990).

Chapter 3. Illegal Markets Step Out of the Shadows

1. Ulbricht in Greenberg (2015).

2. Ulbricht quoted in Bitcoin Forum (2011).

3. Brennan (2012).

4. Bakken et al. (2018).

5. The forum is no longer available, but I saved a copy of it in 2013. All quotes from the Silk Road forums in this chapter are from this copy.

6. Ulbricht wrote in his diary: "Silk Road got its first press, the infamous *Gawker* article. When you look at the historical #s, you can see right when it happened. A huge spike in signups, and the beginning of an upward trend in commerce"; Chen (2011, June 1).

7. On Silk Road reaching $7.5 million, see Aldridge & Décary-Hétu (2014).

8. Beckert & Wehinger (2013); Arlacchi (2002).

9. Lauzon (1998).

10. DiMaggio & Louch (1998).

11. Beckert & Wehinger (2013); Arlacchi (2002).

12. Arlacchi (2002).

13. Reuter (1983). For a more detailed discussion of this, see Ladegaard (2020).

14. Haynie & Duxbury (2024); Ladegaard (2024).

15. In total, I analyzed 3,833 electronically published consumer reports, using qualitative and computational methods. See the above citation for details.

16. Ladegaard (2021).

17. Reuter (1983).

18. Matza & Sykes (1957); Silbey (2005).

19. Griffiths et al. (2006).

20. Sandberg (2013).

21. Schmid & Liechti (2018); Johnstad (2021).

22. Wherry (2012).

23. Parker et al. (2002).

24. Parker et al. (1999).

25. Becker (1953).

26. For more on this, see Ladegaard (2019b).

27. Zelizer (2010).

28. Fligstein & McAdam (2012).

29. For more on this, see Ladegaard (2018c).

30. For an excellent critique of this view, see Zelizer (2010).

Chapter 4. Crackdowns and Adaptations

1. Ladegaard (2018c).

2. Haynie & Duxbury (2024).

3. Woolf (2015, March 18).

4. Ladegaard (2019b).

5. James the moderator then started frequently changing the Bitcoin address, making it difficult to keep track of the total donation volume.

6. Bayat (2013).

7. Zelizer (2010).

8. For details on how I measured darknet trade, see Ladegaard (2020).

9. I downloaded all posts from five darknet market forums and searched for encryption signatures across the dataset.

10. Zimmerman (1995).

11. Rogers (2010).

12. Marantz (2018).

13. For more detailed information about information hub traffic, see Ladegaard (2020).

14. Khazanov (1978).

15. Christin (2013); Aldridge & Décary-Hétu (2014).

16. How these figures were calculated: Early darknet markets required users to leave reviews for their purchases (or empty five-star ratings). Each listing also included the price. This enabled estimation of trade. For more details, see Ladegaard (2020).

17. I collected data on postintervention trade and seller migration from the three largest markets after Silk Road was shut down in October 2013: Silk Road 2, Evolution, and Agora. I collected these data daily from October 2014 until August 2015. Agora lasted throughout the period, but Silk Road 2 was shut down in early November 2014 and Evolution closed in March 2015.

18. Stark (2009).

19. Fligstein & McAdam (2012).

20. Schumpeter & Swedberg (2021); Beckert (2014).

21. McCabe as quoted in Winter (2017, July 20).

22. Garland (1996).

23. Beckert & Wehinger (2013).

24. Stinchcombe (2013 [1965]); Demant et al. (2019).

Chapter 5. Climbing the Great Firewall of China

1. Scott (2020); Sassen (2008).

2. Durkheim's example was the punishment of Socrates. His open questioning of traditional beliefs in Athens made him a criminal by the local law, but the independent thinking he advocated was needed in a changing world (Durkheim [2018]).

3. Vogel (2011); China Heritage (n.d.); Magnus (2018).

4. Pei (2024).

5. Pei (2024).

6. Lei (2018).

7. Roberts (2018); Han (2015).

8. He (2024, May 27).

9. W3Techs (2024).

10. Shen & Shi (2024).

11. Quoted in *The Economist* (2022, June 28).

12. Roberts (2018); Pei (2024).

13. Clinton as quoted in *New York Times* (2000, March 9).

14. Castells (2015); Gillan (2020).

15. The mean number of days in the ladder ecosystem, measured as the difference between a user's first and last GitHub contribution to Shadowsocks or V2Ray projects, is 214 days.

16. *Breakwa11 Blog* (2017).

17. Multiple Authors (n.d.-b).

18. GoAgent (2015, August 25).

19. Plus another two who posted thank-yous on GoAgent's GitHub page.

Chapter 6. Black Markets for Censorship Circumvention

1. Hessler (2022).

2. Based on sixteen airports that a popular airport blogger and tester showcased in an "overview."

3. The calculation is: number of available airports × mean number of Telegram subscribers per airport × the ratio of Telegram subscribers to airport users.

4. Data from reflection.io.

5. Zheng (2017, December 21).

6. Zelizer (2010).

7. Griffiths (2021).

8. Scott (2020).

9. Roberts (2018).

10. On the Iranian government criminalizing VPNs in 2024, see Radio Farda (2024).

11. Griffiths (2021); Lei (2018).

12. Griffiths (2021).

13. Azure (2020).

14. Zuboff (2019).

15. Kottler (2018, March 1).

16. Friedman (2021, January 5).

17. Griffiths (2021).

18. Outline (2024).

19. Jigsaw-Code (2024).

20. According to the organization's tax records.

21. Chandel et al. (2019).

22. Google Trends (2024).

23. Chen & Yang (2019).

24. Roberts (2018).

25. Bayat (2013).

26. Scott (1985).

27. Fincher (2021); Mattingly (2019); Johnson (2018, 2023); Chen (2010); Bakken (2000).

28. Kuo (2021, September 9); Mao (2022, June 7).

29. Giugni et al. (1999).

30. Scott (1985).

31. Dickson (2021).

32. Shambaugh (2008).

33. Brady (2009).

34. Shambaugh (2008).

35. Dickson (2021).

Chapter 7. Deplatforming the Digital Far Right

1. Morrow (2001, December 2).

2. Gambetta & Hertog (2018).

3. Anderson (2008).

4. The Ambassador in Germany (Dodd) to the Secretary of State (1935).

5. Douglas (2003); Bourdieu (1987).

6. I use the term "far right" to describe a broad coalition of groups and movements from populist nationalists to white supremacists. People in this realm differ in many ways, but all talk about shifting demographics as an existential threat to white people, which they typically blame on immigration and policy-making elites. Not every individual in these groups anticipates an impending apocalypse, but in general they voice a longing for a return to a glorified past and/or a desire to build a new and different world, such as an all-white nation.

7. Williams et al. (2021); Squire & Gais (2021, September 29).

8. Miller-Idriss (2022).

9. The Daily Stormer's founder, Andrew Anglin, who was born in 1984, wrote in the site's style guide that he's "a little bit older than the average reader."

10. Hankes (2015, June 21).

11. Roof as quoted in US Attorney's Office, via the Federal District Court (2016, December 10).

12. Those killed by Roof were Clementa C. Pinckney (41), Cynthia Graham Hurd (54), Susie Jackson (87), Ethel Lee Lance (70), Depayne Middleton-Doctor (49), Tywanza Sanders (26), Daniel L. Simmons (74), Sharonda Coleman-Singleton (45), and Myra Thompson (59) (as reported in Kinnard, 2017, January 10).

13. Those killed by Bowers were Joyce Fienberg (75), Richard Gottfried (65), Rose Mallinger (97), Jerry Rabinowitz (66), Cecil Rosenthal (59), David Rosenthal (54), Bernice Simon (84), Sylvan Simon (86), Daniel Stein (71), Melvin Wax (87), and Irving Younger (69) (as reported in Office of Public Affairs, 2023, August 2).

14. Bowers as quoted in United States v. Bowers, Criminal Complaint, No. 18-1396 (W.D. Pa. Oct. 27, 2018).

15. Federal Bureau of Investigation & Department of Homeland Security (2017).

16. Dugan & Fisher (2023); Kearns et al. (2019).

17. Duran (2021).

18. Barkun (2024); Gilbert (2023).

19. Confessore (2023).

20. US Attorney's Office, via the Federal District Court (2016, December 10).

21. Bennett & Segerberg (2012).

22. Berg (2017, December 14).

23. Far-right actors are aware of the legal exceptions to the First Amendment's free speech guarantees. Anglin, for example, notes in his style guide for Daily Stormer contributors that it is illegal to promote violence.

24. E.g., Mattey (2020).

25. US Department of Health and Human Services (2023).

26. Isaac (2024).

27. Sheffield (2017, August 28); BBC News (2017, August 14); Rodriguez (2017, January 23); Coldewey (2017, August 17); Ng et al. (2022).

28. As quoted in Ling (2017, August 15).

29. As quoted in Brustein (2018, October 30).

30. Ladegaard (2019b).

31. See chapter 3.

32. Young (2017).

33. As quoted in Frenkel (2019, March 27).

34. Gersh v. Anglin (2017).

35. Gab has many international users, and despite Torba's thinly veiled support for white supremacism, it is a social media network that is less focused on far-right issues than Stormfront and the Daily Stormer.

36. Rochko (2019, July 4).

37. Makuch (2019, July 11).

38. Thiel & McCain (2022).

39. My measures, based on data purchased from Open Measures, exclude non-English texts and empty repostings of other messages. January 6 is included in the "after" period.

40. Dugan, K. (2017, August 16).

41. Kahneman (2011); Tufekci (2017).

42. Zelizer (2010).

43. Bachelier (2017).

44. Barnes & Goldman (2020, March 10).

45. Hayden & Squire (2021, December 9).

46. Gab AI Inc. (2013).

47. Fitzmaurice et al. (2020).

48. Office of the US Surgeon General (2023); Pettigrew et al. (2011).

49. Ladegaard (2024).

Chapter 8. The Digital Far Right's "Hate Focus"

1. Measured by the mean number of topic keywords per post per day. This finding is corroborated by reviews of Stormfront's most commented threads.

2. Blee & Creasap (2010).

3. This figure excludes the January 6, 2021, siege on the US Capitol. The event meets the terrorism definition used here and did result in the death of five persons. But for reasons discussed in chapter 7, the enormous spike of sign-ups was mostly due to the shutdown of Parler.

4. Moritz-Rabson (2018, October 29).

5. I measured sign-ups by counting and comparing the number of first-time posters per day during the twenty-eight days before the incident and seven days after (including the incident day). I compared weekly periods to reduce the impact of seasonality.

6. Mean days between first and last posts for people who posted for the first time after a violent event or at other times.

7. Quoted in US Attorney's Office, via the Federal District Court (2016, December 10).

8. Kimmel (2018).

9. I examined cases of police brutality that the Associated Press characterized as "high profile." The victims were Eric Garner, Michael Brown, Laquan McDonald, Tamir Rice, Walter Scott, Freddie Gray, Philando Castile, Jordan Edwards, and Breonna Taylor. I added George Floyd to the list and removed Gray because he overlapped with a previous incident. I also removed Edwards because he was preceded by Trump's crackdown on visas and green card applications, which boosted discussion and thus muddied efforts to measure the effect of the police killing. For measures of the effect these incidents had on Stormfront and Gab, I used median rather than mean, as some incidents (e.g., the killing of Floyd) provoked bigger changes than others (Associated Press, 2022, June 9).

10. Törnberg & Törnberg (2021).

11. Blee (2008); Kimmel (2018).

12. E.g., Beauvoir (1989): "No one is more arrogant toward women, more aggressive or more disdainful, than a man anxious about his own virility"; Lankford (2021); Kimmel (2017).

13. Willer et al. (2013).

14. Brines (1994).

15. Global Terrorism Database, University of Maryland (n.d.).

16. Taken at face value, and based on far-right ideas of what it means to be "white," demographic change cannot be genocide, because its definition assumes intent and particular acts that are absent. That is, although demographics are indeed changing in the United States, this is not because some actor intends to eradicate white people. Genocide is defined by the United Nations as "any of the following acts committed with intent to destroy, in whole or in part, a national, ethnical, racial or religious group, as such: killing members of the group; causing serious bodily or mental harm to members of the group; deliberately inflicting on the group conditions of life calculated to bring about its physical destruction in whole or in part; imposing measures intended to prevent births within the group; [and] forcibly transferring children of the group to another group" (UN Office on Genocide Prevention and the Responsibility to Protect, n.d.).

17. This Stormfronter is likely talking about polling numbers in the lead-up to the 2018 midterm elections, which were seen as a test of the people's reactions to Trump's election win two years earlier.

18. Fazio et al. (2015).

19. The Wikipedia entry on Trayvon Martin from a few weeks after he was killed by George Zimmerman in 2012, likely close to the version Roof read, is a dispassionate account of a seventeen-year-old going to the corner store to buy candy during a break in an NBA match. Zimmerman, twenty-eight, saw Martin and called the local police to report that Martin was walking around in the rain, hand in his waistband, looking at houses: "This guy looks like he is up to no good. He is on drugs or something." Martin, who was on the phone with his girlfriend at the time, said a "strange man" was following him. She heard an exchange: "Why are you following me?" from Martin, then "What are you doing here?," presumably from Zimmerman. The police found Martin shot dead. Zimmerman, whose nose was bleeding and jacket stained with grass, said he shot Martin in self-defense after being attacked. Of course Martin's side of the story was never told.

20. Colon (2024).

21. Criminologists would call this a neutralization technique that enables people to reframe their actions. In this case they appeal to "higher loyalties," in the way a man might "justify" vengeful violence as an expression of fatherly love (e.g., "I'm not a violent person, but that man hurt my daughter . . . ").

22. Roediger (2006).

23. Cohn (2014, May 5); Parker et al. (2015, June 11).

24. Panofsky & Donovan (2019).

25. Quoted in Zaitchik (2006).

Chapter 9. *Hyggelig* Hate and the Mainstreaming of
the Digital Far Right

1. Lauzen & Dozier (2005).

2. Pew Research Center (2016, July 20).

3. I found keywords for each topic by building a simple neural net based on text data from Stormfront, Gab, and the Daily Stormer. This enabled inductive word discovery. See the methods section in chapter 1 for details.

4. Kuziemko et al. (2014).

5. Badger et al. (2024).

6. Tversky & Kahneman (1991).

7. Beck (2001); Giddens (1991); Bauman (2013).

8. Gourevitch (2008).

9. Quoted in O'Brien (2017, December).

10. Kang (2014, September 18).

11. Kimmel (2017, 2018).

12. Chayka (2024).

13. Roose (2019, October 9).

14. Daily Stormer (n.d.).

15. Parsons (2015).

16. Ganor (2020); Royal Commission of Inquiry into the Attack on Christchurch Mosques (2020).

17. Quoted in Roose (2019, October 9).

18. Blee & Creasap (2010).

19. Pfohl (2005); Jerolmack & Khan (2014).

20. Robin (2019, January 23).

21. Threads that include one or more of these words and phrases: cooking, cup, favorite song, football, funny, game, joke, jokes, listening, MMA, music, pictures, say something random, this or that, trivia, UFC, word, world cup.

22. Nyhan & Reifler (2010).

23. Simi et al. (2017).

24. A whopping 2,009 Stormfronters wrote at least 1,000 posts. Of these, 442 had at least one year away from the community.

25. Many returnees posted just a few times before or after their hiatus or were absent several nonconsecutive years, both of which make it tricky to measure before-and-after changes in their writing. But ninety-six Stormfronters posted at least one hundred times both before and after a year away from the community, which allows for such a comparison.

26. Wilson (2004).

27. Kimmel (2018).

Chapter 10. Resisting Social Change

1. Scott (2020); Sassen (2008); Giddens (1986).

2. Hobsbawm (2010).

3. Quoted in LaMotte (2024, January 8).

4. Scott (2020).

5. Bauman (2013); Beck (2001).

6. Quoted in Cameron (2023, September 15).

7. Quoted in Knight (2023, May 15).

8. Quoted in Dwyer (2006, August 17); Seo & Harlan (2014, April 18).

9. Vaughan (1996); Ladegaard & Rieger (2024).

10. Garland (1996).

11. Sassen (2008).

12. Garland (1996).

13. Arlacchi (2002); Beckert & Wehinger (2013); Scott (2017); Clastres (2020).

14. Tsing (2024).

15. Quoted in Dread Pirate Roberts (2013, December 5).

16. Scott (2017, 2024).

17. In the words of Beck (1992, p. 186): "the outlines of an alternative society are no longer seen in [political] debates."

18. Quoted in Ladegaard (2018c).

19. Lynch (1999).

20. Garland (2001).

21. Garland (1991, 2001).

22. Bernstein et al. (2010).

23. Shambaugh (2008).

24. Pei (2024).

25. The starting point of modernity is contested, but the start of the Industrial Revolution in the late 1700s is central to sociological discussions of modernity and eventually late/post/second/liquid modernity. E.g., see Hobsbawm (2010).

26. Foucault (2012). Foucault's citation and comment about the document: Archives militaires de Vincennes, A 1,516 91 se. Pièce. This regulation is broadly similar to a series of others that date from the same period and earlier.

27. For more anecdotes on the matter, see Hessler (2020, March 23).

28. Xinhua News (2016, July 1); Mattingly (2019).

29. Chin & Lin (2022).

30. Pei (2024).

31. Scholars of policing and colonialism will be less surprised, however. They've found that many Western social control methods were first developed and used in colonies. See Martin (2018); Go (2020).

32. Filkins (2006, January 1).

33. Nakashima & Warrick (2013, July 14).

34. Schneier (2015).

35. Chin & Lin (2022); Hvistendahl (2018, March 14).

36. Wu (2018, February 16).

37. Rifkin (2014).

38. Roberts (2018); Bauman et al. (2014).

39. Murgia (2024).

40. Nicas et al. (2021, January 13).

41. Scott (1985).

42. Guo (2018).

43. Garrick & Bennett (2018).

44. Childress et al. (2021); Hochschild (2018).

45. Tversky & Kahneman (1991); Norris & Inglehart (2019); Torba (2021, February).

46. Norton & Sommers (2011).

47. Bauman (2000); Scott (2020); Beck (1992).

48. Sassen (2008).

Chapter 11. Embracing Ambiguity

1. Hirschman (2013).

2. Castells (2015); Bayat (2021).

3. Lerner (1985); Nussbaum (2001).

4. Giddens (1991).

5. Scott (1985).

6. Gray (2010); Christie (2016); Godlee & Hurley (2016).

7. Nicolas (2019, February 19).

8. United States v. Ulbricht, 858 F.3d 71 (2d Cir. 2017).

9. Based on my reading of about six hundred DoctorX posts in two public threads titled "Ask a Drug Expert Physician about Drugs & Health" from Silk

Road 1 and 2, published in 2013 and 2014 (the data excludes personal messages, which sometimes amounted to, he said, "dozens a week").

10. United States v. Ulbricht, No. 14 Cr. 68 (S.D.N.Y. May 29, 2015).

11. Centers for Disease Control and Prevention (2024, May 15).

12. Quoted in Ladegaard (2018b).

13. Greenberg (2018, March 8).

14. Ladegaard (2019a).

15. Vickery & Finch (2020); National Academies of Sciences, Engineering, and Medicine (2017).

16. Humphreys & Bovett (2024, March 17).

17. Browning (1992).

18. Orben (2020); Dillon (2004).

19. Dickson (2021).

20. Guo (2018).

21. Bayat (2013).

22. Scott (1985).

23. Although selectively, on the Party's terms, and often mixed with coercion. Dickson (2021).

24. Xi's 2016 speech as quoted in Chin & Lin (2022).

25. Xu (2018); Roberts (2018).

26. Foucault (2012).

27. Miller-Idriss (2022).

28. Petrusich (2020, June 5).

29. Williams (2016, June 12).

30. Pettigrew et al. (2011).

31. Robin (2019, January 23).

32. Black (2013, July 15).

33. Kimmel (2018).

34. Singal (2015, May 29).

35. Benier et al. (2024).

36. Voosen (2023, September 24).

37. Berlin (2013).

38. Kay & King (2020).

39. Ghusn et al. (2022).

40. Centers for Disease Control and Prevention (2024, May 14).

41. Kahneman (2011).

42. Case & Deaton (2020); Norris & Inglehart (2019); Hultman et al. (2019).

43. *The Paris Review interviews*, Vols. 1–4 (2009).

44. Stark (2009).

45. Cerulo (2019).

46. Zuboff (2019).

Epilogue

1. Ong (1982).

2. Carr (2020).

3. Scott (2020).

4. Scott (2017).

5. Fligstein (2018); Giddens (1986); McMillan (2003); Sassen (2008); Scott (2020).

6. Bayat (2013).

7. Confessore (2022, April 30); Robin (2019, January 23).

8. Bobo (2017); Hochschild (2018); Norris & Inglehart (2019).

9. Chayka (2023; 2024, November 13).

10. McGirt (2009, April 1).

11. Wortham (2016, October 25).

12. Kang (2017, January 27); Romm (2017, January 17).

13. Korach (2024, October 5).

14. *The Onion* (2024, December 14); Schleifer (2024, November 13).

15. Bail (2022).

16. Wright (2020).

17. Shirky (2010).

18. Habermas (1991).

Bibliography

Abdulla, R. (2011). The revolution will be tweeted. *Cairo Review of Global Affairs,* 3(1), 41–49.

Aldridge, J., & Décary-Hétu, D. (2014). Not an "Ebay for drugs": The cryptomarket "Silk Road" as a paradigm shifting criminal innovation. Available at SSRN: https://ssrn.com/abstract=2436643. Accessed May 2024.

Alexander, K. (2013, September 26). *Remarks as delivered by General Keith Alexander, director of the National Security Agency.* Intel.gov. https://www.intelligence.gov/ic-on-the-record-database/results/30-remarks-as-delivered-by-general-keith-alexander,-director-of-the-national-security-agency. Accessed May 2024.

The Ambassador in Germany (Dodd) to the Secretary of State. (1935). Foreign Relations of the United States Diplomatic Papers, 1935, The British Commonwealth; Europe, Volume II, Document 305. https://history.state.gov/historicaldocuments/frus1935v02/d305. Accessed May 2024.

Anderson, B. (2008). Imagined communities: Reflections on the origin and spread of nationalism. In S. Seidman & J. C. Alexander (Eds.), *The New Social Theory Reader* (pp. 282–288). Routledge.

Arlacchi, P. (2002). Some observations on illegal markets. In I. Taylor, N. South, & V. Ruggiero (Eds.), *The new European criminology: Crime and social order in Europe* (pp. 221–233). Routledge.

Associated Press. (2022, June 9). A look at high-profile killings by US police. https://apnews.com/article/death-of-daunte-wright-george-floyd-patrick-lyoya-politics-racial-injustice-08c05a3ffd769c0061ff62793286bb90. Accessed June 2024.

Azure 云计算. (2020). *Azure* 紧急提示: 关于自查整改"翻墙"行为的通知! https://web.archive.org/web/20200426173334/https://www.azure.cn /support/announcement/rectification-announcement/index.html. Accessed May 2024.

Bachelier, L. (2017). *[If you're reading this, I am deceased]*. https://web.archive .org/web/20221107111420/http://laurent.bachelier.name/notes-en.txt. Accessed May 2024.

Badger, E., Gebeloff, R., & Bhatia, A. (2024). They used to be ahead in the American economy. Now they've fallen behind. *New York Times*. https:// www.nytimes.com/interactive/2024/10/26/upshot/census-relative-income .html. Accessed December 2024.

Bail, C. (2022). *Breaking the social media prism: How to make our platforms less polarizing.* Princeton University Press.

Bakken, B. (2000). *The exemplary society: Human improvement, social control, and the dangers of modernity in China.* Clarendon Press.

Bakken, S. A., Moeller, K., & Sandberg, S. (2018). Coordination problems in cryptomarkets: Changes in cooperation, competition and valuation. *European Journal of Criminology, 15*(4), 442–460.

Barkun, M. (2013). *A culture of conspiracy: Apocalyptic visions in contemporary America.* University of California Press.

Barkun, M. (2024). Replacement theory on the road to conspiracy. *Conspiracy Theories and Extremism in New Times, 175*.

Barnes, J. E., & Goldman, A. (2020, March 10). Russia trying to stoke U.S. racial tensions before the election, officials say. *New York Times.* https://www .nytimes.com/2020/03/10/us/politics/russian-interference-race.html. Accessed May 2024.

Bauman, Z. (1993). *Postmodernity and its discontents.* New York University Press.

Bauman, Z. (2000). *Modernity and the Holocaust.* Cornell University Press.

Bauman, Z. (2013). *Liquid modernity.* John Wiley & Sons.

Bauman, Z., Bigo, D., Esteves, P., Guild, E., Jabri, V., Lyon, D., & Walker, R. B. (2014). After Snowden: Rethinking the impact of surveillance. *International Political Sociology, 8*(2), 121–144.

Bayat, A. (2013). *Life as politics: How ordinary people change the Middle East.* Stanford University Press.

Bayat, A. (2021). *Revolutionary life: The everyday of the Arab Spring.* Harvard University Press.

BBC News. (2017, August 14). GoDaddy and Google expel Daily Stormer over victim smear. https://www.bbc.com/news/technology-40922029. Accessed May 2024.

Beck, U. (1992). *Risk society: Towards a new modernity*. Sage.

Beck, U. (2001). Interview with Ulrich Beck. *Journal of Consumer Culture*, 1(2), 261–277.

Becker, H. S. (1953). Becoming a marihuana user. *American journal of Sociology*, 59(3), 235–242.

Beckert, J. (2014). Capitalist dynamics: Fictional expectations and the openness of the future. Available at SSRN: https://ssrn.com/abstract=2463995. Accessed May 2024.

Beckert, J., & Wehinger, F. (2013). In the shadow: Illegal markets and economic sociology. *Socio-Economic Review*, 11(1), 5–30.

Benier, K., Faulkner, N., Ladegaard, I., & Wickes, R. (2024). Reducing Islamophobia through conversation: A randomized control trial. *Social Psychology Quarterly*. https://doi.org/10.1177/01902725231217246. Accessed May 2024.

Benkler, Y. (2006, 2010). *The wealth of networks: How social production transforms markets and freedom*. Yale University Press.

Bennett, W. L., & Segerberg, A. (2012). The logic of connective action: Digital media and the personalization of contentious politics. *Information, Communication & Society*, 15(5), 739–768.

Berg, L. (2017, December 14). Charge against Fields upgraded to first-degree murder. *The Daily Progress*. https://web.archive.org/web/20180106211450/http://www.dailyprogress.com/news/local/charge-against-fields-upgraded-to-first-degree-murder/article_77e7fd58-e143-11e7-a17a-bfefa8572139.html. Accessed May 2024.

Berlin, I. (2013). *The crooked timber of humanity: Chapters in the history of ideas*. Princeton University Press.

Bernstein, T. P., Chen, T. M., Goikhman, I., Guan, G., He, D., Hou, X., Ji, Y., Kong, H., Luthi, L., McGuire, E., & Rohlf, G. (2010). *China learns from the Soviet Union, 1949–present*. Rowman & Littlefield.

Biddle, S., Ribeiro, P. V., & Dias, T. (2020, March 16). Invisible censorship. *The Intercept*. https://theintercept.com/2020/03/16/tiktok-app-moderators-users-discrimination/. Accessed May 2024.

Bitcoin Forum. (2011). *Silk Road: Anonymous marketplace. Feedback requested :)*. https://web.archive.org/web/20110605061136/http://forum.bitcoin.org/index.php?action=printpage;topic=3984.0. Accessed May 2024.

Black, D. (2013, July 15). *Derek Black e-mail to Mark Potok*. https://www.splcenter
.org/sites/default/files/derek-black-letter-to-mark-potok-hatewtach.pdf.
Accessed May 2024.

Blee, K. M. (2008). *Women of the Klan: Racism and gender in the 1920s*. University
of California Press.

Blee, K. M., & Creasap, K. A. (2010). Conservative and right-wing movements.
Annual Review of Sociology, 36, 269–286.

Bobo, L. D. (2017). Racism in Trump's America: Reflections on culture,
sociology, and the 2016 US presidential election. *British Journal of Sociology*,
68, S85–S104.

Bond, R. M., Fariss, C. J., Jones, J. J., Kramer, A. D. I., Marlow, C., Settle, J. E., &
Fowler, J. H. (2012). A 61-million-person experiment in social influence and
political mobilization. *Nature, 589*, 295–298. https://doi.org/10.1038
/nature11421. Accessed May 2024.

Bourdieu, P. (1987). *Distinction: A social critique of the judgement of taste*.
Translated by Richard Nice. Harvard University Press.

Brady, A. M. (2009). *Marketing dictatorship: Propaganda and thought work in
contemporary China*. Rowman & Littlefield.

Breakwa11 Blog. (2017). ShadowsocksR. https://web.archive.org/web
/20170607065901/https://breakwa11.blogspot.com/search/label
/ShadowsocksR. Accessed August 2024.

Bremmer, I. (2021, October 19). The technopolar moment: How digital powers
will reshape the global order. *Foreign Affairs*.

Brennan, J. (2012). *Libertarianism: What everyone needs to know*. Oxford
University Press.

Brines, J. (1994). Economic dependency, gender, and the division of labor at
home. *American Journal of Sociology, 100*(3), 652–688.

Browning, C. R. (1992). *Ordinary men: Reserve Police Battalion 101 and the Final
Solution in Poland*. HarperCollins.

Brustein, J. (2018, October 30). Gab, an online haven for white supremacists,
plots its future. *Boston Globe*. https://www.bostonglobe.com/business
/2018/10/30/gab-online-haven-for-white-supremacists-plots-its-future
/eHWJIhgbqaExMD8RooSoN/story.html. Accessed May 2024.

Cameron, C. (2023, September 15). We thought we were saving the planet, but
we were planting a time bomb. *New York Times*. https://www.nytimes
.com/2023/09/15/opinion/wildfires-treeplanting-timebomb.html.
Accessed May 2024.

Caramanica, J. (2011, October 24). SHINee and South Korean K-pop groups at Madison Square Garden. *New York Times*. https://www.nytimes.com/2011/10/25/arts/music/shinee-and-south-korean-k-pop-groups-at-madison-square-garden-review.html. Accessed May 2024.

Carr, D. (2013, February 24). For "House of Cards," using big data to guarantee its popularity. *New York Times*. https://www.nytimes.com/2013/02/25/business/media/for-house-of-cards-using-big-data-to-guarantee-its-popularity.html. Accessed August 2024.

Carr, N. (2020). *The shallows: What the Internet is doing to our brains*. W. W. Norton & Company.

Case, A., & Deaton, A. (2020). *Deaths of despair and the future of capitalism*. Princeton University Press.

Castells, M. (1996). *The information age: Economy, society, and culture* (Vol. 1, *The rise of the network society*). Blackwell.

Castells, M. (2015). *Networks of outrage and hope: Social movements in the internet age*. John Wiley & Sons.

Centers for Disease Control and Prevention. (2024, May 14). *Adult obesity facts*. https://www.cdc.gov/obesity/php/data-research/adult-obesity-facts.html. Accessed May 2024.

Centers for Disease Control and Prevention. (2024, May 15). *Provisional drug overdose death counts*. National Center for Health Statistics. https://www.cdc.gov/nchs/pressroom/nchs_press_releases/2024/20240515.htm. Accessed May and August 2024.

Cerulo, K. A. (2019). *Never saw it coming: Cultural challenges to envisioning the worst*. University of Chicago Press.

Chandel, S., Jingji, Z., Yunnan, Y., Jingyao, S., & Zhipeng, Z. (2019). The golden shield project of China: A decade later—an in-depth study of the great firewall. In 2019 *International Conference on Cyber-Enabled Distributed Computing and Knowledge Discovery (CyberC)* (pp. 111–119). IEEE.

Chayka, K. (2023, November 20). Elon Musk's poisoned platform. *The New Yorker*. https://www.newyorker.com/culture/infinite-scroll/elon-musks-poisoned-platform. Accessed December 2024.

Chayka, K. (2024). *Filterworld: How algorithms flattened culture*. Doubleday.

Chayka, K. (2024, November 13). How Elon Musk rebranded Trump. *The New Yorker*. https://www.newyorker.com/culture/infinite-scroll/how-elon-musk-rebranded-trump. Accessed December 2024.

Chayko, M. (2008). *Portable communities: The social dynamics of online and mobile connectedness*. SUNY Press.

Chen, A. (2011, June 1). The underground website where you can buy any drug imaginable. *Gawker*. https://www.gawkerarchives.com/the-underground-website-where-you-can-buy-any-drug-imag-30818160. Accessed May 2024.

Chen, F. (2010). Trade unions and the quadripartite interactions in strike settlement in China. *China Quarterly*, 201, 104–124.

Chen, Y., & Yang, D. Y. (2019). The impact of media censorship: 1984 or brave new world? *American Economic Review*, 109(6), 2294–2332.

Childress, C., Baumann, S., Rawlings, C. M., & Nault, J. F. (2021). Genres, objects, and the contemporary expression of higher-status tastes. *Sociological Science*, 8, 230–264.

Chin, J., & Lin, L. (2022). *Surveillance state: Inside China's quest to launch a new era of social control*. St. Martin's Press.

China Heritage. (n.d.). *Justified fears, diminished hopes, unflagging faith—revisiting Xu Zhangrun's July* 2018 *jeremiad*. https://chinaheritage.net/journal/justified-fears-diminished-hopes-unflagging-faith-revisiting-xu-zhangruns-july-2018-jeremiad/. Accessed May 2024.

Christie, N. (2016). *Crime control as industry: Towards gulags, Western style*. Routledge.

Christin, N. (2013). Traveling the Silk Road: A measurement analysis of a large anonymous online marketplace. In *WWW '13: Proceedings of the 22nd International Conference on World Wide Web* (pp. 213–224). ACM Digital Library. https://dl.acm.org/doi/10.1145/2488388.2488408. Accessed May 2024.

Clastres, P. (2020). *Society against the state: Essays in political anthropology*. Princeton University Press.

Cohn, D. (2014, May 5). *Millions of Americans changed their racial or ethnic identity from one census to the next*. Pew Research Center. https://www.pewresearch.org/short-reads/2014/05/05/millions-of-americans-changed-their-racial-or-ethnic-identity-from-one-census-to-the-next. Accessed May 2024.

Coldewey, D. (2017, August 17). *Alt-social network Gab booted from Google Play Store for hate speech*. TechCrunch. https://techcrunch.com/2017/08/17/alt-social-network-gab-booted-from-google-play-store-for-hate-speech. Accessed May 2024.

Cole, H., & Griffiths, M. D. (2007). Social interactions in massively multiplayer online role-playing gamers. *Cyber Psychology & Behavior*, 10(4), 575–583.

Colon, D. (2024, November 20). What Musk calls "citizen journalism" is nothing but a weapon for the mass destruction of factual reality. *Le Monde*. https://www.lemonde.fr/en/opinion/article/2024/11/20/what-musk-calls-citizen-journalism-is-nothing-but-a-weapon-for-the-mass-destruction-of-factual-reality_6733433_23.html. Accessed December 2024.

Confessore, N. (2022, April 30). What to know about Tucker Carlson's rise. *New York Times*. https://www.nytimes.com/2022/04/30/business/media/tucker-carlson-fox-news-takeaways.html. Accessed December 2024.

Conger, K., & Frenkel, S. (2021, January 13). Telegram and Signal soar as Trump seeks out new online megaphone. *New York Times*. https://www.nytimes.com/2021/01/13/technology/telegram-signal-apps-big-tech.html. Accessed May 2024.

Copeland, R., & Brown, E. (2018, November 12). Palantir has a $20 billion valuation—and a pretty big problem: It keeps losing money. *Wall Street Journal*. https://www.wsj.com/articles/palantir-has-a-20-billion-valuation-and-a-pretty-big-problem-it-keeps-losing-money-1542042135. Accessed May 2024.

Coscarelli, J. (2020, June 22). Why obsessive K-pop fans are turning toward political activism. *New York Times*. https://www.nytimes.com/2020/06/22/arts/music/k-pop-fans-trump-politics.html Accessed May 2024.

Daily Stormer. (n.d.). Style guide. First published in A. Feinberg (2017, December 13), This is the Daily Stormer's playbook, *HuffPost*. https://www.huffpost.com/entry/daily-stormer-nazi-style-guide_n_5a2ece19e4b0ce3b344492f2. Accessed May 2024.

DDSN Interactive. (2021). *Bill Gates on technology and digital design: 10 powerful quotes*. https://ddsn.com/blog/digital-design-service-technology-quotes/bill-gates.html. Accessed May 2024.

de Beauvoir, S. (1989). *The second sex*. Vintage Books.

Defense Innovation Unit. (n.d.). *Meetings*. https://innovation.defense.gov/Meetings. Accessed May 2024.

Demant, J., Bakken, S.A., Oksanen, A., & Gunnlaugsson, H. (2019). Drug dealing on Facebook, Snapchat and Instagram: A qualitative analysis of novel drug markets in the Nordic countries. *Drug and Alcohol Review*, 38(4), 377–385.

Dickson, B.J. (2021). *The party and the people: Chinese politics in the 21st century*. Princeton University Press.

Dillon, P. (2004). *Gin: The much lamented death of Madam Geneva; The eighteenth century gin craze*. Justin, Charles & Co.

DiMaggio, P., & Louch, H. (1998). Socially embedded consumer transactions: For what kinds of purchases do people most often use networks? *American Sociological Review*, 619–637.

Douglas, M. (2003). *Purity and danger: An analysis of concepts of pollution and taboo*. Routledge.

Dread Pirate Roberts. (2013, December 5). *[Twitter page]*. http://web.archive .org/web/20140110042145/https://twitter.com/DreadPirateSR/status /408768516871831552. Accessed May 2024.

Dugan, K. (2017, August 16). Credit cards are clamping down on payments to hate groups. *New York Post*. https://nypost.com/2017/08/16/credit-cards-are-clamping-down-on-payments-to-hate-groups. Accessed May 2024.

Dugan, L., & Fisher, D. (2023). Far-right and Jihadi terrorism within the United States: From September 11th to January 6th. *Annual Review of Criminology, 6,* 131–153.

Duran, C. (2021). Far-left versus far-right fatal violence: An empirical assessment of the prevalence of ideologically motivated homicides in the United States. *Criminology, Criminal Justice, Law & Society,* 22(2), 33–49.

Durkheim, É. (2018). *The division of labor in society*. Routledge.

Dwyer, J. (2006, August 17). More tapes from 9/11: "They have exits in there?" *New York Times*. https://www.nytimes.com/2006/08/17/nyregion/17tapes .html. Accessed May 2024.

The Economist. (2022, June 28). As censorship in China increases, VPNs are becoming more important. https://www.economist.com/china/2022/06/28 /as-censorship-in-china-increases-vpns-are-becoming-more-important. Accessed May 2024.

Emerson, R.M., Fretz, R.I., & Shaw, L.L. (2011). *Writing ethnographic fieldnotes*. University of Chicago Press.

Fazio, L.K., Brashier, N.M., Payne, B.K., & Marsh, E.J. (2015). Knowledge does not protect against illusory truth. *Journal of Experimental Psychology: General,* 144(5), 993–1002.

Federal Bureau of Investigation & Department of Homeland Security. (2017). *White supremacist extremism poses persistent threat of lethal violence* (IA -0154-17).

Filkins, D. (2006, January 1). 844 in U.S. military killed in Iraq in 2005. *New York Times*. https://www.nytimes.com/2006/01/01/world/middleeast/844-in-us-military-killed-in-iraq-in-2005.html. Accessed May 2024.

Fincher, L.H. (2021). *Betraying big brother: The feminist awakening in China*. Verso Books.

Fischer, C.S. (2023). *America calling: A social history of the telephone to 1940*. University of California Press.

Fitzmaurice, C.J., Ladegaard, I., Attwood-Charles, W., Cansoy, M., Carfagna, L.B., Schor, J.B., & Wengronowitz, R. (2020). Domesticating the market: Moral exchange and the sharing economy. *Socio-Economic Review*, 18(1), 81–102.

Fligstein, N. (2018). *The architecture of markets: An economic sociology of twenty-first-century capitalist societies*. Princeton University Press.

Fligstein, N., & McAdam, D. (2012). *A theory of fields*. Oxford University Press.

Foucault, M. (2012). *Discipline and punish: The birth of the prison*. Vintage.

Frenkel, S. (2019, March 27). Facebook bans white nationalist and white supremacist content. *New York Times*. https://www.nytimes.com/2019/03/27/business/facebook-white-nationalist-supremacist.html. Accessed May 2024.

Fridman, L. (Host). (2022, March 2). *#333—Andrej Karpathy: Tesla AI, self-driving, Optimus, aliens, and AGI*. YouTube. https://www.youtube.com/watch?v=cdiD-9MMpbo. Accessed May 2024.

Friedman, N. (2021, January 5). Advancing developer freedom: GitHub is fully available in Iran. *GitHub Blog*. https://github.blog/2021-01-05-advancing-developer-freedom-github-is-fully-available-in-iran. Accessed May 2024.

Gab AI Inc. (2013). *Form C/A: Amendment to Offering Statement*. US Securities and Exchange Commission.

Gambetta, D., & Hertog, S. (2018). *Engineers of jihad: The curious connection between violent extremism and education*. Princeton University Press.

Ganor, B. (2020). Terrorism is terrorism: The Christchurch terror attack from an Israeli CT perspective.

Garland, D. (1991). Sociological perspectives on punishment. *Crime and Justice*, 14, 115–165.

Garland, D. (1996). The limits of the sovereign state: Strategies of crime control in contemporary society. *British Journal of Criminology*, 36(4), 445–471.

Garland, D. (2001). The culture of control: Crime and social order in contemporary society. University of Chicago Press.

Garrick, J., & Bennett, Y.C. (2018). "Xi Jinping thought": Realisation of the Chinese dream of national rejuvenation? *China Perspectives*, 2018(1-2), 99–105.

Geertz, C. (1973). *The interpretation of cultures: Selected essays*. Basic Books.

Geiger, A.W. (2018, June 4). *How Americans have viewed government surveillance and privacy since Snowden leaks*. Pew Research Center. https://www.pewresearch.org/short-reads/2018/06/04/how-americans-have-viewed-government-surveillance-and-privacy-since-snowden-leaks. Accessed May 2024.

Gersh, T., v. A. Anglin. (2017). Complaint for invasion of privacy, intentional infliction of emotional distress, and violations of the Anti-Intimidation Act. Case No. CV 17-50-M-DLC-JCL. US District Court, District of Montana, Missoula Division.

Ghusn, W., De la Rosa, A., Sacoto, D., Cifuentes, L., Campos, A., Feris, F., Hurtado, M. D., & Acosta, A. (2022). Weight loss outcomes associated with semaglutide treatment for patients with overweight or obesity. *JAMA Network Open*, 5(9), e2231982–e2231982.

Giddens, A. (1986). The nation-state and violence. *Capital & Class*, 10(2), 216–220.

Giddens, A. (1990). *The consequences of modernity*. Stanford University Press.

Giddens, A. (1991). *Modernity and self-identity: Self and society in the late modern age*. Stanford University Press.

Gilbert, D. (2023, May 18). Elon Musk just can't stop posting antisemitic tweets. *Vice*. https://www.vice.com/en/article/elon-musk-george-soros-antisemitic -tweets. Accessed December 2024.

Gillan, K. (2020). Social movements: Sequences vs. fuzzy temporality. In P. Kivisto (Ed.), *The Cambridge handbook of social theory* (Vol. 2, pp. 407–432). Cambridge University Press.

Giugni, M., McAdam, D., & Tilly, C. (Eds.). (1999). *How social movements matter*. University of Minnesota Press.

Global Terrorism Database, University of Maryland. (n.d.). https://www.start .umd.edu/gtd. Accessed June 2024.

Go, J. (2020). The imperial origins of American policing: Militarization and imperial feedback in the early 20th century. *American Journal of Sociology*, 125(5), 1193–1254.

GoAgent. (2015, August 25). *Deleted README.md*. GitHub. web.archive.org /web/20220528055033/https:/github.com/goagent/goagent/commit /e492ed0283f5cde7cf71d7ac47429f64aa48cd13. Accessed May 2024.

Godlee, F., & Hurley, R. (2016). The war on drugs has failed: Doctors should lead calls for drug policy reform. *British Medical Journal*, 355. https://doi.org /10.1136/bmj.i6067. Accessed May 2024.

Google Trends. (2024). https://trends.google.com/trends. Accessed in 2022 and May 2024.

Gourevitch, P. (Ed.). (2008). *The Paris Review interviews* (Vol. 3). Picador USA.

Graham, T., & Andrejevic, M. (2024). A computational analysis of potential algorithmic bias on platform X during the 2024 US election. Working paper.

Gray, J. (2010). *Why our drug laws have failed: A judicial indictment of war on drugs*. Temple University Press.

Greco, A. N. (2023). The impact of legal, intellectual property, and copyright infringement issues: 2000–2022. In *The strategic marketing of science, technology, and medical journals: A business history of a dynamic marketplace, 2000–2020* (pp. 69–91). Springer International.

Greenberg, A. (2015, January 23). Here's the secret Silk Road journal from the laptop of Ross Ulbricht. *Wired*. https://www.wired.com/2015/01/heres -secret-silk-road-journal-laptop-ross-ulbricht. Accessed May 2024.

Greenberg, A. (2018, March 8). Operation Bayonet: Inside the sting that hijacked an entire dark web drug market. *Wired*. https://www.wired.com /story/hansa-dutch-police-sting-operation. Accessed May 2024.

Griffiths, J. (2021). *The great firewall of China: How to build and control an alternative version of the internet*. Bloomsbury Publishing.

Griffiths, R. R., Richards, W. A., McCann, U., & Jesse, R. (2006). Psilocybin can occasion mystical-type experiences having substantial and sustained personal meaning and spiritual significance. *Psychopharmacology, 187*, 268–283.

Grigoropoulou, N., & Small, M. L. (2022). The data revolution in social science needs qualitative research. *Nature Human Behaviour, 6*(7), 904–906.

Grind, K., McMillan, R., & Ovide, S. (2021, February 6). How Big Tech got even bigger. *Wall Street Journal*. https://www.wsj.com/articles/how-big-tech-got -even-bigger-11612587632. Accessed May 2024.

Guo, Y. (2018). *Communist civilization: Reading the China dream*. https://www .readingthechinadream.com/guo-yuhua-communist-civilization.html. Accessed May 2024.

Habermas, J. (1991). *The structural transformation of the public sphere: An inquiry into a category of bourgeois society*. MIT Press.

Halpern, S. (2013). Are we puppets in a wired world? *New York Review of Books, 60*(17), 24.

Han, R. (2015). Manufacturing consent in cyberspace: China's "fifty-cent army." *Journal of Current Chinese Affairs, 44*(2), 105–134.

Hankes, K. (2015, June 21). *Dylann Roof may have been a regular commenter at neo-Nazi website the Daily Stormer*. Southern Poverty Law Center. https:// www.splcenter.org/hatewatch/2015/06/21/dylann-roof-may-have-been- regular-commenter-neo-nazi-website-daily-stormer. Accessed May 2024.

Hansen, J. D., & Reich, J. (2015). Democratizing education? Examining access and usage patterns in massive open online courses. *Science, 350*(6265), 1245–1248.

Hauben, M., & Hauben, R. (1997). *Netizens: On the history and impact of Usenet and the Internet*. IEEE Computer Society Press.

Hayden, M. E., & Squire, M. (2021, December 9). *How cryptocurrency revolutionized the white supremacist movement*. Southern Poverty Law Center. https://www.splcenter.org/hatewatch/2021/12/09/how-cryptocurrency-revolutionized-white-supremacist-movement. Accessed May 2024.

Haynie, D. L., & Duxbury, S. W. (2024). Online illegal cryptomarkets. *Annual Review of Sociology*, 50, 671–690.

He, Jiayan. (2024, May 27). *Goldfish memories*. China Media Project. https://chinamediaproject.org/2024/05/27/goldfish-memories/. Accessed May 2024.

Hessler, P. (2020). Life on lockdown in China. *The New Yorker*.

Hessler, P. (2022). A teacher in China learns the limits of free expression. *The New Yorker*.

Hirschman, A. O. (2013). *The passions and the interests: Political arguments for capitalism before its triumph*. Princeton University Press.

Hobsbawm, E. (2010). *Age of revolution: 1789–1848*. Hachette UK.

Hochschild, A. R. (2018). *Strangers in their own land: Anger and mourning on the American right*. The New Press.

Hultman, M., Björk, A., & Viinikka, T. (2019). The far right and climate change denial. In B. Forchtner (Ed.), *The far right and the environment: Politics, discourse and communication* (pp. 121–135). Routledge.

Humphreys, K., & Bovett, R. (2024, March 17). Why Oregon's drug decriminalization failed. *The Atlantic*. https://www.theatlantic.com/ideas/archive/2024/03/oregon-drug-decriminalization-failed/677678. Accessed May 2024.

Hvistendahl, M. (2018, March 14). A revered rocket scientist set in motion China's mass surveillance of its citizens. *Science*. http://www.science.org/content/article/revered-rocket-scientist-set-motion-china-s-mass-surveillance-its-citizens. Accessed May 2024.

Isaacson, W. (2014). *The innovators: How a group of inventors, hackers, geniuses and geeks created the digital revolution*. Simon and Schuster.

Isaac, M. (2024, April 24). Meta says it plans to spend billions more on A.I. *New York Times*. https://www.nytimes.com/2024/04/24/technology/meta-profit-stock-ai.html. Accessed May 2024.

Isaacson, W. (2011). *Jobs*. Simon and Schuster.

Jerolmack, C., & Khan, S. (2014). Talk is cheap: Ethnography and the attitudinal fallacy. *Sociological Methods & Research*, 43(2), 178–209.

Jigsaw-Code. (2024). *Outline releases: Security audits*. GitHub. https://github.com/Jigsaw-Code/outline-releases/tree/master/security_audits. Accessed May 2024.

Johnson, I. (2018). *The souls of China: The return of religion after Mao*. Vintage.

Johnson, I. (2023). *Sparks: China's underground historians and their battle for the future*. Oxford University Press.

Johnstad, P. G. (2021). Day trip to hell: A mixed methods study of challenging psychedelic experiences. *Journal of Psychedelic Studies, 5*(2), 114–127.

Kahneman, D. (2011). *Thinking, fast and slow*. Macmillan.

Kang, C. (2017, January 27). Google, in post-Obama era, aggressively woos Republicans. *New York Times*. https://www.nytimes.com/2017/01/27/technology/google-in-post-obama-era-aggressively-woos-republicans.html. Accessed December 2024.

Kang, J. C. (2014, September 18). ISIS's call of duty. *The New Yorker*. https://www.newyorker.com/tech/annals-of-technology/isis-video-game. Accessed May 2024.

Kay, J., & King, M. (2020). *Radical uncertainty: Decision-making beyond the numbers*. W. W. Norton & Company.

Kearns, E. M., Betus, A. E., & Lemieux, A. F. (2019). Why do some terrorist attacks receive more media attention than others? *Justice Quarterly, 36*(6), 985–1022.

Kinnard, M. (2017, January 10). Roof's victims were united by tragedy—and faith. *AP News*. https://apnews.com/general-news-a165c4f7a54d443f8034bf7ba605d3d4. Accessed September 2024.

Korach, N. (2024, October 5). "Cowardice": *Washington Post* blasted for not endorsing in 2024. *Vanity Fair*. https://www.vanityfair.com/news/story/washington-post-blasted-not-endorsing-2024.Accessed December 2024.

Kottler, S. (2018, March 1). February 28th DDoS incident report. *GitHub Blog*. https://github.blog/2018-03-01-ddos-incident-report. Accessed June 2024.

Khazanov, A. M. (1978). Characteristic features of nomadic communities in the Eurasian steppes. In W. Weissleder (Ed.), *The nomadic alternative: Modes and models of interaction in the African-Asian deserts and steppes* (pp. 119–126). De Gruyter Mouton.

Kimmel, M. (2017). *Angry white men: American masculinity at the end of an era*. Hachette UK.

Kimmel, M. (2018). *Healing from hate: How young men get into—and out of—violent extremism*. University of California Press.

Knight, S. (2023, May 15). How a disaster expert prepares for the worst. *The New Yorker*. https://www.newyorker.com/magazine/2023/05/22/lucy-easthope-profile-disaster-response. Accessed May 2024.

Kramer, A. D., Guillory, J. E., & Hancock, J. T. (2014). Experimental evidence of massive-scale emotional contagion through social networks. *Proceedings of the National Academy of Sciences*, 111(24), 8788–8790.

Kuo, L. (2021, September 9). Xi Jinping's crackdown on everything is remaking Chinese society. *Washington Post*. https://www.washingtonpost.com/world/asia_pacific/china-crackdown-tech-celebrities-xi/2021/09/09/b4c2409c-0c66-11ec-a7c8-61bb7b3bf628_story.html. Accessed May 2024.

Kurzweil, R. (2010). *The singularity is near*. Duckworth Books.

Kuziemko, I., Buell, R. W., Reich, T., & Norton, M. I. (2014). "Last-place aversion": Evidence and redistributive implications. *Quarterly Journal of Economics*, 129(1), 105–149.

Ladegaard, I. (2018a). Hosting the comfortably exotic: Cosmopolitan aspirations in the sharing economy. *Sociological Review*, 66(2), 381–400.

Ladegaard, I. (2018b). Instantly hooked? Freebies and samples of opioids, cannabis, MDMA, and other drugs in an illicit e-commerce market. *Journal of Drug Issues*, 48(2), 226–245.

Ladegaard, I. (2018c). We know where you are, what you are doing and we will catch you: Testing deterrence theory in digital drug markets. *British Journal of Criminology*, 58(2), 414–433.

Ladegaard, I. (2019a). Crime displacement in digital drug markets. *International Journal of Drug Policy*, 63, 113–121.

Ladegaard, I. (2019b). "I pray that we will find a way to carry on this dream": How a law enforcement crackdown united an online community. *Critical Sociology*, 45(4–5), 631–646.

Ladegaard, I. (2020). Open secrecy: How police crackdowns and creative problem-solving brought illegal markets out of the shadows. *Social Forces*, 99(2), 532–559.

Ladegaard, I. (2021). Strangers in the sheets: How Airbnb hosts overcome uncertainty. *Socio-Economic Review*, 19(4), 1245–1264.

Ladegaard, I. (2024). Cleansing frames: How digital "consumer reports" of cannabis and psychedelics normalise drug-taking and neutralise its counter-cultural potential. *Sociology*, 58(1), 100–117.

Ladegaard, I., & Rieger, A. (2024). How "ceremonial openness" prevents organizational change: An analysis of corporate earnings calls in the oil and gas industry, 2007–2020. *Social Problems*, 71(3). https://doi.org/10.1093/socpro/spae045. Accessed May 2024.

LaMotte, S. (2024, January 8). Nanoplastics found in bottled water, study finds. CNN. https://www.cnn.com/2024/01/08/health/bottled-water-nanoplastics-study-wellness/index.html. Accessed May 2024.

Lankford, A. (2021). A sexual frustration theory of aggression, violence, and crime. *Journal of Criminal Justice, 77*, 101865.

Laterza, V. (2021). Could Cambridge Analytica have delivered Donald Trump's 2016 presidential victory? An anthropologist's look at big data and political campaigning. *Public Anthropologist, 3*(1), 119–147.

Lauzen, M.M., & Dozier, D.M. (2005). Maintaining the double standard: Portrayals of age and gender in popular films. *Sex Roles, 52*, 437–446.

Lauzon, E. (1998). The Philip Zimmerman investigation: The start of the fall of export restrictions on encryption software under First Amendment free speech issues. *Syracuse Law Review, 48*, 1307.

Lazer, D.M., Baum, M.A., Benkler, Y., Berinsky, A.J., Greenhill, K.M., Menczer, F., . . . & Zittrain, J.L. (2018). The science of fake news. *Science, 359*(6380): 1094–1096.

Lei, Y.W. (2018). *The contentious public sphere: Law, media, and authoritarian rule in China.* Princeton University Press.

Leon, H. (2019, October 28). Scariest takeaways on the current state of smartphone surveillance from Edward Snowden. *The Observer.* https://observer.com/2019/10/edward-snowden-smartphone-surveillance-joe-rogan-podcast. Accessed August 2024.

Lerner, H. (1985). *The dance of anger: A woman's guide to changing the patterns of intimate relationships.* Harper & Row.

Levy, S. (2011). *In the plex: How Google thinks, works, and shapes our lives.* Simon & Schuster.

Lianos, M. (2003). Social control after Foucault. *Surveillance and Society, 1*(3), 412–430.

Ling, J. (2017, August 15). Neo-nazi site the Daily Stormer moves to the dark web, but promises a comeback. *Vice.* https://www.vice.com/en/article/gydmdj/neo-nazi-site-the-daily-stormer-moves-to-the-darkweb-but-promises-a-comeback. Accessed May 2024.

Lynch, M.J. (1999). Beating a dead horse: Is there any basic empirical evidence for the deterrent effect of imprisonment? *Crime, Law and Social Change, 31*, 347–362.

Mann, J., Sargeant, B.L., Watson-Capps, J.J., Gibson, Q.A., Heithaus, M.R., Connor, R.C., & Patterson, E. (2008). Why do dolphins carry sponges?. *PloS one, 3*(12), e3868.

Magnus, G. (2018). *Red flags: Why Xi's China is in jeopardy*. Yale University Press.

Makuch, B. (2019, July 11). The Nazi-free alternative to Twitter is now home to the biggest far-right social network. *Vice*. https://www.vice.com/en/article/mb8y3x/the-nazi-free-alternative-to-twitter-is-now-home-to-the-biggest-far-right-social-network. Accessed May 2024.

Mao, F. (2022, June 7). Li Jiaqi: China Lipstick King sparks Tiananmen questions. *BBC News*. https://www.bbc.com/news/world-asia-china-61715843. Accessed May 2024.

Marantz, A. (2018). Reddit and the struggle to detoxify the internet. *The New Yorker*, 19, 18.

Martin, J. (2014). Lost on the Silk Road: Online drug distribution and the "cryptomarket." *Criminology & Criminal Justice*, 14(3), 351–367.

Martin, J. (2022, September 14). Why Black women love Korean TV dramas: "They see us." *Washington Post*. https://www.washingtonpost.com/lifestyle/2022/09/14/black-women-korean-tv-drama-k-drama. Accessed May 2024.

Martin, J. T. (2018). Police and policing. *Annual Review of Anthropology*, 47(1), 133–148.

Marwick, A. E. (2013). *Status update: Celebrity, publicity, and branding in the social media age*. Yale University Press.

Mattey, C. (2020). *In harm's way: Smart regulation of digital and network technologies*. Aspen Institute.

Mattingly, D. C. (2019). *The art of political control in China*. Cambridge University Press.

Matza, D., & Sykes, G. (1957). Techniques of neutralization: A theory of delinquency. *American Sociological Review*, 22(6), 664–670.

McGirt, E. (2009, April 1). How Chris Hughes helped launch Facebook and the Barack Obama campaign. *Fast Company*. https://www.fastcompany.com/1207594/how-chris-hughes-helped-launch-facebook-and-barack-obama-campaign. Accessed December 2024.

McHugh, C. (2024, November 11). What Democrats don't understand about Joe Rogan. *Politico*. https://www.politico.com/news/magazine/2024/11/11/how-trump-won-the-podcast-bros-00188518. Accessed December 2024.

McLuhan, M. (2017). The medium is the message. In D. Mortensen (Ed.), *Communication theory* (pp. 390–402). Routledge.

McMillan, J. (2003). *Reinventing the bazaar: A natural history of markets*. W. W. Norton & Company.

McPherson, M., Smith-Lovin, L., & Cook, J. M. (2001). Birds of a feather: Homophily in social networks. *Annual Review of Sociology*, 27(1), 415–444.

Miller-Idriss, C. (2022). *Hate in the homeland: The new global far right.* Princeton University Press.

Moritz-Rabson, D. (2018, October 29). Why is Gab down? Site used by accused Pittsburgh synagogue shooter is offline. *Newsweek.* https://www.newsweek .com/gab-shuts-down-pittsburgh-synagogue-offline-tree-life-suspect -robert-bowers-1191684. Accessed May 2024.

Morrow, L. (2001, December 2). The last word: Shockley at Stanford. *Los Angeles Times.* https://www.latimes.com/archives/la-xpm-2001-dec-02-tm-10501 -story.html. Accessed June 2024.

Multiple Authors. (n.d.-b). *Xray-core.* GitHub. https://github.com/XTLS/Xray-core. Accessed August 2024.

Murgia, M. (2024, September 27). Signal's Meredith Whittaker: "I see AI as born out of surveillance." *Financial Times.* https://www.ft.com/content/799b4fcf -2cf7-41d2-81b4-10d9ecdd83f6. Accessed December 2024.

Nakashima, E., & Warrick, J. (2013, July 14). For NSA chief, terrorist threat drives passion to "collect it all." *Washington Post.* https://www.washingtonpost .com/world/national-security/for-nsa-chief-terrorist-threat-drives-passion -to-collect-it-all/2013/07/14/3d26ef80-ea49-11e2-a301-ea5a8116d211_story .html. Accessed August 2024.

National Academies of Sciences, Engineering, and Medicine. (2017). *The health effects of cannabis and cannabinoids: The current state of evidence and recommendations for research.* National Academies Press.

Nelson, L. K. (2020). Computational grounded theory: A methodological framework. *Sociological Methods & Research, 49*(1), 3–42.

Nelson, L. K., Getman, R., & Haque, S. A. (2022). And the rest is history: Measuring the scope and recall of Wikipedia's coverage of three women's movement subgroups. *Sociological Methods & Research, 51*(4), 1788–1825.

New Scientist & Press Association. (2018, April 5). Facebook admits data scandal may have hit 87 million users. *New Scientist.* https://institutions .newscientist.com/article/2165685-facebook-admits-data-scandal-may -have-hit-87-million-users. Accessed May 2024.

New York Times. (2000, March 9). Clinton's words on China trade: "It is the smart thing." https://www.nytimes.com/2000/03/09/world/clinton-s -words-on-china-trade-is-the-smart-thing.html. Accessed August 2024.

Ng, L. H. X., Cruickshank, I. J., & Carley, K. M. (2022). Cross-platform information spread during the January 6th capitol riots. *Social Network Analysis and Mining, 12*(1), 133.

Nicas, J., Isaac, M., & Frenkel, S. (2021, January 13). Millions flock to Telegram and Signal as fears grow over Big Tech. *New York Times*. https://www .nytimes.com/2021/01/13/technology/telegram-signal-apps-big-tech.html. Accessed May 2024.

Nicolas, D. (2019, February 19). The unstoppable rise of Sci-Hub: How does a new generation of researchers perceive Sci-Hub? *LSE Impact Blog*. https:// blogs.lse.ac.uk/impactofsocialsciences/2019/02/19/the-unstoppable-rise -of-sci-hub-how-does-a-new-generation-of-researchers-perceive-sci-hub. Accessed May 2024.

Norges Bank Investment Management. (2024). Market value. Norges Bank Investment Management. https://www.nbim.no/en/the-fund/Market- Value. Accessed May 2024.

Norris, P., & Inglehart, R. (2019). *Cultural backlash: Trump, Brexit, and authoritarian populism*. Cambridge University Press.

Norton, M. I., & Sommers, S. R. (2011). Whites see racism as a zero-sum game that they are now losing. *Perspectives on Psychological Science, 6*(3), 215–218.

Novos, I. E., & Waldman, M. (2013). *Piracy of intellectual property: Past, present, and future. Review of Economic Research on Copyright Issues, 10*(2), 1–26.

Nussbaum, M. C. (2001). *Upheavals of thought: The intelligence of emotions*. Cambridge University Press.

Nyhan, B., & Reifler, J. (2010). When corrections fail: The persistence of political misperceptions. *Political Behavior, 32*(2), 303–330.

O'Brien, L. (2017, December). The making of an American Nazi. *The Atlantic*. https://www.theatlantic.com/magazine/archive/2017/12/the-making-of-an- american-nazi/544119. Accessed May 2024.

Office of Public Affairs. (2023, August 2). *Jury recommends sentence of death for Pennsylvania man convicted for Tree of Life Synagogue shooting*. US Department of Justice. https://www.justice.gov/opa/pr/jury-recommends-sen- tence-death-pennsylvania-man-convicted-tree-life-synagogue-shooting. Accessed May 2024.

Office of the Surgeon General. (2023). *Our epidemic of loneliness and isolation: The US Surgeon General's advisory on the healing effects of social connection and community*. US Department of Health and Human Services.

Ong, W. (1982). *Orality and literacy: The technologizing of the word*. Methuen & Co.

The Onion. (2024, December 14). Trump locks bathroom door so Elon Musk can't follow him in. https://theonion.com/trump-locks-bathroom-door-so- elon-musk-cant-follow-him-in. Accessed December 2024.

Open Technology Fund. (2023). *OTF's budget for the 2023 fiscal year*. https://www.opentech.fund/news/otfs-budget-for-the-2023-fiscal-year. Accessed May 2024.

Orben, A. (2020). The Sisyphean cycle of technology panics. *Perspectives on Psychological Science, 15*(5), 1143–1157.

Ottoni, E. B., & Izar, P. (2008). Capuchin monkey tool use: Overview and implications. *Evolutionary Anthropology: Issues, News, and Reviews, 17*(4), 171–178.

Outline. (2024). *Outline VPN—Access to the free and open internet*. https://getoutline.org/. Accessed May 2024.

Panofsky, A., & Donovan, J. (2019). Genetic ancestry testing among white nationalists: From identity repair to citizen science. *Social Studies of Science, 49*(5), 653–681.

The Paris Review interviews, Vols. 1–4 (2009). Picador.

Parker, H., Aldridge, J., Measham, F., & Haynes, P. (1999). Illegal leisure: The normalisation of adolescent recreational drug use. *Health Education Research, 14*(5), 707–708.

Parker, H., Williams, L., & Aldridge, J. (2002). The normalization of "sensible" recreational drug use: Further evidence from the North West England longitudinal study. *Sociology, 36*(4), 941–964.

Parker, K., Horowitz, J. M., Morin, R., & Lopez, M. H. (2015, June 11). *Chapter 1: Race and multiracial Americans in the U.S. Census*. Pew Research Center. https://www.pewresearch.org/social-trends/2015/06/11/chapter-1-race-and-multiracial-americans-in-the-u-s-census. Accessed June 2024.

Parrado, E. A. (2011). How high is Hispanic/Mexican fertility in the United States? Immigration and tempo considerations. *Demography, 48*(3), 1059–1080.

Parsons, E. F. (2015). *Ku-Klux: The birth of the Klan during Reconstruction*. UNC Press Books.

Pei, M. (2024). *The sentinel state: Surveillance and the survival of dictatorship in China*. Harvard University Press.

Petrusich, A. (2020, June 5). K-pop fans defuse racist hashtags. *The New Yorker*. https://www.newyorker.com/culture/cultural-comment/k-pop-fans-defuse-racist-hashtags. Accessed May 2024.

Pettigrew, T. F., Tropp, L. R., Wagner, U., & Christ, O. (2011). Recent advances in intergroup contact theory. *International Journal of Intercultural Relations, 35*(3), 271–280.

Pew Research Center. (2016, July 20). *In political correctness debate, most Americans think too many people are easily offended.* https://www.pewresearch.org/short-reads/2016/07/20/in-political-correctness-debate-most-americans-think-too-many-people-are-easily-offended/. Accessed May 2024.

Pew Research Center. (2016, November 4). *Americans' views about privacy, surveillance and data-sharing.* https://www.pewresearch.org/internet/2016/11/04/americans-views-about-privacy-surveillance-and-data-sharing. Accessed May 2024.

Pfohl, S. (2005). New global technologies of power: Cybernetic capitalism and social inequality. In M. Romero & E. Margolis (Eds.), *The Blackwell companion to social inequalities* (pp. 546–592). Blackwell.

Preece, J., & Ghozati, K. (2001). Observations and explorations of empathy online. In R. R. Rice & J. E. Katz (Eds.), *The internet and health communication: Experience and expectations* (pp. 237–260). Sage.

Radio Farda. (2024). https://www.radiofarda.com/a/iran-announce-vpn-illegal-internet-khamenei/32827817.html. Accessed May 2024.

Reagan National Defense Forum. (2019, December 20). *Conversation with Jeff Bezos.* The Ronald Reagan Presidential Foundation & Institute. https://www.reaganfoundation.org/reagan-institute/scholarship/podcasts/reaganism/reagan-national-defense-forum-conversation-with-jeff-bezos/. Accessed May 2024.

Reuter, P. (1983). *Disorganized crime: The economics of the visible hand.* MIT press.

Rheingold, H. (2000). *The virtual community: Homesteading on the electronic frontier.* MIT Press.

Rifkin, J. (2014). *The zero marginal cost society: The internet of things, the collaborative commons, and the eclipse of capitalism.* St. Martin's Press.

Roberts, M. (2018). *Censored: Distraction and diversion inside China's Great Firewall.* Princeton University Press.

Robin, C. (2019, January 23). The plight of the political convert. *The New Yorker.* https://www.newyorker.com/books/under-review/the-plight-of-the-political-convert. Accessed June 2024.

Rochko, E. (2019, July 4). Statement on Gab's fork of Mastodon. *Mastodon Blog.* https://blog.joinmastodon.org/2019/07/statement-on-gabs-fork-of-mastodon. Accessed May 2024.

Rodriguez, S. (2017, January 23). Gab CEO explains how the social network plans to handle 2021 inauguration. *Inc.* https://www.inc.com/salvador-rodriguez/gab-apple-inauguration.html. Accessed May 2024.

Roediger, D. R. (2006). *Working toward whiteness: How America's immigrants became white; The strange journey from Ellis Island to the suburbs*. Hachette UK.

Rogers, E. M. (2010). *Diffusion of innovations*. Simon and Schuster.

Romero, S. (2018, December 31). Wielding rocks and knives, Arizonans attack self-driving cars. *New York Times*. https://www.nytimes.com/2018/12/31/us/waymo-self-driving-cars-arizona-attacks.html. Accessed May 2024.

Romm, T. (2017, January 17). Google's Schmidt met with Kushner in Republican outreach. *Politico*. https://www.politico.com/story/2017/01/googles-schmidt-reaches-out-to-republicans-233729. Accessed December 2024.

Roose, K. (2019, October 9). What does PewDiePie really believe? *New York Times*. https://www.nytimes.com/interactive/2019/10/09/magazine/PewDiePie-interview.html. Accessed May 2024.

Rosenberg, M. (2018, April 22). Cambridge Analytica and Facebook: The scandal and the fallout so far. *New York Times*. https://www.nytimes.com/2018/04/22/business/media/cambridge-analytica-aleksandr-kogan.html. Accessed July 2024.

Royal Commission of Inquiry into the Attack on Christchurch Mosques. (2020). *Executive summary*. https://christchurchattack.royalcommission.nz/the-report/executive-summary-2/executive-summary/. Accessed June 2024.

Sanchez, G. H. (2019, August 21). These photos show the intense passion of true K-pop fans. *BuzzFeed News*. https://www.buzzfeednews.com/article/gabrielsanchez/the-intense-trending-passion-of-true-k-pop-fans. Accessed May 2024.

Sandberg, S. (2013). Cannabis culture: A stable subculture in a changing world. *Criminology & Criminal Justice, 13*(1), 63–79.

Sassen, S. (2000). Territory and territoriality in the global economy. *International Sociology, 15*(2), 372–393.

Sassen, S. (2008). *Territory, authority, rights: From medieval to global assemblages*. Princeton University Press.

Scheiber, N. (2017, April 2). How Uber uses psychological tricks to push its drivers' buttons. *New York Times*. https://www.nytimes.com/interactive/2017/04/02/technology/uber-drivers-psychological-tricks.html. Accessed May 2024.

Schleifer, T. (2024, November 13). At Mar-a-Lago, "Uncle" Elon Musk puts his imprint on the Trump transition. *New York Times*. https://www.nytimes.com/2024/11/13/us/politics/musk-trump-transition-mar-a-lago.html. Accessed December 2024.

Schmid, Y., & Liechti, M. E. (2018). Long-lasting subjective effects of LSD in normal subjects. *Psychopharmacology, 235*, 535–545.

Schmidt, E. (2020, February 27). I used to run Google. Silicon Valley could lose to China. *New York Times.* https://www.nytimes.com/2020/02/27/opinion/eric-schmidt-ai-china.html. Accessed May 2024.

Schneier, B. (2015). *Data and Goliath: The hidden battles to collect your data and control your world.* W. W. Norton & Company.

Schüll, N. D. (2012). *Addiction by design: Machine gambling in Las Vegas.* Princeton University Press.

Schumpeter, J. A., & Swedberg, R. (2021). *The theory of economic development.* Routledge.

Scott, J. C. (1985). *Weapons of the weak: Everyday forms of peasant resistance.* Yale University Press.

Scott, J. C. (2017). *Against the grain: A deep history of the earliest states.* Yale University Press.

Scott, J. C. (2020). *Seeing like a state: How certain schemes to improve the human condition have failed.* Yale University Press.

Scott, J. C. (2024). Intellectual diary of an iconoclast. *Annual Review of Political Science, 27*, 1–7.

Seo, Y., & Harlan, C. (2014, April 18). South Korean ferry passengers told to stay put after captain abandoned ship. *Washington Post.* https://www.washingtonpost.com/world/asia_pacific/south-korean-ferry-passengers-told-to-stay-put-after-captain-abandoned-ship/2014/04/18/bb52e73c-c6ef-11e3-9f37-7ce307c56815_story.html. Accessed May 2024.

Shambaugh, D. L. (2008). *China's Communist Party: Atrophy and adaptation.* University of California Press.

Sheffield, M. (2017, August 28). Stormfront, the internet's oldest major racist website, has domain suspended. *Salon.* https://www.salon.com/2017/08/28/stormfront-internets-oldest-major-racist-website-has-domain-suspended. Accessed May 2024.

Shen, F., & Shi, W. (2024). Censorship and freedom of expression in China. In J. Steel & J. Petley (Eds.), *The Routledge companion to freedom of expression and censorship* (pp. 138–152). Routledge.

Shirky, C. (2010). *Cognitive surplus: Creativity and generosity in a connected age.* Penguin UK.

Silbey, S. S. (2005). After legal consciousness. *Annual Review of Law and Social Sciences, 1*(1), 323–368.

Simi, P., Blee, K., DeMichele, M., & Windisch, S. (2017). Addicted to hate: Identity residual among former white supremacists. *American Sociological Review, 82*(6), 1167–1187.

Singal, J. (2015, May 29). How a grad student uncovered a huge fraud. *The Cut.* https://www.thecut.com/2015/05/how-a-grad-student-uncovered-a-huge -fraud.html. Accessed May 2024.

Small, M.L. (2011). How to conduct a mixed methods study: Recent trends in a rapidly growing literature. *Annual Review of Sociology, 37*, 57–86.

Squire, M., & Gais, H. (2021, September 29). *Inside the far-right podcast ecosystem, part 4: Far-right podcasting, past and present.* Southern Poverty Law Center. https://www.splcenter.org/hatewatch/2021/09/29/inside-far-right-podcast- ecosystem-part-4-far-right-podcasting-past-and-present. Accessed May 2024.

Stark, D. (2009). *The sense of dissonance: Accounts of worth in economic life.* Princeton University Press.

Statista. (2024, March 26). *Leading tech companies worldwide 2024, by market cap.* https://www.statista.com/statistics/1350976/leading-tech-companies -worldwide-by-market-cap/. Accessed May 2024.

Steel, C.M. (2009). Child pornography in peer-to-peer networks. *Child Abuse & Neglect, 33*(8), 560–568.

Stinchcombe, A.L. (2013 [1965]). Social structure and organizations. In J.G. March (Ed.), *Handbook of organizations* (pp. 142–193). Rand McNally.

Sunstein, C.R. (2009). *Republic.com 2.0.* Princeton University Press.

Thiel, D., & McCain, M. (2022). *Gabufacturing dissent: An in-depth analysis of Gab.* Stanford Internet Observatory.

Timotija, F. (2024, December 14). Apple CEO visits Mar-a-Lago, joining list of tech execs seemingly courting Trump. *The Hill.* https://thehill.com /technology/582927-apple-ceo-visits-mar-a-lago-joining-list-of-tech -execs-seemingly-courting-trump. Accessed December 2024.

Torba, A. (2021, February). *Gab.com/a.* Accessed June 2024.

Törnberg, A., & Törnberg, P. (2021). "Wake-up call for the white race": How Stormfront framed the elections of Obama and Trump. *Mobilization: An International Quarterly, 26*(3), 285–302.

Tsing, A.L. (2024). *Friction: An ethnography of global connection.* Princeton University Press.

Tufekci, Z. (2014). Engineering the public: Big data, surveillance and computa- tional politics. *First Monday* 19(7). https://doi.org/10.5210/fm.v19i7.4901. Accessed May 2024.

Tufekci, Z. (2017). *Twitter and tear gas: The power and fragility of networked protest*. Yale University Press.

Turkle, S. (2012). *Alone together: Why we expect more from technology and less from each other*. Basic Books.

Tversky, A., & Kahneman, D. (1991). Loss aversion in riskless choice: A reference-dependent model. *Quarterly Journal of Economics, 106*(4), 1039–1061.

United States v. Bowers, Criminal Complaint, No. 18-1396 (W.D. Pa. 2018).

United States v. Ulbricht, No. 14 Cr. 68 (S.D.N.Y. May 29, 2015).

United States v. Ulbricht, 858 F.3d 71 (2d Cir. 2017).

UN Office on Genocide Prevention and the Responsibility to Protect. (n.d.). *Genocide*. https://www.un.org/en/genocideprevention/genocide.shtml. Accessed June 2024.

US Attorney's Office, via the Federal District Court. (2016, December 10). Full Dylann Roof confession. *New York Times*. https://www.nytimes.com/video/us/100000004815369/full-dylann-roof-confession.html. Accessed May 2024.

US Department of Health and Human Services. (2023). *Surgeon General issues new advisory about effects social media use has on youth mental health*. https://www.hhs.gov/about/news/2023/05/23/surgeon-general-issues-new-advisory-about-effects-social-media-use-has-youth-mental-health.html. Accessed May 2024.

US Department of Homeland Security. (2020, December 22). *Data security business advisory: Risks and considerations for businesses using data services and equipment from firms linked to the People's Republic of China*. https://www.dhs.gov/sites/default/files/publications/20_1222_data-security-business-advisory.pdf. Accessed May 2024.

Van Dijk, J. (2020). *The digital divide*. John Wiley & Sons.

Van Krieken, R. (1990). The organization of the soul: Elias and Foucault on discipline and the self. *European Journal of Sociology/Archives Européennes de Sociologie, 31*(2), 353–371.

Varoufakis, Y. (2024). *Technofeudalism: What killed capitalism*. Melville House.

Vaughan, D. (1996). *The Challenger launch decision: Risky technology, culture, and deviance at NASA*. University of Chicago Press.

Vickery, A. W., & Finch, P. M. (2020). Cannabis: Are there any benefits? *Internal Medicine Journal, 50*(11), 1326–1332.

Vogel, E. F. (2011). *Deng Xiaoping and the transformation of China*. Harvard University Press.

Vogels, E. A. (2021, July 20). *56% of Americans support more regulation of major technology companies.* Pew Research Center. https://www.pewresearch.org /short-reads/2021/07/20/56-of-americans-support-more-regulation-of -major-technology-companies. Accessed May 2024.

Voosen, P. (2023, September 24). NASA delivers bounty of asteroid samples to Earth. *Science.* https://www.science.org/content/article/nasa-delivers -bounty-asteroid-samples-earth. Accessed May 2024.

W3Techs. (2024). *Historical overview of content languages for websites.* https:// w3techs.com/technologies/history_overview/content_language/ms/y. Accessed August 2024.

Waters, R. (2019, December 8). Jeff Bezos warns US military it risks losing tech supremacy. *Financial Times.* https://www.ft.com/content/b38c5cf6-198a -11ea-97df-cc63de1d73f4. Accessed May 2024.

Web Technology Surveys. (2024). *Historical yearly trends in the usage statistics of content languages for websites.* https://w3techs.com/technologies/history _overview/content_language. Accessed June 2024.

Wherry, F. (2012). *The culture of markets.* Polity.

Willer, R., Rogalin, C. L., Conlon, B., & Wojnowicz, M. T. (2013). Overdoing gender: A test of the masculine overcompensation thesis. *American Journal of Sociology,* 118(4), 980–1022.

Williams, H. J., Evans, A. T., Ryan, J., Mueller, E. E., & Downing, B. (2021). *The online extremist ecosystem: Its evolution and a framework for separating extreme from mainstream.* Rand.

Williams, Z. (2016, June 12). Echoes: Beating the far right, two triple brackets at a time. *The Guardian.* https://www.theguardian.com/technology/shortcuts /2016/jun/12/echoes-beating-the-far-right-two-triple-brackets-at-a-time. Accessed May 2024.

Wilson, T. D. (2004). *Strangers to ourselves: Discovering the adaptive unconscious.* Harvard University Press.

Winter, T. (2017, July 20). AlphaBay, Hansa shut, but drug dealers flock to dark web DreamMarket. NBC News. https://www.nbcnews.com/news/us-news /alphabay-hansa-shut-drug-dealers-flock-dark-web-dreammarket-n785001. Accessed May 2024.

Wolf, M. (2017, November 14). Taming the masters of the tech universe. *Financial Times.* https://www.ft.com/content/45092c5c-c872-11e7-aa33 -c63fdc9b8c6c. Accessed May 2024.

Wolfram, S. (2023). What is ChatGPT doing: . . . and why does it work?. Wolfram Media.

Wortham, J. (2016, October 25). Obama Brought Silicon Valley to Washington. *New York Times Magazine*. https://www.nytimes.com/2016/10/30/magazine /barack-obama-brought-silicon-valley-to-washington-is-that-a-good-thing .html. Accessed December 2024.

Woolf, N. (2015, March 18). Bitcoin "Exit scam": Deep-web market operators disappear with $12m. *The Guardian*. www.theguardian.com/technology/2015 /mar/18/bitcoin-deep-web-evolution-exit-scam-12-million-dollars. Accessed May 2024.

Wright, E. O. (2020). *Envisioning real utopias*. Verso Books.

Wu, T. (2018, February 16). The tyranny of convenience. *New York Times*. https:// www.nytimes.com/2018/02/16/opinion/sunday/tyranny-convenience.html. Accessed May 2024.

xAI. (2024, November 26). About xAI. https://x.ai/about. Accessed November 2024.

Xinhua News. (2016, July 1). Chinese President Xi says G20 should strengthen role of innovation, open economy. Xinhuanet. https://web.archive.org/web /20221008101246/http://www.xinhuanet.com//english/2016-07/01 /c_135481121.htm. Accessed May 2024.

Xu, Z. (2018). *China's moment*. Reading the China Dream. https://www .readingthechinadream.com/xu-zhangrun-chinas-moment.html. Accessed May 2024.

Young, J. (2017). Merton with energy, Katz with structure: The sociology of vindictiveness and the criminology of transgression. In K. Hayward (Ed.), *Cultural criminology* (pp. 153–177). Routledge.

Zaitchik, A. (2006). *How Klan lawyer Sam Dickson got rich*. Southern Poverty Law Center. https://www.splcenter.org/fighting-hate/intelligence-report /2006/how-klan-lawyer-sam-dickson-got-rich. Accessed May 2024.

Zelizer, V. A. (2010). *Economic lives: How culture shapes the economy*. Princeton University Press.

Zheng, S. (2017, December 21). Man jailed for 51/2 years, fined US$76,000 for selling VPN software in China. *South China Morning Post*. https://www .scmp.com/news/china/policies-politics/article/2125326/man-jailed-51 /2-years-fined-us76000-selling-vpn. Accessed August 2024.

Zimmerman, P. R. (1995). *PGP frequently asked questions with answers*. Internet Archive Way Back Machine, https://web.archive.org/web/20160103011955 /http://www.faqs.org/faqs/pgp-faq/part1/. Accessed January 2016.

Zuboff, S. (2019). *The age of surveillance capitalism: The fight for human future at the new frontier of power*. Profile Books.

Index

9/11 attacks, 28–29, 122, 149–50, 186, 215

Abacus, 211–12
activism, 131, 206, 225; Arab Spring
 uprisings, 23, 205; Black Lives
 Matter (BLM), 23, 130, 217; Chinese
 anticensorship community, 5–6,
 80–81, 87–92, 99–101, 105–6,
 108–11, 199–200, 214–15; Chinese
 blank paper protests, 82, 214;
 counteractivists, 125–26, 216–18,
 230; Hong Kong protests, 108–10;
 incremental forms of, 80–84;
 Iranian anticensorship community,
 5, 99–106, 114, 214, 241; of K-pop
 fans, 22–23, 217; resistance to
 far-right groups, 216–20; of Silk
 Road consumers, 53, 60; Tiananmen Square protests, 110; Tor
 Project, 5, 39, 42–43, 45, 55, 105–7,
 114, 126. *See also* social movements
Agora, 70*fig.*, 71–72, 240, 247n17
airports (firewall ladders with server
 access), 241, 248n2, 249n3; banning
 political activity, 110–12; Chinese
 market for, 94–98, 101, 104–5, 107,
 214–15, 230; distribution of labor

and, 98, 109*fig.*; Iranian protesters
 and, 101–3, 105. *See also* firewall
 ladders; virtual private networks
 (VPNs)
Alexander, Keith, 28–29, 196
Alipay, 101
Alphabet, 29, 233; Waymo, 31. *See also*
 Big Tech; Google
Amazon, 30–32, 234; Silk Road
 compared to, 4, 39, 45; Web
 Services, 130. *See also* Big Tech
Anglin, Andrew, 124, 127, 138, 173,
 250n9, 251n23; antisemitism of,
 128–29, 135, 163, 170–71; critiquing
 colonialism, 169; cryptocurrency
 and, 126, 132, 134–36; misogyny of,
 164. *See also* Daily Stormer
anonymity, 11–12, 14, 21, 81–82, 108,
 122, 139, 179, 187; cryptocurrency
 and, 39, 42–43, 132, 134–35; Silk
 Road and, 3, 39, 42, 45, 54, 207,
 240; on Stormfront, 18, 132, 135,
 162–63; Tor and, 5, 39, 42–43, 45,
 105, 126. *See also* encryption;
 pseudonymity

anti-Blackness, 146–47, 201–2, 217; Emanuel African Methodist Episcopal Church shooting, 121, 123–24, 143–45, 159. *See also* hate speech; police brutality; racism

anticensorship communities: Chinese, 5–6, 80–81, 87–92, 99–101, 105–6, 108–11, 199–200, 214–15; Iranian, 5, 99–106, 114, 214, 241

anticensorship tools. *See* airports; firewall ladders; Shadowsocks; V2Ray

antisemitism, 121, 135, 149, 152, 166, 169–71, 217; eugenics and, 119–20, 157, 201; Tree of Life Synagogue shooting, 6, 122, 124, 127, 141, 143, 150–51, 159. *See also* hate speech; Nazi Party; neo-Nazism

Apple, 31, 166, 198; banning Gab, 126–27, 131; Shadowsocks and, 86–87. *See also* Big Tech

artificial intelligence (AI), 25, 33–34, 121, 166, 222–23; encryption and, 43–44; revolution in, 8–9, 22, 32; social control and, 196–97

Baidu, 107

Bezos, Jeff, 30, 234. *See also* Amazon

Big Tech, 27, 30–31, 34–35, 104, 187; deplatforming far-right media, 131–32, 139, 173; US government and, 226, 233–35. *See also individual companies*

Bitcoin, 42–43, 126; donations to Gab, 136–37; donations to Stormfront, 132–36; microlending, 50–51, 114; Silk Road and, 39–40, 56, 58, 247n5

Black, Derek, 219

Black, Don, 120, 127, 133, 142, 158, 219, 231. *See also* Stormfront

Black Lives Matter (BLM), 23, 130, 217

BlackMarket, 61–63, 240

Bluesky, 234–36

Bowers, Robert, 124, 150, 159, 179; casualties of, 250n13; hate speech on Gab, 121–22, 127, 141

Brin, Sergey, 105. *See also* Google

Cambridge Analytica, 32

Cameron, Claire, 185

Carlson, Tucker, 123, 231, 233–34

Caudevilla, Fernando "DoctorX," 207–11, 256n9

censorship: anticensorship tools (*see* airports; firewall ladders; Shadowsocks; V2Ray); case selection and, 240–41; by Chinese government, 5, 77–82, 89–92, 97–98, 105, 108–10, 114, 198–99, 215; incremental action against, 80–84; mainstreaming circumvention of, 105–6, 109–12, 214–15. *See also* anticensorship communities

Charlottesville, Virginia: "Unite the Right" rally (2017), 123–28, 132, 134–35, 231

child pornography, 12–13, 205, 239; prohibited on Silk Road, 41, 211

China, People's Republic of: airport technology in, 94–98, 101, 104–5, 107, 214–15, 230; anticensorship community in, 5–6, 80–81, 87–92, 99–101, 105–6, 108–11, 199–200, 214–15; blank paper protests, 82, 214; case selection, 240–41; changing internet content (Chinese language), 77–79*fig.*; globalizing anticensorship technology, 98–99, 114–15; Great Firewall, 80, 85, 92, 95, 97–98, 103, 105, 107–12, 214–16; National Intelligence Law of 2017, 29–30; Telecom 4G network, 87, 89;

Tiananmen Square massacre, 77, 110; VPN crackdown, 5, 78–80, 92, 98, 101, 108; Western tech companies in, 103–6; Xi Jinping, 194, 200, 215. *See also* Chinese Communist Party (CCP)

Chinese Communist Party (CCP): nationalist narrative, 200; political reform and, 194–95, 214–16; surveillance for social control, 29, 77–81, 98–99, 111–15, 187, 194–96; Zero-COVID strategy, 82, 195, 197, 214. *See also* China, People's Republic of

Christchurch, New Zealand, mosque shooting, 172

Christian culture: as code for whiteness, 121, 131–32, 137, 159, 201

Cisco, 103

Clinton, Bill, 22, 79, 115, 233

Cloak, 100

Clowwindy, 18, 80, 83–84, 86–93, 108, 112. *See also* Shadowsocks

Communications Decency Act (US), 125

community: around ladder technology, 82–90, 99, 104–10, 113–15, 127, 129–30, 241; being "alone together" in, 22; Chinese anticensorship community, 5–6, 80–81, 87–92, 99–101, 105–6, 108–11, 199–200, 214–15; darknet trade and, 49–53, 55–60, 69, 73; far-right extremism and, 15, 120–22, 130–32, 138, 147, 162–63, 166, 169, 177; *hyggelig* hate and, 162–63, 173–75, 179; information hubs and, 66–71, 218, 229–30, 240; Iranian anticensorship community, 5, 99–106, 114, 214, 241; of K-pop fans, 22–23, 217; nomadism and, 71–74; open

secrecy and, 3–5, 11–15, 49, 55, 81–84, 90–91, 101, 108, 111–15, 138, 205–7, 225–26, 229. *See also individual websites*

COVID-19 pandemic, 31, 108, 110, 134, 185, 194; China's Zero-COVID strategy, 82, 195, 197, 214

cryptocurrency, 11–12, 39, 42–43, 132–36, 189. *See also* Bitcoin

Cure53, 105

Daily Stormer, 15, 120–21, 142, 242, 254n3; cryptocurrency donations to, 126, 132, 134–35; deplatforming of, 125–29; hatred toward Black men on, 157–59, 167*fig.*; hatred toward Jewish people on, 128–29, 135, 163, 167, 169–71, 217; hatred toward women on, 147, 163–64; "Unite the Right" rally (2017, Charlottesville, Virginia) and, 124–26, 128, 135. *See also* Anglin, Andrew

Darknet Heroes League, 211

darknet trade, 97, 108, 188, 206, 211, 247n16; case selection, 239–41; community in, 49–53, 55–60, 69, 73; consumer drug reviews in, 46–49, 190; deterrence and, 191–94, 229; encryption in, 42–44, 85; information hubs and, 66–71, 218, 229–30, 240; marketing in, 45–46, 51; of MDMA, 192, 208–10, 212; nomadism in, 71–74; threats to, 56, 61, 66–67*fig.*, 69–70*fig.*, 72–74, 229. *See also* cryptocurrency; Silk Road

data collection, 154, 218, 228; by airport providers, 97, 112; author's methods of, 14–18, 68, 95, 142, 177, 239–42, 247nn9,16,17, 248n2, 249n3, 254nn3,21; Big Tech experiments with, 31–34; data-generation

data collection *(continued)*
industries, 13; digital trails and, 4, 10, 25, 45, 225; by Dutch National Police on Hansa, 211; in information hubs, 68–71; National Security Agency (NSA) and, 28, 35, 196–97, 245n48; Netflix and, 26–27; in space exploration, 220–21. *See also* surveillance
DDoS (distributed denial of service) attacks, 42, 70, 97
DeepDotWeb, 69
DelBene, Kurt, 30
Dickson, Sam, 157–58
digital divide, 8–9
digital trails, 4, 10, 25, 45, 225
Discord, 126
Distributed Denial of Secrets, 218
DNStats, 69–70*fig.*
Dread, 230
drug trade, 11, 188–89, 198, 229; cannabis, 45–49, 211–13; case selection, 239–40; conducted by law enforcement, 97; consumer reviews in, 46–49, 190; deterrence and, 191–94; harm reduction efforts online, 207–13; MDMA, 45, 192, 209–10, 212; overdose epidemic, 97, 210–13, 223; psychedelics, 3, 14, 42–43, 46–49, 210; resistance through, 206–7; safer online, 41–42, 44–46, 51–52. *See also* darknet trade; Silk Road
Duke, David, 120, 158. *See also* Ku Klux Klan (KKK)
Durkheim, Émile, 77, 80, 115, 248n2

Easthope, Lucy, 185
eBay, 4, 39, 206
e-commerce. *See* darknet trade; drug trade; *individual websites*

Eichmann, Adolf, 162
Emanuel African Methodist Episcopal Church (Charleston, South Carolina), shooting at, 121, 123–24, 143–45, 159. *See also* Roof, Dylann
encryption, 3–4, 11, 14, 42, 81, 137, 189, 206, 218, 247n9; in China, 88, 100, 108; for identity verification, 44, 61–66, 67*fig.*, 71–73, 85–86; manual, 43–44, 86, 198; surveillance capitalism and, 199, 225, 234
eugenics, 119–20, 157–60, 201
Evolution, 56, 71–72, 240, 247n17
Expressvpn, 78–79

Facebook, 107, 125, 165, 172, 233–34; banning white supremacism, 128; experiments with, 27–28, 236; This Is Your Digital Life, 32. *See also* Meta
far-right extremism, 17, 35, 178, 204, 235–36, 243n15, 251nn23,35, 253n16; anti-Blackness in, 121, 123–24, 143–47, 159, 201–2, 217; antisemitism in (*see* antisemitism); case selection, 239, 241–42; Christian culture as code for, 121, 131–32, 137, 159, 201; community and, 15, 120–22, 130–32, 138, 147, 162–63, 166, 169, 177; connection to Ku Klux Klan (KKK), 15, 120, 140, 147, 158; conspiratorial talk in, 16, 123, 148–52, 173–77, 231–32; cryptocurrency and, 12, 126, 132, 134–37, 189; growth through open secrecy, 5–6, 15, 122–23, 129, 138–39, 172–73, 179, 187, 189, 226, 230; humor in, 121, 123, 170–73, 179, 254n21; *hyggelig* hate and, 162–63, 173–75, 179; misogyny in, 121, 147–48, 163–65, 178; neo-Nazism

and, 120–21, 123–24, 134–36, 173,
201; perceptions of mainstream
media in, 146, 148–50, 153–57;
resistance to, 216–20; terminology
note, 250n6; as terrorist threat,
122–24; "Unite the Right" rally
(2017, Charlottesville, Virginia)
and, 123–28, 132, 134–35, 231; white
nationalism and, 16, 161, 163, 171,
176, 201. *See also* Daily Stormer;
Gab; hate speech; Stormfront;
white supremacist extremism;
white victimhood
Fields, James Alex, Jr., 125
firewall ladders, 214–15, 238, 241,
248n15; community around, 82–90,
99, 104–10, 113–15, 127, 129–30, 241;
developers' perspectives on, 83–92,
97–103, 106, 110–12; labor
distribution and, 81–83, 85. *See also*
airports; Shadowsocks; V2Ray
Floyd, George, 145–47, 160, 252n9
Forrest, Katherine, 191–92, 209–12
Fortuna, Vinicius, 106
Foucault, Michel, 195–97

Gab, 201, 230–32, 235, 254n3; as
alternative economy, 136–39, 166;
conspiratorial talk on, 173–76;
deplatforming of, 6, 126–27, 129–32,
139, 141–43, 173; GabPay, 137; hate
focus of, 6, 121–22, 127, 141–42, 147,
157, 159–60, 166–68, 175–76;
switching to Mastodon code,
129–30; traffic data, 15, 129–32,
142*fig.*, 143, 146–47, 159–60, 242,
243n15, 251n35, 252n9. *See also*
Torba, Andrew
Gates, Bill, 8, 233
GitHub, 6, 18, 129, 189–90, 248n19;
Shadowsocks and V2Ray projects

on, 82–84, 86–88, 90–91, 99–100,
104, 248n15; US sanctions on, 104
GoAgent, 84, 89–90, 248n19
GoDaddy, 125–26
Google, 5, 25, 29–30, 114, 155;
deplatforming Daily Stormer, Gab,
125–27; Jigsaw, 105; leaving China,
104–7; Outline VPN, 106; Play, 96,
127; Translate, 100; Trends,
107–10. *See also* Alphabet; Big Tech
Great Firewall, 80, 85, 92, 95, 97–98,
103, 105, 107–12, 214–16
Grenfell Tower fire (London, UK),
185–86
gun shows, 161–62

hackers, 17, 44, 56, 67*fig.*, 86, 216;
Clowwindy, 18, 80, 83–84, 86–93,
108, 112; Distributed Denial of
Secrets, 218; Hacker News, 92;
services for hire, 42
Hansa, 211
hate speech, 6, 15, 121–22, 125, 127,
140–46, 176, 201–2, 252nn1,9; *hygge*
and, 162–63, 173–75, 179; toward
Black men on Daily Stormer, Gab,
Stormfront, 147–48, 157–60, 163,
167–68, 174, 177; toward Jewish
people on Daily Stormer, Gab,
Stormfront, 128–29, 135, 148–53, 155,
157, 163, 166–71, 174, 177, 217;
toward Muslim people on Daily
Stormer, Gab, Stormfront, 149–51,
163, 167*fig.*, 168; toward women on
Daily Stormer, Gab, Stormfront,
147–48, 163–65
Hauben, Michael, 20–21, 30
Hauben, Rona, 20–21, 30
He, Jiayan, 78
Heyer, Heather, 125–26
Hoffman, Reid, 30

Nazi Party, 119; Holocaust, 151–53, 155, 184, 202, 217

neo-Nazism, 120–21, 123–24, 134–36, 173, 201. *See also* antisemitism; far-right extremism

Netflix, 26–27, 110, 113

Nuremberg Laws, 201

Obama, Barack, 147, 233

Open Measures, 218, 242, 251n39

open secrecy, 68, 199; in case selection, 239–42; community and, 3–5, 11–15, 49, 55, 81–84, 90–91, 101, 108, 111–15, 138, 205–7, 225–26, 229; definition, 3; diminishing state power, 10, 18, 60, 111–12, 203, 240; diminishing state sovereignty, 10, 13–14, 187–90, 225–26; drug trade and, 41–42, 45–46, 49, 55, 60, 74, 192–93, 211; growth of far-right extremism and, 5–6, 15, 122–23, 129, 138–39, 172–73, 179, 187, 189, 226, 230; for social change, 216, 220, 225–26, 229–30, 234

open-source code, 6, 12, 32, 81, 98, 129–30, 166; in ladder community, 84–85, 111–12, 215

Parler, 126, 130–31, 252n3

PayPal, 131–33

piracy networks, 12–13, 105, 107, 207, 239

police brutality, 131, 143–44, 159, 200, 202; killing of Breonna Taylor, 146–47, 252n9; killing of George Floyd, 145–47, 160, 252n9

Pretty Good Privacy (PGP), 43, 64, 85. *See also* Zimmerman, Philip

privacy, 33, 61, 65, 83, 86, 104, 179; loss of appeal, 198–99; Pretty Good Privacy (PGP), 43, 64, 85. *See also* anonymity; data collection; encryption; pseudonymity; surveillance; VPNs

pseudonymity, 14, 18, 21, 45, 129, 187; encryption and, 3–4, 11, 71, 108; software developers and, 12, 80, 82, 84, 92, 99, 103, 108, 230. *See also* anonymity

Python, 8, 14–15

Qian, Xuesan, 197, 221

racism, 16, 142*fig.*, 162, 167*fig.*, 175, 178–79; "Christian culture" and, 121, 131; eugenics, 119–20, 157–60, 201; Ku Klux Klan (KKK), 15, 120, 140, 147, 157–58, 171; police brutality and, 131, 143–47, 159–60, 200, 202, 252n9; terrorism and, 141, 220; white victimhood and, 123, 144–48, 150–53, 157–58, 171, 201–2, 204. *See also* hate speech; white supremacist extremism

Raymond, Victoria, 83, 89, 91–93, 112. *See also* V2Ray

Reagan National Defense Forum (2019), 30

Reddit, 69–70*fig.*, 229–30, 233, 240, 242

Rifkin, Jeremy, 198–99

Roof, Dylann, 18, 122–24, 154–55, 179, 253n19; casualties of, 250n12; Stormfront and, 121, 143–45, 159

Russia: AI boom and, 8; mass-media governance in, 99, 114; web content in Russian, 79*fig.*

sanctions (US), 104

Schmidt, Eric, 29–30, 104–5. *See also* Alphabet; Google

Shadowrocket, 96

Shadowsocks, 80–81, 94, 108, 248n15; Apple products and, 86–87; banned by Microsoft, 104; forks (copies) of, 91, 91*fig.*; Google Outline and, 105–6; in growth of ladder community, 82, 93; ShadowsocksR (Breakwa11), 83–84; translations of, 99–102. *See also* Clowwindy

Sheep, 56, 67*fig.*

Shockley, William, 119–20, 158, 221

Signal, 199, 234

Silk Road, 3–5, 45–46, 229; author's use of, 42, 239–40, 246n5; banning child pornography, 41, 211; community and, 49–53, 56–61, 127; cryptocurrency and, 39–40, 56, 58, 136, 247n6; harm reduction efforts on, 207–12; the Hub and, 58–59, 69, 247n5; identity verification concerns and, 61–66; nomadism and, 71–72; promotion of, 39, 51–53, 246n6; shutdown of, 54–55, 59–61, 68, 72–73, 192, 240, 247n17; subreddits, 69. *See also* Silk Road 2; Ulbricht, Ross

Silk Road 2, 4, 12, 69, 189; author's use of, 240, 247n17; encryption for identity verification on, 64–65; the Hub and, 58–59, 69, 247n5; moderator, Libertas, 59–60, 69; nomadism and, 71–72

Snowden, Edward, 28, 197, 199

social media, 26, 28, 102–3, 120, 154, 164; Arab Spring and, 23; Barack Obama and, 233; Donald Trump and, 166, 170, 232, 234; drug trade and, 12, 39, 54, 67–69, 74, 189, 198, 229; Elon Musk and, 122–23, 156, 232, 234; prosocial change and, 10, 35, 189, 216–18, 235–36, 239–41; *The Social Network*, 31. *See also individual platforms*

social movements, 51, 85, 178–79; censorship circumvention as nonmovement, 109–12, 214–15; far-right extremism as, 124–25, 147, 157, 160, 165, 172, 217, 232; social movement scholarship, 10, 15, 23, 80–81, 113, 172, 240. *See also* activism

Soros, George, 123, 232

Southern Poverty Law Center, 219

sovereignty, state/national, 31, 187; undermined by open secrecy, 10, 13–14, 187–90, 225–26. *See also* state power

Soviet Union Communist Party, 194

Spencer, Richard, 124

state censorship. *See* censorship

state control, 3, 186, 199, 202–3, 206, 241; artificial intelligence (AI) and, 196–97; Chinese Communist Party (CCP) and, 29, 77–81, 98–99, 111–15, 187, 194–96, 214–15; of labor distribution, 113, 152, 189, 228; undermined by open secrecy, 11, 110–12, 187–90, 225–26; Western methods of, 187, 196, 200–201, 213, 256n31

state power, 28–29, 183–84, 191, 214–16; of Big Tech, 30–32, 35; undermined by open secrecy, 10, 18, 60, 111–12, 203, 240. *See also* sovereignty, state/national

state surveillance. *See* surveillance

Stormfront, 242, 243n15, 251n35, 253n17, 254n3; anonymity and, 18, 132, 135, 162–63; conspiratorial talk on, 148–52, 174–77, 231–32; cryptocurrency donations to, 132–36; deplatforming of, 126–29; Don Black and, 120, 127, 133, 142,

V2Ray, 80–84, 89, 91, 94, 106–8, 248n15. *See also* Raymond, Victoria

virtual private networks (VPNs), 78–80, 92, 94, 98–107

Vpnclub, 103

war on drugs (US), 52–53, 207, 211, 224

WeChat, 94, 101, 109

West, global, 6, 54, 77, 113, 199, 215; Chinese airport technology and, 92, 95; data collection in, 29, 196; extremism and, 120, 134, 148–49, 158, 160, 163, 166, 200–201, 241; methods of state control in, 187, 196, 200–201, 213, 256n31; US technological supremacy, 30; Western tech presence in China, 103–6

white supremacist extremism, 5, 23, 124, 134, 155, 161, 169, 171, 217; Gab and, 122, 129, 137–38, 140, 147, 157, 230–31, 251n35; note on terminology, 250n6; repudiated by Derek Black, 219; Stormfront and, 128–29, 140, 144–45, 147, 151–52, 157,

164–65, 231, 251n35. *See also* far-right extremism; hate speech; racism

white victimhood, 159–61, 168–69, 217; racism and, 123, 144–48, 150–53, 157–58, 171, 201–2, 204

Wikipedia, 24, 110, 154–55, 216, 235, 253n19

wildfires, 184–85

Witty, Patrick, 215

Wolf, Martin, 31

Wolfram, Stephen, 25

Xray, 84

X/Twitter, 103, 126, 171, 189, 232, 235–36

Yahoo!, 103–4

YouTube, 106, 170, 172, 222

Zimmermann, Philip, 43. *See also* Pretty Good Privacy (PGP)

Zuckerberg, Mark, 233–34. *See also* Meta

Founded in 1893,
UNIVERSITY OF CALIFORNIA PRESS
publishes bold, progressive books and journals
on topics in the arts, humanities, social sciences,
and natural sciences—with a focus on social
justice issues—that inspire thought and action
among readers worldwide.

The UC PRESS FOUNDATION
raises funds to uphold the press's vital role
as an independent, nonprofit publisher, and
receives philanthropic support from a wide
range of individuals and institutions—and from
committed readers like you. To learn more, visit
ucpress.edu/supportus.

www.ingramcontent.com/pod-product-compliance
Lightning Source LLC
Chambersburg PA
CBHW020830270326
41928CB00006B/482